CLOTH

THAT DOES

NOT DIE

THE MEANING
OF CLOTH IN
BÙNÚ SOCIAL LIFE

CLOTH

THAT DOES

NOT DIE

THE MEANING
OF CLOTH IN
BÙNÚ SOCIAL LIFE

ELISHA P. RENNE

A McLellan Book

UNIVERSITY OF WASHINGTON PRESS

SEATTLE AND LONDON

This book is published with the assistance of a grant from the McLellan Endowed
Series Fund, established through the generosity of Martha McCleary McLellan
and Mary McLellan Williams.

Printed in the United States of America
Design and composition by Wilsted & Taylor

LIBRARY OF CONGRESS CATALOGING-IN-PUBLICATION DATA

Renne, Elisha P.
    Cloth that does not die : the meaning of cloth in Bùnú social life / Elisha P.
Renne.
      p. cm.
    Includes bibliographical references (p.   ) and index.
    ISBN 0-295-97392-7 (acid-free paper)
    1. Textile fabrics, Yoruba—Nigeria—Bunu District—Social aspects.
2. Yoruba (African people)—Social life and customs.
3. Hand weaving—Nigeria—Bunu District.   I. Title.
DT515.45.67R45   1994
746.1′4′08996333—dc20   94-12014
                                                        CIP

For my parents

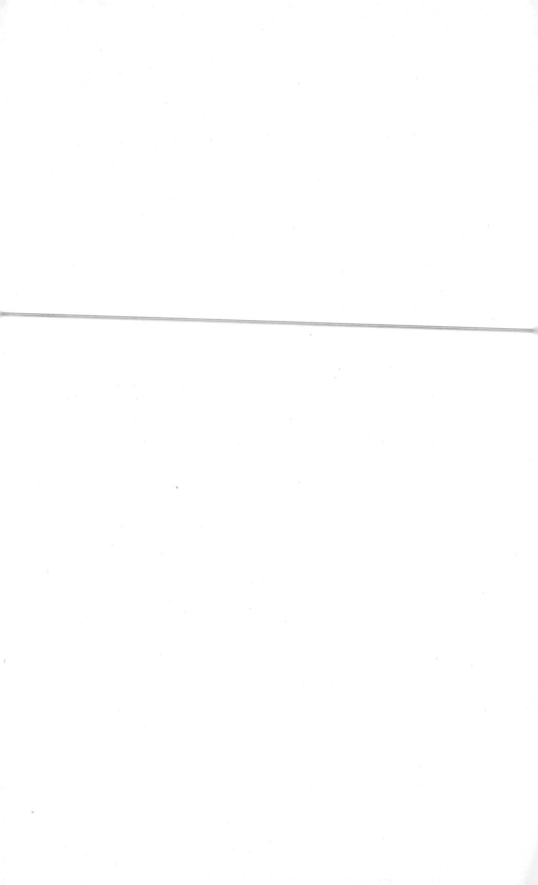

CONTENTS

ILLUSTRATIONS

FOREWORD

The title of these exceptional essays is taken from a Bùnú Yorùbá incantation, and expresses a fundamental human paradox. As it ages,
Bùnú cloth frays and gradually disintegrates, mirroring the impermanence of human life. Yet like the Yorùbá belief that each child
born represents the rebirth of an ancestor, the actions of cloth in ritual and exchange are thought to create a bridge from the past that
becomes the basis for future social and political claims to land, titles,
and authority. Thus, cloth does not die but, like children, must be
continually reproduced through time. Each complex stage of its production—preparation of the fibers, spinning, dyeing, and weaving
—is equated with aspects of human reproduction. Because cloth
is described as a second skin, it becomes ever more potent as it ab-
sorbs the body's moisture and smells. These beliefs are made public
through the colors of particular cloths and the details of their designs
and are expressed in the way fabrics are worn, given to others, mag-
ically fortified, and passionately safeguarded for future generations.
Elisha Renne's research is remarkable in revealing the endurance of
such animated cloth in this central Nigerian society; handspun cloth
is produced there much less frequently now than in the past, yet its
powerful and dangerous properties still occupy the thoughts of those
who covet these special treasures.

Renne's deeply textured ethnographic focus on Bùnú Yorùbá cloth
takes the reader beyond description into the underside of lived experience. Following the paths of locally handspun and "foreign"
cloth, Renne provides an intimate vision of politics, gender, kinship,
kingship, and the spirit world in action. What she learns about the

rules of social life—what one ought to do—also exposes the decep-
tions and craftiness, the sorrows and fears, that underlie the strat
egies people use when they face everyday challenges and times of
crises.

This tension is poignantly expressed when Bùnú villagers talk
about the fabric's two-sided significance. One side faces outward, reflecting openness and hopes for social harmony. The other, facing inward against the body, symbolizes private concerns, which over time
may become destructive and lead to witchcraft. Renne explores the
dynamics of this side of social life with rare sensitivity, tracking
quarrels over the political ascendancy of chiefs and kings, the rivalry
of kin group alignments, and the magical powers of hunters and diviners. How cloth is woven, handled, argued over, revered, lost, or
historically displaced reveals the context in which villagers lay claim
to authority over others.

Renne eloquently shows that to study cloth is to study the pulse
of society—its conflicts and joys and the dislocations wrought by
colonialism, neocolonialism, modernism, and postmodernism. She
describes how "tradition" itself is redefined when fashionable new
pan-Yorùbá cloths favored by the young vie with highly valued but increasingly rare marriage and funeral cloths favored by the old. Bùnú
cloth is the focus for political and generational conflicts as older villagers assert their authority through control of these ancestral
cloths, while many younger villagers challenge these traditions and
hence the authority of their elders. Such conflicts, however, are not
unidimensional. Those who counter the authority of elders by wearing Bob Marley tee-shirts to a masquerade ritual where Yorùbá dress
prevails have aspirations that they recognize are contradictory. Even
as they seek images of modernity, they remain committed to preserving the distinctiveness of their own local identity in other domains;

at marriages, for instance, "foreign" cloth cannot substitute for women's handspun cloth.

These struggles over cultural identity have a long, tangled history, much of it prefigured in competition over cloth production. With the imposition of the British Protectorate, the colonial plan was to make northern Nigeria into a vast raw cotton–producing satellite for British textile companies and at the same time establish Nigerian markets for the finished fabrics. In discussing this history, Renne describes how Bùnú women's production of handspun cloth was undermined by "cotton imperialism." But the dialogue about cloth production that took place between Bùnú villagers and British colonial officers included Bùnú women as well as men. As a result, women aggressively shifted their own economic goals and directly encouraged the decline of cotton and cloth production. Renne shows how homespun cloth became a vehicle for social change among women, even as the cloth itself remained the political marker of "tradition" for the present and the future.

These chapter essays reveal the conflicting properties attributed to cloth. Handspun cloth represents the inalienability of social identity and at the same time the fragility of "tradition," authority, and power. Renne beautifully portrays the range of meanings accorded treasured fabrics and the transmission and transformation of these meanings over time. For the Bùnú, "cloth does not die." For the reader, thanks to Renne's insightful research, Bùnú cloth emerges as an extraordinary object, the key material possession linking ancestors with economics, the politics of kings and chiefs with women's social control, and the legacies of "tradition" with modernity.

Annette B. Weiner
January 1995

PREFACE

I at least have much to do in

unravelling certain human lots,

and seeing how they were woven

and interwoven . . .

George Eliot, Middlemarch

I first arrived in the confluence area of central Nigeria in November 1987 to study the production of handwoven cloth and the political organization of the Owé Yorùbá of Kàbbà. Approaching the town of Kàbbà by road, I was struck by the beauty of the landscape with its stark inselbergs, solitary hills of rock jutting abruptly from the flat savannah. These rocks were marked by irregular, vertical white striations as if a sacrificial liquid had been poured from on high, indicative of some spiritual presence. The town itself was less evocative of such romantic musings. It looked like many other Yorùbá towns, with its innumerable rectangular, concrete houses with rusting iron roofs, interspersed with the occasional elegant two-story structures of the local elite and myriad shops and small bars. Despite its lack of distinction, Kàbbà was nonetheless intriguing. I had read about its long unsettled chieftaincy dispute and knew of its reputation as the source of Kàbbà cloth. Through connections with Nigerians living in the States, I arranged to move in with a family and soon after began asking about weavers and examples of handwoven cloth used in chieftaincy.

As is the case with many anthropology Ph.D. projects, what I had set out to study was not what I found. With one exception, the only women weaving in Kàbbà were Ebira women, temporary residents from Okene to the northwest. Furthermore, very few locally hand-woven cloths were being kept, and even the cloth regalia used by opposing factions in the ongoing chieftaincy dispute consisted largely of strip-woven cloth purchased outside Kàbbà.

It would have been interesting to study why locally woven cloth had so thoroughly disappeared from Kàbbà, but instead I decided to visit some villages in neighboring Bùnú District where people assured me that handweaving was still being done. One day, after an outing with a friend to Lokoja, instead of taking the good road through Okene on which we had come, we drove back to Kàbbà on the disintegrating one that intersected several villages along the southern border of the Bùnú District.

The first village we stopped in was Àpàá-Bùnú. Although a few older women enthusiastically confirmed that they still wove, I was disappointed with the plain cloth that I saw on one loom. At Òkè-Bùkún, another Bùnú village closer to Kàbbà, Sarah James, the one remaining weaver there, invited me to return to talk about weaving. I halfheartedly agreed.

When my research assistant, Esther Eniọlọ́runfẹ́, a young Kàbbà woman, and I returned a week later, Sarah invited us inside her house while she looked in her room for cloths to show us. As we waited in the house's central passageway, a young woman sat with us, nursing her baby, and an older man sat in an adjacent room, smoking a pipe. Sarah emerged from her bedroom holding several handwoven cloths, including one black one with narrow bands of red and white and uncut warp ends. This one, she explained, was *àdófì* cloth that every Bùnú woman should have in order to perform traditional marriage. She had just woven this cloth as she was about to perform her own traditional marriage. Yet Sarah was at least fifty years old and already a grandmother. The young woman nursing was her daughter and the man in the next room was the young woman's father. I wondered about Sarah's marriage and why the handwoven marriage cloth *àdófì* was crucial when handweaving itself was on the decline in Bùnú. The obvious importance that Bùnú women placed on performing traditional marriage seemed a compelling reason to examine what traditional marriage meant for Bùnú women and men, in light of the many changes in their social world over the last hundred years. Rather than study cloth and political hierarchy, I decided to focus on the transformation of Bùnú traditional marriage practice in relation to divorce and changing customary court rulings during the colonial and postcolonial periods.

Despite this research shift, cloth nonetheless provided a useful way of talking about marriage, as older women liked to describe cloths they had woven or used when they had married. Also, my interest in seeing examples of the different types of cloths and in learning to weave made my extended stay in Bùnú District more comprehensible to village residents. As one man put it, "Practica [learning to weave] is part of your coursework."

Early in December 1987 I packed my things from Kàbbà and took a room in a family house in the southern Bùnú village of Àpàá-Bùnú, where I lived for nine months. Esther Eniọlọ́runfẹ́ stayed with me most of the time, helping as much with etiquette as with language. We began interviewing older women about traditional marriage, their work as weavers, and why things had changed. During this time, preparations for a marriage and a commemorative funeral were taking place. We attended these events, recording songs, photographing the participants, and generally talking to people about what was happening. This combination of participating in village events, open-ended interviewing, and just hanging out was augmented by trips to other villages in Bùnú, particularly to Aíyétóró-Kírí in the north and to Ọ̀llẹ̀ in central Bùnú. There I stayed with a family related to the one I lived with in Àpàá. I also attended traditional marriage performances in these places, which, like the distinctive dialects, were performed somewhat differently from those in the south.

Actually, this peripatetic research style, which included waiting hours for public transport and holding babies during flat tire repair, was similar to the experience of many Bùnú villagers who would often travel to visit relations elsewhere in the District. Later, it was through my Bùnú connections that I was able to gain access to local colonial court records pertaining to divorce, which I supplemented with research at the Nigerian National Archives, Ìbàdàn and Kaduna, and at the Church Missionary Society Archives at the University of Birmingham.

While concentrating on traditional marriage and the introduction of divorce in colonial courts, I was also accumulating bits and pieces of information about cloth. For example, when I asked about village disputes settled out of court, I found that formerly the cloths of two quarrelling women would be torn in half as part of the settlement. At first I was not aware of the amount of information I was accumulating. Later, I realized that cloth use and references pervaded Bùnú social life in ways I had hardly imagined. My initial disappointment at not finding women weaving quantities of intricately patterned cloths for use in chieftaincy ritual was replaced by an appreciation of the significance of plain, white cloth. I returned to Bùnú in June–July 1990 and December 1991 to fill in some of the missing pieces and ask further questions.

The following chapters are the result of these cumulative observations. They examine the use of cloth by a particular group of people, in a particular time and place from the perspective of a particular individual. While this discussion of cloth focuses on its use in constituting and representing interpersonal and group relations, another study might have investigated the distinction made in Bùnú between cloth woven for rituals and those woven as commodities and how villagers' increasing participation in a cash-based economy affected cloth production. Or a study of the social implications and historical connections of red chieftaincy cloth used by the Bùnú and by neighboring groups with different forms of political organization might have been pursued. However, as the final line in one Bùnú song reminds listeners, "cloth has many uses." It can have many studies as well.

ACKNOWLEDGMENTS

This study would not have been possible without the help of many people. I would first like to thank the women and men of Bùnú District. Many who helped are cited in individual interview excerpts. To them and others not individually named, I am grateful.

I also thank my many friends in Kàbbà, particularly F. O. Ọbásàjú, J. F. Ọbásàjú, Victoria Ọbásàjú, and other members of their family, without whose help this project would never have begun. The research assistance of Esther Eniọlọ́runfẹ́, John Ẹ̀bájẹ́mítọ́, and Peter Ọnayésemí was also essential. I am indebted to the former Oyi Local Government staff, who facilitated my stay in the area; to the former Kàbbà-Bùnú Local Government chairman, Philip E. Ọlọ́runípa; and to the members of the Traditional Council of Chiefs for their approval of initial work in Bùnú District.

At the University of Ìbàdàn, the staff of the Institute of African Studies was a constant source of help. I am especially grateful to Bọ̀lanle Awé, who sponsored my initial research affiliation at the university, to S. O. Babáyẹmí, and to Cornelius O. Adepégbá, who advised me during my stay. Members of the Department of History,

University of Ìbàdàn, in particular, LaRay Denzer, Adé Ìjágbèmí, R. A. Adéléyę, and O. Adewoyè also provided encouragement and insights, as did Glenn Webb of the Department of Anthropology. Historians at other institutions—E. J. Alagoa, University of Port Harcourt, and Adé Ọbáyẹmí, University of Ìlọrin—gave excellent advice and comments.

I also thank the members of the staff at the National Archives of Nigeria at Ìbàdàn and Kaduna and at the Christian Missionary Society Archives at the University of Birmingham for their assistance. At the Museum of Mankind, London, and at the Department of History and Applied Arts, Royal Museum of Scotland, Edinburgh, staff members kindly helped with the inspection of their Nigerian textile collections. Wendy Cosford and Jenny Braid, at the Australian National University, Canberra, gave valuable editorial advice, while Kay Dancey of the cartography section of the Department of Human Geography graciously contributed the map of Bùnú.

Last but hardly least, I would like to thank Annette B. Weiner and Constance R. Sutton, New York University, and Joanne B. Eicher, University of Minnesota, for their invaluable guidance. Joanne Eicher first encouraged me to work in Nigeria with its rich textile traditions and has continued to be supportive of my subsequent work there. Connie Sutton recommended that I look at the role of women in Nigerian cloth production and trade, which led to my working in Kàbbà. Annette Weiner stimulated me to consider cloth use and production in their political and cultural context, with their more general implications for gender and power relations. I would also like to thank another member of the Department of Anthropology, New York University, T. O. Beidelman, for his pithy criticism.

I am grateful to Diana Fane, Bill Siegmann, and the staff of the Department of African, Oceanic, and New World Art at the Brooklyn Museum who contributed suggestions and moral support during write-up and to Simon Ottenberg who encouraged me to submit the manuscript for publication. Thanks also to Naomi Pascal, Julidta Tarver, and Marilyn Trueblood at the University of Washington Press for their patience and advice.

Finally, I express my special appreciation to Bruce Cleary, Barbara Bianco, and Susan Bergh for their comments, corrections, and kindnesses.

This study was made possible by a grant from the National Science Foundation (BNS-8710282), a Foreign Language Area Studies program grant, and a James Arthur fellowship awarded by the Graduate School of Arts and Sciences, New York University. Unless otherwise indicated, all photographs were taken by the author.

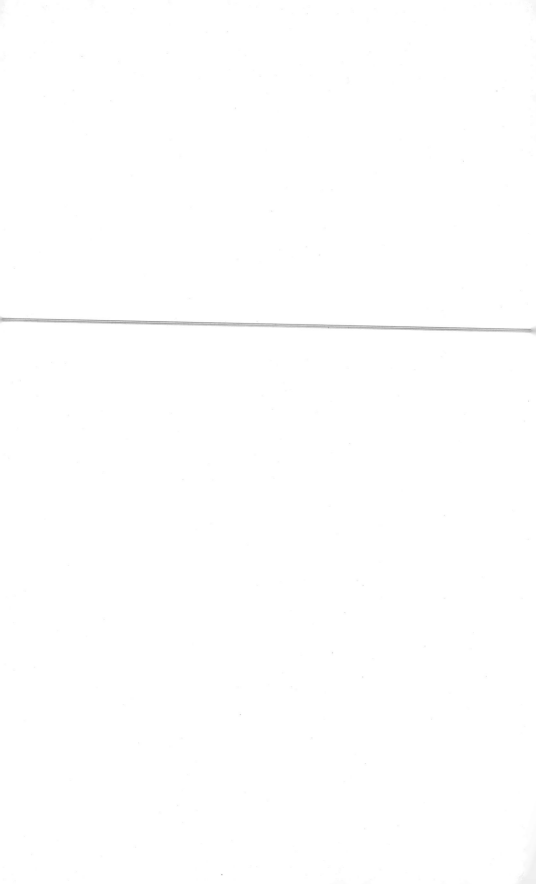

CLOTH
THAT DOES
NOT DIE

THE MEANING
OF CLOTH IN
BÙNÚ SOCIAL LIFE

ONE

INTRODUCTION

When you have money,

some people will be angry;

When you have cloth,

some people will be angry;

When you have children,

some people will be angry;

Cloth has many uses.

Bùnú Yorùbá song

The Bùnú Yorùbá people of central Nigeria mark every critical junc-
ture in an individual's life, from birthing ceremonies to funeral celebrations, with handwoven cloth. In rituals such as that for
installing a chief or for traditional marriage, cloth is used to express
changes in the status of individuals as well as in the social connections of kin, affines, and other supporters. As dress, it ranks chiefs
and distinguishes them from commoners. In tailored and untailored
forms, it may be used to demarcate gender as well as educational status.[1] Further, handwoven cloth is worn to distinguish ritual events
from everyday affairs where commercial, industrially woven cloth
prevails. Using cloth, Bùnú villagers concretely construct and repro-
duce ideas about their social world.

Until recently, cloth weaving and dyeing were also a major facet of
Bùnú economic life, as they were for many other Yorùbá-speaking
groups in southwestern Nigeria (Boser-Sarivaxévanis 1975; Lamb
and Holmes 1980; Picton and Mack 1979). Women processed, spun,
dyed, and wove cotton that was grown by men. Many of these cloths

were sold by women in large local markets, and profits from cloth sales were a primary source of income. As in Incan, Indian, and medieval Mediterranean societies, where cloth production and consumption were major factors in local economies, handwoven cloth in Bùnú had important social, political, and religious implications for both ritual and everyday affairs.[2]

This industry no longer exists. Yet handwoven cloths are being kept for ritual use and a few older women still weave them. Why, if cloth is rarely woven today, does it continue to play such a vital role in Bùnú social life? In attempting to answer this question, I consider cloth use and production in Bùnú society from approximately 1900 to the present.

The many distinctive cloths used in Bùnú reflect various aspects of village society. In a way, then, this book is as much about a small group of people associated with a particular past and place in central Nigeria as it is about cloth. Indeed, I argue that focusing on things such as cloth may be as rewarding a way to understand the changing complexity of social life as organizing material according to more abstract categories such as family or political organization.[3] The study of such everyday objects can often provide special insights since "the aspects of things that are most important to us are hidden because of their simplicity and familiarity" (Wittgenstein 1978: 129). An analysis centering on a concrete object may, ironically, be one of the best ways to approach the fleeting quality of social relations in "the everyday world of lived experience" (Jackson 1989:13).

Furthermore, cloth has specific characteristics appropriate to the analysis of certain aspects of social life, particularly the relationship between the individual and society. Because of its skinlike proximity to the human body, cloth is intimately associated with the individual. By absorbing bodily substances such as saliva, mucus, and sweat, it may be thought to assimilate attributes, such as saintliness, of a particular wearer.[4] Yet cloth is also the product of social life; its construction reflects contemporary technologies and tastes that are based on knowledge accumulated from past generations. In this sense, wearing cloth links the individual with others, past and present, situating the person in society. The dual position of the individual in society, who is "contained in sociation and, at the same time, finds himself confronted by it" (Simmel 1971:17), may be emphasized by playing upon the two-sided quality of cloth. A wearer's sociality may be publicly expressed by the side of cloth facing outward, while an individual's private concerns and intentions are associated with its other side, facing inward.

This Janus-faced quality of cloth, which suggests the opposition inherent in group and individual interests, nonetheless underscores the fact that both sides are of a piece. A person is distinct from society despite personal effacement, as when masquerade costumes and uniforms are used to disguise or minimize individual identity and project a generalized social role. Cloth may also be used to hide individual deformity and disease, representing the kind of socially duplicitous but judicious behavior praised in this Yorùbá *oríkì* poem (Barber 1991:140):

Bí ò sí aṣọ	If there were no cloth
Mo ní à bá ṣiṣe	We would surely be at fault
Bí ò sí aṣọ	If there were no cloth
À bá ṣiwà hù	Our blemishes would be exposed
Bíi kókó, bí oówo	Like lumps, like boils
Bí íkù	Like swollen hips
Bí àgbáàrín	Like grape-sized swellings . . .

Alternatively, an individual may wear diaphanous silk or fine linen which simultaneously covers and reveals, suggesting the good intentions of a wearer who has nothing to hide.

It is this oscillation between group and individual identities and interests, in part, that propels social life. Individuals seek a sense of community while striving to achieve personal goals, which, for many reasons, they may only partially realize. These conflicting aims do not reflect different phases of structural order and disorder ending in a communal harmony (Turner 1969). Rather, they reflect the ways in which social and individual aspirations provide a continuous counterpoint for each other, resulting in a tension that is never ultimately resolved. This tension is illuminated by a further consideration of the conjunction of ideas and particular qualities of cloth.

IDEAS, THINGS, AND THE
QUALITIES OF CLOTH

Emile Durkheim, who stressed the benefits of society for the individual, observed the importance of material things in conveying specific ideas and sentiments. Things exhibit a certain dialectical quality in that they are invested with meaning but may themselves be integral to the reproduction of ideas that contribute to group unity in time and space. For example, old cloths kept and handed down from ancestors are associated with past beliefs and practices. Their value is derived from this connection with the past and with the number of individuals previously associated with these cloths. Such accrued value is referred to as "inalienable wealth" by Weiner (1985) who discusses how "ancestral" objects legitimate present-day claims to authority in ways which newly made objects, no matter how costly or prestigious, are unable to do.[5] One of the central problems in societies where "ancestral" things such as cloth are retained is the necessity of "keeping-while-giving" (1992), whereby the need to maintain sociability through exchange must be countered by the keeping or replacing of cloths on which individual and group identities rest.

Further, in many societies cloth is often used in ceremonies of birth and rebirth to represent the beginning of social and spiritual identity for individuals. Moments after birth, infants may be swaddled, covered, and carried with special cloth that provides both a womblike security and a social identity. Corpses may be wrapped with an abundance of cloths that, it is believed, will support them in the next world (Darish 1989:135) while reinforcing the status of kinspeople who remain in this one.

Cloth may also be used to support the moral and ideological assertions of religious groups. In West Africa, Muslims wear tailored garments associated with Allah (Perani 1989) rather than untailored cloths. These cut and tailored garments contrast with uncut cloths woven on looms with a revolving warp, implying circular continuity (Schneider and Weiner 1986:180). This circularity is suggestive of reincarnation, associated with indigenous religious beliefs about rebirth. In another West African context, literate Christian converts who were freed slaves chose to wear costly European dress, enhancing their new position as political elites in southern Nigerian (Mann 1986) and Sierra Leonean (Spitzer 1974) societies. Furthermore, cloths associated with the past and reproduced exactly through an intentional "conspicuous archaism" (Cort 1989) may be employed by a modern, educated elite to adapt to economic, political, and religious change and simultaneously to maintain a sense of continuity and timelessness. Thus cloth is used in asserting competing group claims, in reconstructing traditions, and in constructing new beliefs.

Cloth not only covers human bodies and is passed on through time, it is also wrapped around trees and rocks (Feeley-Harnick 1989; Mack 1989) and draped over houses (Blier 1987; Smith 1982). Used in these ways, it suggests a common connection and compatibility of scale among natural, domestic, and personal domains (Jackson 1989). These connections are also reinforced by the metaphors based

on cloth and by a weaving imagery common in many languages. As a
symbol of interconnectedness, one speaks of cloth that "ties people
together," of the "interweaving of the social fabric," and of the "warp
and weft of social life" (Weiner and Schneider 1989:2).

Yet cloth has contradictory and ambiguous associations as well as
beneficial ones. As the Bùnú song that begins this chapter suggests,
the good fortune—money, cloth, and children—of some is cause for
the resentment and anger of others. The song expresses what Simmel (1971:91) called an "awareness of dissonance" in social life, an
appreciation of the contradictory side of interpersonal and group relations in which conflict coexists with general social ideals. The ambiguous position of the individual who must continually juggle self-
and group interests is reflected in the suggestively sinister overtone
of the song's final line, "Cloth has many uses." These uses may be for
good or ill. Like the gift that should project selfless generosity but
also entails competitive challenge, cloth used to represent social
unity and harmony may also be used to defeat rivals and to express
conflict. Thus, while cloth may be socially beneficial—as a source of
economic power, as a symbol of family and group unity, as a marker
of political ranks, and as a link between the living and the dead—it
has other, more subversive, sides. Cloth may conceal malevolent intentions (Schneider and Weiner 1986:179) and be used to threaten
(Brett-Smith 1989), as well as represent more positive ideals. The
multiple and contradictory ideas associated with "the many uses of
cloth" make it a particularly appropriate vehicle for examining the
complicated ambiguity of human intentions and social life.

"CLOTH ONLY WEARS,

IT DOES NOT DIE"

The fact that cloth is impermanent, that it shreds and frays, expresses ambiguity as well. An awareness that material things such as

cloth may be lost, wear out, or decay may be used to express the difficulty of maintaining social continuity in the face of disruptive change and the finiteness of death. Unless specially preserved, cloths—like human bodies—eventually disintegrate and disappear. Yet despite their propensity to wear and decay, objects such as cloth may be kept because of their ability to "confound time" (Kuchler 1988:629) in other ways. Indeed, the actual quality of durability or hardness is not necessarily the basis of this immortality, for as Kuchler (1988) has observed in the case of Malangan wood and fiber sculpture, memories associated with a particular object that has rotted or burnt may equally serve this purpose. In some cases, the ability of cloth to absorb and emit odors makes it a particularly evocative source of memories—as was Şóyínká's mother's handwoven aṣọ òkè cloth: "Wild Christian's bedroom . . . was a riot of smells, a permanent redolence of births, illnesses, cakes, biscuits and petty merchandise. This varied from the rich earth-smell of aṣọ òkè [handwoven cloth], to camphor balls and hundreds of unguents" (Şóyínká 1988:77–78).

Bùnú villagers use cloth to evoke memories by representing ancestors as masquerades and recreating the political claims of particular kin groups in chieftaincy rituals. Cloth may also be employed medicinally to confound time—its use is believed to prolong an individual's life by countering disease—reflected in the Bùnú Yorùbá incantation Gbígbó k'áṣọ í gbó, éè kú—"Cloth only wears, it does not die." This incantation may be intoned when particular medicinal substances are given to patients. Its imagery suggests that while individuals and cloths may wear out, children and new cloths will replace them. The incantation relates cloth to ideas about individual mortality, social continuity, and the circularity of time and of space—represented by the regeneration of ancestral spirits in individual bodies and by connections between earthly and spirit worlds. Using cloth, Bùnú villagers address the problem of how to maintain continuity in social life, despite the disruption of conflict, disease, and death.

The ideas of individual human bodies "wearing" into dust, of undying souls returning to the spirit world, and of worn but undying cloth appear to be conflated. In order for the recycling of souls and cloth to continue, old bodies and cloth must wear out and be reproduced. Thus the impermanence of cloth and human bodies is the very quality by which undying social continuity is achieved. This paradox is the key to understanding the continued importance of handwoven cloth in Bùnú social life through which individuals and groups extend identities and claims through time.

CLOTH IN WEST AFRICA
AND NIGERIA

As early as the eleventh century, cloth was used to distinguish political and social ranks among members of West African royal courts: "Among the people [of the Kingdom of Ghana] who follow the king's religion only he and his heir apparent (who is the son of his sister) may wear sewn clothes. All other people wear robes of cloth, silk, or brocade, according to their means" (al-Bakri, cited in Levtzion and Hopkins 1981:80).[6]

Cloth production and trade were important economic factors for many precolonial West African kingdoms and groups (Gilfoy 1987; Sundstrom 1974). At the end of the fifteenth century, Portuguese merchants traded European cloth along the coast of West Africa. By the early sixteenth century, a yard of cloth had become a principal unit of exchange.[7]

Along the southern Nigeria coast, the cloth trade continued to expand with important ramifications for indigenous weavers. Dutch and English merchants began purchasing huge quantities of locally produced cloth from trading stations in the Kingdom of Benin.[8] Consisting of three or four joined pieces, these cloths were known as *mouponoqua* by Nigerian traders and as "Benin cloth" by Europeans. However, they were most likely the products of women weavers from other coastal groups and from the Nigerian interior rather than from Benin itself (Landolphe 1823; Ryder 1965). These plain indigo blue or blue and white striped cloths were bartered for gold, ivory, and slaves in Ghana, Gabon, and Angola (Ryder 1969:94). Cloth continued to be used as a primary measure of value, but the indigenous cloth "piece," or *pagne*, replaced European cloths as the standard measure (Fourneau and Kravetz 1954; Ryder 1969:208).

In southern Nigeria, even after the beginning of the eighteenth century when trade in indigenous cloth had declined,[9] further European trade on the coast and exploration of the interior, along with missionary endeavors, ensured the continued use of cloth in African-European encounters. In the eighteenth and nineteenth centuries, it headed the lists of items essential for maintaining good relations with Nigerians.[10]

While a number of European merchants recorded information about cloth trade on the Nigerian coast from the sixteenth century on, less is known about cloth production and trade for the comparable period in central and northern Nigeria. Yet nineteenth-century explorers, such as Clapperton, Barth, and the Lander brothers, suggest that cloth production and trade played a prominent role in the economic life of the kingdoms of northern Nigeria. This prominence is evidenced by Barth's enthusiastic description of the cloth trade of Kano and its environs:

There is really something grand in this kind of industry, which spreads to the north as far as Murzuk, Ghat, and even Tripoli; to the west, not only to Timbuktu, but in some degree even as far as the shores of the Atlantic, the very inhabitants of Arguim dressing in the cloth woven and dyed in Kano; to the east, all over Bornu, although there it comes in contact with the native industry of the country; and to the south it maintains a rivalry with the native industry of the Igbira and Igbo, while toward the southeast it invades the whole of Adamawa. . . .   (1857, 1:511)

Barth's mention of the "rivalry with the native industry of the Igbira [Ebira]" is relevant here as it probably refers to the cloth production of their immediate neighbors, the Bùnú and Owé Yorùbá of Kàbbà, as well.[11] Unfortunately, there is little documentation of the cloth trade around Kàbbà during this period (see chapter 7). Yet Frobenius, who visited the large market at Bida in 1912, observed that the production of cloths that came from Bùnú and Kàbbà was "enormous," exceeding Nupe women's cloth production in volume.[12]

The economic vitality of the West African cloth trade generally was also evidenced by the presence of European representatives of textile firms who collected samples of West African cloths to be manufactured in Europe and then exported to specific African markets (Steiner 1985).[13] An important part of British colonial policy centered on promoting the production of raw materials such as cotton and exporting British manufactured textiles back to the colonies (Johnson 1974). These cotton-growing and cloth-selling schemes failed in southern Nigeria, initially because of the low prices offered by British cotton firms and because of the competition for raw cotton by Nigerian weavers whose products continued to be in demand because of their lower price and durability. Later, economic disruption caused by the 1929 world depression and the world war, along with competition from Japanese and Indian textiles, undercut British textile imports during the colonial period.

At present, Nigerian textile manufacturing firms produce large amounts of commercial cloth. While the number of weavers has declined, handweaving continues in Nigeria, particularly by men

weavers in Ìlọrin and Ìsẹ́yìn and by women weavers of Okene and Akwete.[14] The use of handwoven cloth as prestige dress (Boyer 1983;
Lloyd 1953) was bolstered by a 1978 ban on textile imports, which
was formulated in part to encourage industrial and handwoven textile production in Nigeria. Further, governmental agencies and the
press have promoted the wearing of handwoven cloth as both pa-
triotic and fashionable, thus extending its economic, political, and
cultural importance in Nigerian social life.[15]

The diversity of West African and Nigerian textile traditions has
been treated in several general surveys on cloth types and looms.[16]
While the cultural importance of cloth in West African societies—
in funerals, in chieftaincy installation, in spirit possession, as bridewealth payments, and as currency—has been noted,[17] the social significance of cloth and its production has received relatively little
attention in West African textile literature.[18]

This study focuses on the social relationships formed and maintained through the use and production of cloth in one central Nigerian society. However, it also includes information about specific
cloth types, their production and marketing, thus complementing
studies of women's handweaving production elsewhere in southwestern Nigeria where similar loom terminology was used and long-
distance cloth trading was also common. This study of Bùnú cloth
contributes to our general knowledge of handweaving in the Yorùbá-
speaking areas of southwestern Nigeria as well as to the particularities of Bùnú history, geography, and society.

BÙNÚ YORÙBÁ SOCIETY

The Bùnú Yorùbá people are one of several small ethnic groups living
near the confluence of the Niger and Benue rivers in central Nigeria.[19] The Bùnú and three neighboring groups (the Owé, Ìjùmú, and

Yàgbà), who speak a dialect of the Yorùbá language, are collectively known as the Northeast or O-kun Yorùbá, the term *o-kun* referring to a common greeting used in the area (Krapf-Askari 1965:9). These groups are sometimes called "fringe Yorùbá" because of their location on the periphery of the Yorùbá-speaking heartland to the southwest. They are also "fringe" in the sense that while they share some characteristics with southwestern Yorùbá groups, they are distinct from them in several ways.

Situated in savannah country to the north of the tropical rainforests associated with the south, the area gets a shorter rainy season as well as smaller quantities of rain, which limits agricultural options and, hence, economic surplus available to northeast Yorùbá farmers. Furthermore, their inland position limited them to overland trade as opposed to the riverine or intercreek trade that favored the economic positions of groups such as the Ìjèbu Yorùbá to the south. These geographical limitations on the accumulation of wealth and on mobility are reflected in the less hierarchical forms of political organization and traditional religious cosmology in Bùnú compared with southwestern Yorùbá groups. There are no specific royal clans or lineages, for example, because appointment to royal office is based on rotation among three clan groupings. Nor is there the elaborate pantheon of gods and goddesses associated with southwestern Yorùbá groups. Nonetheless, the Bùnú and other northeast groups speak a similar language and share common cultural practices such as Ifá divination, and some claim a common origin.

Bùnú District consists of hilly savannah, interspersed with heavily timbered forests. While colonial officials were interested in tapping Bùnú's natural resources, other developments such as the building of roads and schools came later to Bùnú than Kàbbà (in Kàbbà District), which was the divisional capital, and the more cen-

View of Aíyétóró-Kírí-Bùnú in northern Bùnú.

trally located Yàgbà and Ìjùmú (Gbẹ̀ddẹ) districts. Bùnú with its sparse population and poor roads is relatively undeveloped compared to other northeast Yorùbá districts. Because of their isolated location and particular history, the residents of Bùnú District have tended to maintain certain traditional practices including handweaving.

History. In precolonial times, Bùnú consisted of several small kingdoms,[20] each with a large town or village ruled by a head chief or king (*olú*) and council of chiefs. Individual settlements were said to be founded by individual hunters whose descendants formed large villages and, at times, walled towns (Krapf-Askari 1966a; Ọbáyẹmí 1978a). Their small size does not imply that these settlements were static, for both trade and warfare linked these groups with large kingdoms to the south, east, and north—at Benin, Idah, and Bida, respectively.

During the mid-nineteenth century, horsemen from the powerful Nupe kingdom centered at Bida to the north invaded the entire area (James 1914, NAK; Bridel 1931, NAK). Shortly thereafter the Nupe established a tribute system in Bùnú whereby people, agricultural produce, and cloth[21] were given in return for protection from further raiding (Mason 1970:205; Ọbáyẹmí 1978b). One of the results of Nupe raids in Bùnú in the nineteenth century was migration, particularly in the southern part of the district where villagers moved to more defensible positions near Ebiraland. These forced and voluntary migrations had important cultural ramifications for the Bùnú Yorùbá, who have incorporated certain Nupe and Ebira cultural practices.

In 1897, a constabulary force of a British firm, the Royal Niger Company, routed the Nupe from northeast Yorùbá areas. In 1900, Bùnú District, rather arbitrarily organized, came under the political control of the British colonial Protectorate of Northern Nigeria. Since independence in 1960, Bùnú District has become one of two districts that make up the Kàbbà-Bùnú Local Government Area, a countylike administrative unit in Kogí State, Nigeria.[22]

Social and Economic Organization. Currently, most Bùnú towns and villages are located next to the two main roads that bisect the district. Affiliation with a particular Bùnú village and associated rights to farmland and chieftaincy titles are ideally based on descent reckoned patrilineally from an ancestral male village founder. In reality, historical, political, and economic exigencies have led individuals to make bilateral claims in these matters. However, patrilineal identity is reinforced by virilocal residence after marriage since most children are born among their father's people. Married women, nonetheless, retain rights within their own patrilineal homes, which are often in nearby villages where they frequently visit. In general, individuals maintain ties with both patrilineal and matrilateral kin.

During the 1920s when British colonial officials assessed the district, Bùnú village economy consisted of subsistence agriculture, cloth production, and trade, with a distinct sexual division of labor. Women wove and traded cloth, while men farmed and hunted. This situation gradually changed during the colonial period as better roads and transport made alternative economic opportunities available. At the end of the twentieth century, Bùnú village women and men are principally engaged in cash-crop production along with subsistence agriculture, growing yams, cassava, sorghum, and maize on separate farm plots. Agricultural products are usually sold by women who take produce to major urban markets. Women have continued their role as traders although many have ceased weaving as an economic pursuit, partly because of the difficulties of acquiring materials and labor.

While farmland continues to be plentiful in Bùnú District, labor was also the factor mentioned by farmers as the primary constraint on production. Since farm labor and financial support are often supplied by one's children and other family members (see Caldwell 1976; Peel 1983:120), older Bùnú villagers face the problem of how to establish and maintain the loyalty of kin. This is difficult in light of migratory pressures, such as employment, which lure young people to urban centers. However, Bùnú villagers who have migrated to cities

often return during holiday periods when masquerade performances, chieftaincy installations, and marriages take place. Generational connections are maintained, in part, through the use of
material things handed down, which include marriage cloths and
chieftaincy regalia.

Local Political Organization. In Bùnú, village projects and dispute
settlements are generally addressed locally, often by a group of older
men who, through payments, village philanthropy, and common con-
sent, acquire the title of chief. These men are responsible for organizing village-wide ritual performances and deciding whether
strangers may reside in a village. They also serve as an interface between Nigerian federal and state government officials and Bùnú
villagers.

Acquiring a chieftaincy title offers individual Bùnú men leadership opportunities in local political affairs. There are three grades (or
levels) of chieftaincy positions that require successively larger
amounts of cash, as well as family and community support, to acquire. Most adult men living in Bùnú villages have taken first-level
titles; those with the second level are fewer, and the highest political
office in Bùnú—the third-level title known as *olú* or king—is rare
nowadays.[23]

Presently, in all but a few Bùnú villages, chiefs are exclusively
male. This monopoly of chieftaincy by men was not always the case.
In the past, a woman could also take a chieftaincy title, which gave
her authority to officiate in women's affairs and participate in decisions made by male chiefs. Now there are few women chiefs and
Bùnú women acquire status through the performance of the traditional marriage ritual, *gbé obitan.*

Religious Practice. Chieftaincy ritual in the past was closely related to belief in nature spirits (*ẹbọra*). Chiefs were responsible for the well-being of groups and communities through sacrifice to these spirits (Krapf-Askari 1966a:4), conceptualized as both amorphous and invisible. *Ẹbọra* spirits are believed to reside "under the water," in stones, or in other natural sites such as trees, rocks, hills, or termite mounds. Specific spirits are frequently associated with particular patrilineages, patriclans, or villages. While today most Bùnú Yorùbá are practicing Christians,[24] many continue to acknowledge the existence of these spirits, thus reaffirming group identity and continuity. Patrilineal identity has also been maintained through sacrifices and prayers made to ancestral spirits at the graves of deceased patrilineal members. Also, generalized ancestral figures are represented by *egúngún* masqueraders, who may perform during funeral celebrations and at other annual events.

The living may communicate with ancestral or nature spirits through the efforts of an Ifá diviner, known as a *babaláwo*, "father of the secret." These men are consulted in everyday and ritual affairs for advice on a wide range of concerns. Many Bùnú residents continue to believe in the ability of diviners to communicate with spirits and in the efficacy of their predictions. Except for the most strict of Christian practitioners, these beliefs are not viewed as a contradiction but rather as additional and complementary means of addressing the difficult problems of living.

Bùnú villagers have modified past practices—including chieftaincy organization, traditional marriage, farming, and religious ritual—to the conditions of living in modern Nigeria. Similarly, handwoven cloth, now infrequently produced, has not been abandoned but rather its use has been adapted. For despite economic, religious, and political changes in Bùnú society that militate against the pervasive use of handwoven cloth as in the past, the desire to prevent illness and death, to avoid the enmity of others, to be generous while preserving one's own resources, these problems still persist. Cloth, perceived as protecting individuals and connecting groups with the past, continues to be used in attempts to solve these problems.

TWO

WATER, SPIRITS,

AND PLAIN WHITE CLOTH

They dressed me in a spotless

robe of material so soft and

white that I felt I had been

wrapped in a cloud.

Okri, The Famished Road

In *African Textiles*, one of the primary publications on the subject, the authors note that "plain white cloth, woven of either hand- or machine-spun cotton yarn, is the ubiquitous product of West African looms . . . it should not be forgotten that probably the greater volume of cloth produced in West Africa is plain white" (Picton and Mack 1979:103).

This image of ubiquitous, mass-produced, plain white cloth hardly suggests the power of white cloth to heal bodies, placate spirits, and metaphorically transcend the world of humans, connecting it with the spirit world. What, for example, are we to make of an incident from southeastern Nigeria described by Mary Kingsley in the 1890s?

An old blind slave was found in the bush, and brought to the Mission [near Creek Town]. . . . She was in a deplorable state . . . but her whole mind was set upon one thing with a passion. . . . What she wanted was a bit, only a bit, of white cloth.   (1988:490–91)

Because white cloth was associated with indigenous religious practices, the missionaries refused to give her this cloth. Kingsley continues:

The old woman, however, kept on pleading and saying the spirit of her dead mistress kept coming to her asking and crying for white cloth, and white cloth she must get for her, and so at last, finding it was not to be got at the Mission station, she stole away one day, unobserved, and wandered off into the bush, from which she never reappeared.

In order to understand why an old woman might die looking for "a bit of white cloth" and why missionaries might prohibit its use, I examine the production and use of white cloth by the Bùnú villagers living to the north and west of the region described by Kingsley.

In Bùnú society until recently,[1] production of white cloth encoded a pattern of social relations between women and men, old and young. Men owned the black cotton seed, which they planted, selling the resulting white cotton fiber to women. Young girls were taught to clean the bolls and remove the seeds, returning the seed to men.[2] These girls then spun thread which older girls and women wove into white cotton cloth. Several types of cloth were woven, all in plain weave and of varying size, weight, and density. Single narrow strips (6 to 8 inches) were woven for use as head bands and waist ties. Wider panels (20 inches) were woven and then sewn together to make large cloths used as wrappers. These cloths ranged in color from grayish off-white to creamy white, depending on the color and cleanliness of the cotton used in spinning.

While the social relations associated with white-cloth production have changed—young girls no longer spin and women may purchase industrial thread at urban markets—white cloth continues to be woven to some extent by older women. In fact, now that few women weave, industrially woven white cloths may be substituted for hand-woven ones, the idea of whiteness taking precedence over traditional production. However, for some things, handwoven white cloth, preferably of handspun cotton, must be used.

White cloth is also used to represent relationships between indi-

viduals and society. The disorderly conduct of individuals in the social world—evidenced by miscarriages, crying fits, and frequent
arguments and illnesses—may be remedied by wearing white cloth
prescribed by diviners. Bodily illness is often associated with disorder in the cosmos, as when evil nature-spirits (*àlùjònú*) are believed
to enter the bodies of pregnant women, causing deformities in unborn children. White cloth is also used in the natural domain, for example, when it is wrapped around the trunks of certain sacred trees
to placate spirits that are believed to reside within them (Awólàlú
1979:49). Thus, the production and use of white cloth in Bùnú society would appear to embody beliefs about the "essential unity of
personal, social and natural domains of Being" (Jackson 1983:143).

There are both ritual and everyday ways in which white cloth pal-
pably communicates these ideas and values. The particular qualities
of white cloth—for example, its color, absorbency, and susceptibility
to decay—make it an evocative symbol for mediating relations among
individuals, social groups, and spirits. Yet its opacity and impermanence also suggest less benign associations, such as hiding and de-
sertion. White cloth, ideally used to facilitate harmonious social and
natural relations, may also be used to subvert them. While cloth may
be used to represent and to placate spirits, it is not always clear
whether these spirits are harmful or helpful. Similarly, the harmonious social relations that the use of white cloth seeks to promote may
not be beneficial for all involved (for example, in relations of domination and subordination).

This appreciation of the ambiguity of social life, where the ideals
of a common good are continually and necessarily being constrained
by countervailing interests,[3] is associated with white cloth. Indeed,
the ambiguous and polysemic associations made with white cloth
may help to explain its continued use by many Bùnú women and men
despite changing beliefs about the regeneration of life and immor-

tality, curing and human agency, and the spirit world. Contrary to Kingsley's European missionaries, many Bùnú Christians continue to use white cloth in religious practice in the hope that it will facilitate conception, cure, and consensus, much as they hope that prayer will provide solutions to these problems of human existence. Yet it is believed that these practices will not always accomplish the desired ends because of conflicting spiritual claims made by others. The longing for the efficacy of white cloth and prayer is tempered by a knowledge that spiritual power may be used for good or ill.[4]

WHITENESS, WATER,
AND THE SPIRIT WORLD

In Bùnú villages, as in other parts of Africa, three colors are named: black (*dúdú*), red (*pupa*), and white (*funfun*).[5] White includes transparent, liquid things such as rain, snail trails, mucus, and tears, as well as shades of white, ecru, and light gray, represented by other bodily substances such as milk, semen, saliva, urine, and genital secretions. Water is perceived as white, and whiteness implies wateriness.[6] For example, when a British district officer brought his new bride to a Bùnú village in the early 1920s, older women begged to touch her white skin. Having touched her, one exclaimed, "It is just like water" (Niven 1982:65). Another district officer's wife had a similar experience, revealing the connection made between her whiteness, heaven, and rain:

At one small village I created a painful impression, apparently; the headmen, who came to the usual interview, lay on the ground, their heads wrapped tightly in their gowns, and groaned aloud, in abject fear. . . . The scare subsided happily, before we left, and they recorded their opinion that I had come straight from heaven, and besought me not to permit it to rain for a day or two.   (Larymore 1911:17)

Similarly, because of their white skin, albinos are often associated with the spirit world (Agbor 1989:32, Larymore 1911:19; Verger 1968:1452), which is conceptualized as "under water" or "in heaven"; the sky, like water, also is described as white (Buckley 1985:57). White cloth, sometimes referred to as *aṣọ ẹbọra* (spirit cloth), is also related to spirits that come from water because of its whiteness.

EJÍNUWỌN SPIRITS,
CHILDREN OF WATER

Bùnú villagers associate the spirit world under water with a particular cult known as *ejínuwọn*, "children of water."[7] This cult consists largely of women who have had trouble conceiving children, who had children who died young, or who themselves were born after several previous siblings died.[8] They are believed to have spirit-doubles who live under water (or at other natural sites) and who routinely trouble them. These spirits may cause them to cry uncontrollably, to quarrel with their neighbors, and to die unexpectedly. Women said that it was a particular whiteness in the eye that indicated one was *ejínuwọn*, a fact that could be confirmed by a diviner.

It is especially important that divination be performed prior to marriage so that proper steps may be taken to protect an *ejínuwọn* bride from "going back" to the spirit world (i.e., dying), which they are prone to do at this time. An *ejínuwọn* bride should wear white on the eve of her marriage because the black marriage cloth, *àdófì*, may cause her to become ill. A woman describes the consequences of not taking these necessary precautions:

They went to Ìkàrẹ́ to buy cloth [for her marriage]. . . . But the bride had forgotten all the things she was supposed to do, so she started shaking and was very sick. Since she was doing traditional marriage her husband should have given her a white sheep, a white cloth, a white chicken, but they all forgot.

Then an *ejínuwọn* woman came and asked, "Have you done her *ejínuwọn* sacrifice before the wedding began?" So the bride's mother went to buy many things. . . . If not, the cold or sickness would have gotten worse and she would have died.   (M. Ọmọ́le, Àghèdẹ-Bùnú)

White cloth is used here as sacrifice in the sense of an exchange. It is acquired to be given to one's *ejínuwọn* spirit, though it does not necessarily indicate a spirit's immediate presence. Indeed, in this instance, the bride's coldness suggests lifelessness, that her own spirit (*ẹlẹ́da*) had left her body and gone back to the spirit world.

Ejínuwọn spirits may come to claim their cloth at any time, which explains the sudden disappearance of white cloth frequently mentioned by *ejínuwọn* women:

I used the first white cloth bought for me by my husband as a cover when I slept. One night I woke up and could not see the cloth. I lit my lantern to search for it, but could not find it. In the morning, I sent a person to consult Ifá. Ifá said that *ejínuwọn* spirits had taken it away.
(D. Kọ́láwọlé, Àgbèdẹ-Bùnú)

Implicit in this comment is the idea that in exchange for white cloth, *ejínuwọn* spirits allow women to live peacefully by leaving them alone.

Ejínuwọn women have the power to attract these spirits by using a set of three, named white cloths, generically known as *àkì*. The cloths are given specific names according to their use—*òjá* is worn around the waist, *àkọjá* is worn over the shoulder and across the breast, and *àkì* is worn around the head. *Ejínuwọn* women may commission the weaving of these three cloths, which are worn during all-night spirit possession dances. These cloths, consisting of a single strip of handwoven handspun cotton, should be woven in one day,[9] after which their long fringes are tied with old Nigerian coins, cowrie and periwinkle shells, and metal bells. The use of these objects sug-

Mrs. Comfort Olútìmáyìn wearing white on the eve of her marriage. Note the àbò yẹyè *(ridiculous marriage basket) and small white chicken to her right, both indications of her spirit status.*
Àgbèdẹ-Bùnú, June 1988.

gests both wealth (coins and cowries served as currency), distance, and spiritual relations (Hocart 1970b:101). None of these objects is indigenous to Bùnú; they must be acquired through trade from far-away places. Unlike other white cloths used by *ejínuwọn* women, which may disappear at any time, these cloths are buried with their owner. As one woman put it, "It doesn't disappear because it already belongs to the spirit. It is the spirit that says one should possess *àkì*" (D. Kọ́láwọlé).

When an *àkì* cloth is tied around an *ejínuwọn* woman's head, it is said to give her supernatural vision: "You will see things as if you are dreaming. If the sick person needs to make a sacrifice, you will know it and will tell her the type of things she has to offer" (D. Ḳ́oláwọlé). Through association with spirits made possible by the use of white *àkì* cloth, the appropriate sacrifice is known and a cure is effected. However, not every woman has this ability, as "she must be a real *ejínuwọn* and not just an ordinary one" (D. Ḳ́oláwọlé).

WHITE CLOTH, SPIRITS, AND HEAVEN

Apart from *ejínuwọn* spirits "under water," whiteness is associated with other spirits said to reside in heaven.[10] While the Bùnú believe in a Supreme Being, Olọ́run (literally, the "owner of heaven"), this relationship is distant and rather vaguely defined.[11] Other Yorùbá groups to the southwest with more elaborate mythologies describe Olọ́run or Olódùmarè as Alálàfunfun-Òkè—"The One clothed in white, Who dwells above."[12] Olódùmarè is also described as an "Essentially White Object, White Material without Pattern" (Ìdòwú 1962:154).

White cloth, associated with spirits in the sky, is used with a complex of objects for inducing rain. These objects are placed in a pot, the neck of which is tied with white cloth.[13] White palm wine is added and the pot's contents are stirred to a foam. If the white foam overflows the pot, stones formed from lightning (*ẹdun pàra*, lightning celts) are added and rain will fall. The whiteness of the palm wine, foam, and cloth are related to the whiteness of the sky; the pot overflowing represents the desired effect of rainfall, which is underscored by the addition of lightning celts. The wrapping of the pot's neck with white cloth also implies spiritual intercession, as when the white *àkì* cloth is tied around an *ejínuwọn* woman's head, inducing possession by her spirit.

Thus the gap between the heavens, the spirit world, and earth may be bridged by the use of white things.[14] This is dramatically illustrated in one Bùnú story of a wife who threw her spindle of spun cotton up to heaven, climbing up the white thread as it unwound, thus escaping from an evil senior wife. Likewise, the man who introduced the powerful women's cult, òfósì, to Bùnú by bringing a special medicine pot wrapped with white cloth, is said to have disappeared after climbing white coils of smoke to heaven (Kennett 1931:437).

Whiteness is related to travel in the opposite direction (i.e., from the spirit world to earth) as when the presence of ancestral and nature spirits is induced by hanging out white cloth, which, as Kingsley described for Calabar shrines, "attracts wandering spirits . . . like earwigs" (1988:495). White cloth may also be used to repel other spirits that may harm a community, house, or farm. A piece is tied to a long pole tied to a tree. After this, "It will not be well with the enemy," as one diviner described it (B. Jethro, Ìsàdó-Kírí-Bùnú). This practice is related to the way in which white cloth, hung around two poles, demarcates the encompassed space, which is then free from evil spirits. White cloth is perceived as attracting beneficial spirits while repelling and reducing the effects of malevolent ones.

One cloth called òrun padà is woven specifically to mediate between ancestor spirits and humans. This predominantly white cloth must be woven in one day, a restriction that applies to several other cloths categorized as spirit cloth. Òrun padà cloth is used in a ritual for divining the identity of ancestors reborn in young children, known as ó mú ni mọ pákó (Verger 1973). A child so identified may wear this cloth at any time, though eventually it becomes threadbare and disappears: "Òrun padà can disappear because it is for the spirit. If you miss it, you should not worry because the owner has come to collect it" (M. Zaccheus, Àkútúpá-Kírí-Bùnú). The owner

Young Bùnú girl wearing the
white ancestral cloth, ọrun padà.
Àkútúpá-Kírí-Bùnú, April 1988.

is the ancestral spirit reborn in the child. Several individuals, men
and women, reported the disappearance of these cloths, which
they attributed to spirits, including one man who put his own *ọrun*
padà cloth in his box, only to find it gone when he looked for it
again.

These images of cloth suggest lines of connection between the world of humans and that of spirits—white thread descending from heaven, white cloth attracting good spirits while repelling evil ones, and white cloth used for the reincarnation of ancestral spirits. The image of *òrun padà*—woven for a particular individual, then worn to shreds and disappearing—poignantly expresses the recycling of ancestor spirits in individual bodies that become frail and turn into dust. Paradoxically, the impermanence of old cloth, which disintegrates and disappears, entails its replacement with a new one, which in turn contributes to a sense of continuity (Kuchler 1988). Indeed, the disappearance of white ancestral and spirit cloths parallels the way in which spirit-souls inhabiting temporal bodies can "go back" at any time. These spirits are then reborn in the new bodies of descendants, much as old white cloths are replaced by identically woven new ones.

WHITE CLOTH AND
CONTINUITY IN TIME

The idea of endless continuity is reinforced by the processes of spinning and weaving. In spinning, a continuous thread miraculously emerges from an amorphous mass of white fluff. Bùnú women also weave on looms on which the warp threads literally revolve, exemplifying circularity. Cloths are often removed without cutting, accentuating the unending quality of these pieces. When eventually the unwoven warp is cut in order to use the cloth, the fringes are left, again suggesting continuity rather than the finiteness of cut and hemmed edges (Schneider and Weiner 1986:180).

An emphasis on cloth's absorbent quality also underscores this sense of connection and continuity. Cloth and threads attract spirits, soak up prayers to ancestors sprayed on their surfaces, and absorb bodily substances such as blood and urine.[15] Because of their intimate association with bodies and bodily substances, cloths are likened to wombs carrying children[16] and to outer skins. Indeed, Bùnú masquerades consist entirely of cloth (Àrèmú 1982.6). This imagery of wrapped fetuses, bodies, and spirits is most commonly depicted in rites of passage at death, birth, and marriage.[17] A corpse is wrapped in a white cloth when buried, before being reborn as an ancestor. Brides who are known to have difficult *ejínuwọn*,or spirit-doubles, will be wrapped in white cloth on the eve of the performance of traditional marriage. In some parts of Yorubaland, a new wife's virginity may be tested by the use of a white cloth, which is later used to carry her first-born child (Ajísafẹ́ 1924:57). White cloth is used to wrap individuals traversing the boundaries of the spirit and human worlds.

SOCIETY, INDIVIDUALS, AND WHITE CLOTH

While white things are used ritually to connect the spiritual and social worlds and represent collectively held beliefs about the unitary nature of the society and the world, individuals may use white cloth in more idiosyncratic ways. When individuals are quarrelsome, cry inexplicably, are frequently sick, or bear many children who die, their problems are said to be caused by displeased spirits that call for individual attention. Diviners ascertain exactly which type of spirit is troubling an individual and may prescribe white cloth. For example, a sickly child who is an *àbíkú* spirit will be wrapped in white cloth. When I had a series of terrifying dreams about strange men and expanses of water, I was told by a diviner that my *ejínuwọn* spirit was troubling me and to sleep under white cloth. As an extra precaution, I was to rest my head on it as well. One man, who had badly cut his hand, dressed in white to honor the ancestral spirit of his maternal grandfather when he recovered. A woman whose spirit was divined to have been brought to the village by a hunter commissioned a special hunter's shirt made of white cloth (*àwòdẹ*) for herself.

One herbalist told me that as a precautionary measure, all women should wear white cloth because of their various spirits. Several women did say that they became ill as a result of not properly accommodating spirit-doubles. One woman described a common sign of this jeopardized state—fainting and feeling cold even though it was sunny outside. The remedy for such seizures is to wrap the victim in white cloth. Thus illness is often associated with individual spirits out of control, resulting in socially disruptive behavior that can be made right with white cloth.

The extreme form of this antisocial behavior is the premature death of women and children whose spirit-doubles cause them to "go back" to the spirit world under water or in heaven. In several Bùnú stories told by men, women are portrayed as having skin "as slippery as okra" or "slippery like fish." In such instances cloth may be used to represent the difficulties and tenuousness of personal relations.[18] In one story, a new wife is rescued from a stream in which the residing spirits have threatened to change her into a fish. Her husband, a king, rejoicing at her recovery, showers her with gifts, including sumptuous cloths for her to wear. However, as the cloths are arranged on her body, they slide off her slippery, wet skin. The king picks up the cloths and encircles her with both the fallen cloths and his arms.

WHITE CLOTH AND

CONTRADICTORY INTENT

Much as individual Bùnú villagers draw upon larger societal associations between whiteness, water, and spirit, individuals with different conceptions of the cosmos may nonetheless appropriate these associations for their own uses. J. O. Babalọlá, one of the founders

of the evangelical Christ Apostolic Church movement, had his own
vision about setting the world aright and about the rebirth of spirit.
That church's revival movement, known as *Omi Ìyè* (water of life),
swept through southwestern Nigeria during the social and economic
difficulties of the 1930s:

Babalọlá clad in white shorts and shirt, with Bible and handbell, preached
to the people to renounce evil practices and witchcraft, and to bring out
for burning all their idols and juju, for God was powerful enough to
answer all their needs, and to cure them.   (Peel 1968:91)

Thousands came to hear him speak, to partake of the life-giving
water he was dispensing,[19] and to convert to Christianity. Babalọlá
astutely relied on a configuration of symbols (white cloth and water)
and techniques for healing that, while used differently, resonated
with prior beliefs about the creation of life, the longing for harmony
in social and personal relations, and the longing for a sense of unity
in the cosmos.

When Babalọlá came to Kàbbà in 1930, many Bùnú people attended, not all with benevolent intentions. According to one Bùnú
woman who was there: "Some witches came with their special whistles and tried them on him but they didn't work so some became birds
and flew away—some had their whistles burnt" (R. Mọni, Àpàá-
Bùnú). Another participant described the euphoria of many, who
threw their charms and medicine into the huge bonfire as Babalọlá
prayed that the disease, death, and drought attributed to witches and
sorcerers would no longer harm them (F. Ọbásàjú, Kàbbà). Their actions expressed their longing for a renewed sense of order during a
period of disease and economic distress, in a world perceived as "falling apart," a result of the changes in the social, economic, and political order brought about by colonial rule. Some "flew away," rejecting
the new authority of those with Christian solutions based on prayer
and revelation inspired by Biblical texts. However, many converted,

acknowledging their disaffection with old beliefs that did not seem effective in solving problems of a different social and political order. Yet after Babalǫlá left, people continued to become ill and die. While remaining Christians, some people again attempted to control some forms of illness and death that were impervious to prayer through Ifá divination and the use of white cloth.

Because of white cloth's particular qualities—its unpatterned whiteness, its absorbency, and its propensity to disappear—it continues to be perceived by many as linking spiritual, social, and personal domains. It is used metaphorically to wrap, tie, or cover when some sort of disjunction between these domains—the cause of certain illnesses, nightmares, and lack of rain—is divined. Yet some characteristics of white cloth, such as its opacity, suggest ways in which these beneficial uses may be subverted. Some of the ambiguities of white cloth use have been mentioned, such as when white cloth is tied to a pole as protection from the malevolence of others. The diviner's remark that "all would not go well with the enemy" suggests more than simple protection, despite moral justification, from evil intentions.

Indeed, when white cloth is hung around two poles to demarcate space associated with spirit, there is no assurance that the spirit invoked is necessarily good. The opacity of white cloth may hide and protect evil as well as good intentions. For example, I was told that a man whose belongings had been stolen went to the owner of a particularly dangerous spirit, known as *sìgìdì*, in order to avenge his loss. When he entered the room where the clay figure representing the *sìgìdì* was kept, the figure itself was hidden by a white cloth, emphasizing the spiritual quality of the *sìgìdì*. The danger and destruction associated with this spirit, however, is indicated by its description as "a suffocating spirit" causing nightmares (Morton-Williams 1960:6).[20]

Moreover, while white cloth can absorb "sprayed" saliva and beneficial prayers intoned to calm a disruptive spirit-double, it can also absorb more sinister messages which can cause its wearer to fall ill. If the cause of an illness is so divined, the victim's cloth must be burnt entirely in order for a cure to be effective (O. Ezekiel, Aíyétórò-Kírí-Bùnú).

Finally, the social equality suggested by the use of patternless, generically named white cloth by *ejínuwon* spirit-cult members is belied by their use of distinctively named white *àkì* cloths. While the use of three types of *àkì* cloth does not identify individual *ejínuwon* spirits during possession as in Hausa Bori spirit possession, their restricted ownership does distinguish those who possess them from other *ejínuwon* women. This distinction is underscored by one woman's comment that only "real *ejínuwon*" as opposed to "ordinary ones" attain special curing insights during possession. It suggests how the use of *àkì* cloth contributes to ranking within *ejínuwon* cults, despite the fact that the plainness of *ejínuwon* cloths suggests commonality and cult unity. These contradictory tendencies of ranking and individual interest as opposed to egalitarianism and the common good are reflected in the uses of plain, white cloth.[21]

White cloth embodies beliefs about and longing for unity and harmony in the world. Bùnú associate white cloth with the whiteness of heaven, the watery spirit world, whiteness of skin and eye, mother's milk, semen, and vaginal fluids. Turner (1967:90) has suggested that these primary bodily substances and experiences "are the *fons* and *origo* of all classification." I want to emphasize another aspect of these bodily phenomena, namely their temporality and tenuousness. Breast milk may cease to flow, watery semen may flow involuntarily (Buckley 1985:75), and tears may fail to fall from dry eyes. White cloth relates this tenuousness of bodily substances to the problematics of social relations, individuals' bodies, and spirits. For spirits may harm or help, water may invoke images of fertility or slippery evasiveness, and one's closest kin may love or curse. These contradictory relationships are poignantly reflected in the ambiguous nature of cloth, which may be used both to support and protect, but which also may harm and conceal. The difficulties of knowing whom to trust and whom to suspect in the face of these contradictions is reflected in the use of cloth as medicine (chapter 3).

THREE

CLOTH

AS MEDICINE

He recalled again the shock
which had accompanied his letter
of appointment. And his father
had been cautious—they will try
to kill you, he warned. If they can,
they will harm you. So you must
come home first and let us
prepare the necessary
protection. . . .
Ṣóyínká, Ìsarà

Through its association with the whiteness of skin, water, and the sky, white cloth conveys a sense of unity and interconnectedness among personal, social, and natural domains. Some types of illness, conceptualized as a disruption in the connection between these spheres, may be remedied through the use of white cloth. However, as is suggested by the above excerpt from the novel Ìsarà by Wọlé Ṣóyínká, there are people—envious, avaricious, or mean-spirited—who wish others harm, and this sense of harmonious holism is not so easily maintained. One must sometimes take defensive action against the threatening powers of others with their own medicinal arsenals, using things and substances which will offer protection. Thereafter, one would not be "afraid to shake hands with them, not even caring what kind of dye-blackened rings they wore on their fin-

gers" (Șóyínká 1989:101). Șóyínká does not specify what protective
substances, referred to as medicine (ogùn), were employed in the
case he cites. In Bùnú, cotton cloth (or thread or lint) is frequently
used in such instances. Neither the idea of medicinal protection
against the intentions of others nor the use of cloth as a pharma-
ceutical specific are commonly associated by westerners with medical practice.[1] Yet many Bùnú villagers do make these associations. In
this chapter I focus on how cloth used as medicine reflects Bùnú notions of illness and cure and why cloth would be deemed an appropriate material for addressing particular complaints. I also consider
the ambiguous social roles of those who use cloth medicinally and of
diviners who prescribe it.

By examining Bùnú ideas about illness and cure from the perspective of cloth, this chapter also emphasizes the importance of
metaphor in healing (Jackson 1989:147) and how ideas about cure
and disease are related to social relations and religious belief (Bloch
1973; Evans-Pritchard 1956; deHeusch 1981; Turner 1967, 1969).
Because cloth is used to represent connections between the social
and spiritual world, it should not be surprising that it is used in cases
of illness believed to result from disruption of these connections.
Cloth is also perceived as an appropriate object for altering bodily
states because of its physical proximity to the human body, its ability
to absorb bodily secretions, and its likeness to skin (Schneider and
Weiner 1986:179).[2] In Bùnú, bodily disorder may be physically remedied through wrapping and wiping with cloth and by filling inci-
sions with cloth derivatives such as ash. Further, cloth which has
been worn is said to absorb the perspiration and essence of its owner
and thus may serve as a skinlike substitute for an individual in certain forms of therapeutic sacrifice.[3] Yet this close association of cloth
with its wearer may also be dangerous. The corner of a cloth stolen

from its owner may serve as a surrogate for others with less benevolent intentions. An incantation over a piece of purloined cloth may cause illness or death to its owner.[4]

Cloth is also used metaphorically to represent a connection between bodily health and social states. For example, the act of covering the body with cloth is often conflated with the idea of having social support. The saying Èniyàn l'aṣọ mi, "people are my cloth," refers to the way that people's family and friends protect and support them.[5] A person without social ties and without cloth is unsupported and exposed. Such people may be literally thought of as mad.[6] Indeed, the epitome of antisocial beings, witches (àjé) and wizards (oṣó), are also described as "cloth-less" or naked when they fly about at night. Yet such individuals—who are believed to cause illness and death by their nightly sojourns—will be dressed during the day like everyone else, cloth providing the means for their deceptive behavior.

ILLNESS, SOCIAL RELATIONS, AND CLOTH AS CURE

Cloth is often used as medicine for protection in morally ambiguous situations in which one individual might well wish another harm. An understanding of the ambivalence felt by Bùnú villagers toward individuals of extraordinary achievement and wealth helps to explain its use in such cases.

Why some people should be successful while others suffer misfortune is mysterious. While respected and envied, the former are also threatening because they are suspected of acquiring their success at the expense of others. Successful people may even be suspected of being witches or wizards, using medicines that immobilize or kill rivals, though these measures are not as common as in the past according to one man. Instead:

Some are now looking for a way of getting good things from life. Some who have four eyes [*olójúmẹ́rin*, literally, "owners of four eyes," i.e., witches and wizards] are now using the power they possess to better their condition, for example, that their own children should not be cheated by others. They train their children in schools and some people try to protect their children with the use of medicine so that if such children travel, they will come back safely. (Z. Olú, Àpàá-Bùnú)

Those who employ medicine to harm others are morally frowned upon. Yet there are times when the use of such medicines to enhance one's power is socially accepted, at least indirectly. As the above quotation suggests, people whose power is suspected to derive from witchcraft and the use of offensive medicines may also educate their children and build block houses with iron roofs. They are respected for contributing to the development of the town or village.

What seems to be expressed in this ambivalence toward achievement is the idea that the forces that make success possible for some may also, by necessity, be the source of ill fortune or disease for others. Suspicions about the sources of power of those with wealth and office are also reflected in attitudes about illness and infertility whose causes are similarly uncertain. When one co-wife has abundant children and another has recurring miscarriages, people may suspect that medicine is being used.

This ambiguous attitude toward the morality of success is illustrated more clearly by the use of a type of medicine called *ogùn sòra* prepared with white cloth by Bùnú diviners. As is the case with some types of cloth used as medicine, this medicine protects a person by turning harmful medicine back on its perpetrator. It also has a built-in "tamper-proof" mechanism that prevents it from being used directly to harm someone else. If a person owning this medicine uses it to wish illness on another, the illness will befall the owner instead. In fact, keeping such medicine is thought to be dangerous for the owner, who must take care not to misuse it for fear of the consequences. While the suspicion that someone may be trying to harm you justifies the use of *ogùn sòra* medicine, it is a poignant reminder that no one is free from wishing ill toward others and that one is culpable for harm done, regardless of whether it was intentional or not. The particular danger associated with misusing *ogùn sòra* medicine suggests that there is a fine line between the use of medicine with the intention of protecting oneself and its use for harming another.

People need to use protective medicine because others use harmful ones. The idea of balancing opposing harmful and protective forces resonates with Ọ̀yọ́ Yorùbá ideas about maintaining bodily health. In his discussion of Yorùbá traditional medicine, Buckley (1985) argues that good health results from the proper balance of worms and germs in the body. Thus, many diseases are believed to be caused by an excess of worms and germs, not by their absence. Further, it is often the excessive behavior (eating too much sweet food, having too many sexual partners, etc.) of an individual that results in an imbalance and the onset of disease (Buckley 1985:49–51). This conception of health as the balance of two opposing states is key to understanding cure. If an excess of worms, germs, food, or sex is believed to cause a certain type of illness, the illness may be cured by changing one's behavior or by using medicines to counter these excesses (Buckley 1985:47–48), just as the effects of medicines used by those wishing harm may be countered by the use of medicines that protect or appease.

CLOTH AS

PROTECTIVE MEDICINE

This idea of balancing opposing things in cure is literally reflected in the use of black and white threads in medicine. When these opposing colors are combined, things happen. The earth's black surface is penetrated by rain, described as white, resulting in agricultural fecun-

Aṣọ ìpò cloth (ọ̀já, àbatá, and ìfalẹ̀) hung in front of the house of the late Chief David Láràiyetàn. The pot at the lower right was used as a drum by ọ̀fòsì women's cult members as they danced and sang in front of the cloths during funeral observances.

Àpáá-Bùmú, December 1987.

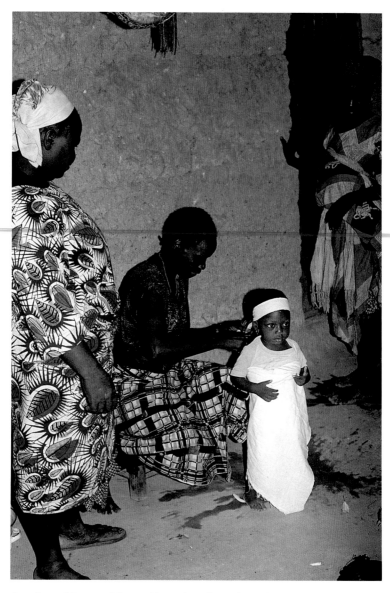

Daughter of Peter and Grace Ọlọ́runfẹmí, being dressed with white cloth by the ejínuwọn cult leader, Mrs. Deborah Kọ́láwọlé, while the child's maternal and paternal grandmothers look on.
Àpàá-Bùnú, July 1988.

Mrs. Mésin Mọni wearing a women's hunter's shirt (àwọdẹ).
Àpàá-Bùnú, December 1987.

Family members of the bride count the marriage cloths in the wife's marriage basket (àbò) *to make sure the requisite number are present.*
Àkútúpá-Kírí-Bùnú, April 1988.

Bùnú brides wearing their àdófì *cloth wrappers on a "trip to the market" during the performance of traditional marriage.*
Àkútúpá-Kírí-Bùnú, April 1988.

The Bùnú masquerade known as Iyelúgbó with its "handler," during performance at Òkè-Bùkún-Bùnú, April 1988.

Chief Selewa Àyìnmódè, the Olú-Kírí, wearing regalia of a northern Bùnú king.
Aíyétórò-Kírí-Bùnú, January 1988.

Wives Janet and Kẹ́hìndé Ògúníbì (center and right) distributing water about the town as part of traditional marriage performance. They are wearing the marriage cloth awẹ̀rẹ̀ *as wrappers, with* ojúedewó *cloths on their shoulders and* ọrun padà *cloths on their heads.*
Àgbẹ̀dẹ-Bùnú, December 1987.

Grace and Joel Baiyésheá wearing outfits made of aṣọ òyìnbó, *industrially woven cloth. The woman's wrapper and top are made of black printed cotton while the man's pants, top, and hat are made of a cotton twill cloth called One Gambari.*
Àgbèdẹ-Bùnú, *December 1991.*

dity; and the white semen of men penetrates the black bodies of women, resulting in children (Buckley 1985:56). Men, associated with white cloth, and women, associated with black (Àrèmú 1982:9), come together to make new life.

Similarly, opposing black and white threads wrapped together activate the medicine they cover. As one Bùnú diviner described it: "One can wrap black and white threads around some herbs, which will make the medicine powerful. . . . When you put them together, [you know that] white cannot be black and black cannot be white. So if you say you want to do something for your child, it will happen. . . . When I say something, it can't be something else" (Z. Olú). When I asked why black and white thread worked in this way, several people mentioned the word *ahínimóni*, which means something that acts like a catalyst, triggering a reaction. *Ahínimóni* is used to describe a range of actions which set off opposing forces, causing them to "fight." Thus, a child whose behavior provokes two adults to quarrel is described as *ahínimóni*.[7] Black and white threads do not cure or protect by themselves but rather activate substances that do.

One man described the preparation of a particular medicine called *àdàbò*, which incorporates black and white threads. *Àdàbò* is used for protection against illness and death by countering and deactivating harmful medicines prepared by others. Its preparation and use illustrate several principles of certain types of Bùnú protective medicine. Black and white threads cover an egg wrapped with special leaves.[8] The thread-wrapped egg is covered with clay and then thrown at a wall. If the egg sticks, the medicine will not work; however, if it falls from the wall, the egg is removed, the thread unwound, and the patient eats the cooked leaf and egg mixture. Thereafter, the person is protected from the effects of harmful medicines.

There are three aspects to the use of this medicine: imitation, activation, and incorporation (MacGaffey 1977:174). First, it imitates the desired effect. Just as the mud-egg does not stick to the wall, the evil intentions of others will not "stick" to the person using the medicine. Second, by wrapping the egg and leaves in black and white threads, the power of the medicine is activated. Third, the activated ingredients are ingested, becoming a part of the patient whom they protect.

Much as bodies are protected by ingesting herbs and eggs whose medicinal powers are activated by black and white thread, so houses and bodies are also protected by medicinal amulets (*èle*) wrapped with black and white thread, which are placed above doorways and around necks or waists, respectively. These amulets protect houses and individuals and their property[9] by threatening harm to thieves and others. Black and white threads may also be used to activate invisible substances within bodies. Known as *mágùn*, literally, "don't mount," these substances are said to protect against other forms of antisocial behavior such as adultery. Black and white threads laid on a threshold, and consequently stepped over by a woman, activate this *mágùn* substance within her (Awólàlú 1979:77–78; Ìbéjìgbà 1988). Any man other than her husband who has intercourse with her will become deathly ill, though the woman herself is unaffected. The man may possibly die unless he confesses and an herbal antidote is administered. Thus, while black and white threads activate medicine that protects against evil intentions, theft, and adultery, the consequences of its use may be life-threatening to the guilty party (Jacobson-Widding 1979).

CLOTH AS MEDICINE
THAT PLACATES

Sacrifice in the context of healing serves a similar purpose to black and white threads. As one traditional healer remarked, "Sacrifice is what makes medicine work" (O. Baiyéré, Tẹ̀dó-Kírí-Bùnú). Any cloth prescribed by a diviner, though it need not be a black and white one, may be used as a sacrifice.[10] Sacrifice, which includes killing animals and distributing meat as well as giving something of value such as a precious cloth, is also related to the idea of placating opposing forces. Cloth may be given as "sacrifice" to the physically unfortunate. Lepers and the blind were most commonly mentioned, these people being associated with the spiritual domain (Evans-Pritchard 1956; Jackson 1989). In exchange, they convey blessings that counter the opposing intentions of others, thus allowing for protection or efficacious cure.

Many ailments associated with sacrifices of cloth are also associated with particular parts of the body, namely the head and the womb, possibly because these are conceptualized as the sites of spiritual presence in the body. The head, *orí*, is the site of a person's spirit, which determines one's destiny (also *orí*), while the womb (*inú*, inside, or *ilé-ọmọ*, literally, house of the child) is perceived as a sort of halfway house for a child who is between the spirit and human worlds. These parts of the body are believed to be both vulnerable and amenable to spiritual intervention through the sacrifice of cloth.

One diviner eloquently expressed the importance of making sacrifice in facilitating conception and childbirth:

It is like a door locked against a person who wants to enter. If the door is not opened, the person will remain outside. It is like that for a woman who is looking for a child. Ifá may tell her that if she does not make the prescribed sacrifice, the child will be locked out. . . . If she heeds the advice of Ifá, she will have a child.   (Z. Olú)

Ifá diviners, because of their ability to "see both sides" of doors, will know the appropriate sacrifice to make. Because cloth relates individual bodies of the personal domain with the spirit domain from which children are believed to come, diviners often prescribe it as sacrifice to mediate between these two domains. If a woman has trouble conceiving, she may go to a diviner who will prescribe a cure:

If a woman hasn't borne children and wants to have them, the oracle may tell her to use white cloth to carry an animal on her back. Ifá will tell the woman to go to a certain place, carrying that animal. When she gets there, she should remove the animal and the cloth, giving them out to a blind person or leper. She will then become pregnant.   (B. Jethro)

In this case, a woman imitates the desired end, the birth of a child to be carried on her back with cloth. The cloth and the object carried (it can be an animal or anything that the diviner prescribes) are then given out, in other words, sacrificed, so that through the counter-blessings of the afflicted, a child can be conceived.

Once a woman is pregnant, she may continue to use white cloth, either wearing it or sleeping on it as a pillow, particularly if she is a member of the water spirit cult, *ejínuwọn*. Such use protects a woman from *ejínuwọn* spirits who are believed to be a source of disturbance during childbirth. Cloth may also be given out during labor to prevent these problems:

At the time of giving birth, an *ejínuwọn* woman may have made a promise to go back [to the spirit world, i.e., to die]. People will look for a certain leaf (*tùwàre*) which when burnt smells very bad to *ejínuwọn* spirits. They will then hate the laboring woman and will not allow her to join them. But if they ask for anything—it may be cloth, a chicken, pigeon or goat—it must be given.   (M. Zaccheus)

Cloth may also be given as an exchange with human beings whose ill will causes them to interfere with young women's fertility or ability to bear live children. Conceptualized as witches or wizards—the former often described as older women, the latter older men—these people are said to have spirits that attack members of their own family at night.[11] For example, to prevent recurring still-births, cloth is given to an older postmenopausal woman at the performance of a protective ritual using the black marriage cloth, *ojúedewó*. In performing this ritual, a pregnant woman will prepare three steamed white, guinea-corn cakes. Wearing *ojúedewó* cloth, she takes the cakes to the market where she eats them. At the same time, she is rubbed with red camwood and marked with white chalk. She then goes to the stream and bathes, removing the *ojúedewó* and changing into another cloth, which she wears during the trip back to her house. There, a cloth that she had worn during her last unsuccessful pregnancy is given to an elderly person in her family, usually a woman. Afterwards, it is said that she will bear healthy children.

The black marriage cloth and red camwood are references to traditional marriage, which is performed in part to enhance the fertility of women (see chapter 4). The white chalk refers to spiritual intervention of some kind. The fact that this cloth is given to a family member, usually an older woman, is significant. It suggests that the woman's still-births were attributed to the grudges or jealousies of family members. Belying the expectations of benevolent behavior on the part of one's closest relations, this giving of cloth expresses the belief that they may actively, if secretly, be working against you. These ambiguous actions are countered by the giving of cloth.

Cloth may be used as a sacrificial substitute for the life of an individual. One woman described an incident in which a diviner advised her that some people were trying to harm her children. The woman swore that she would be willing to sacrifice anything to save them: "Later, when I opened my box to use one of my marriage cloths, I found that all had been eaten by termites. I sent someone to an Ifá diviner who said that I should be thankful, that what I had said, God had accepted. That was why my children were spared" (O. Ezekiel). This episode underscores the close connection made between cloth and the vitality of children. Cloth is used as sacrifice in exchange for spiritual blessings or protection, which are believed to bring children to barren women and, later, to insure children's lives, health, and longevity in the face of opposing wishes of co-wives and others who may threaten them.

Cloth may also be prescribed for afflictions that threaten a member of a descent group or household more generally. Several people described taking a sick family member's cloth (or a cloth from anyone of their lineage living in the same house) and burning or burying it. Similarly, a sick person could be told by a diviner to take a cloth and wipe it over their body. The cloth would then be given out or abandoned on a road and the affected person would recover. Or, on the other hand,

if someone is sick and the disease is not ordinary [i.e., it is the result of witchcraft], they [the family] will go to a diviner and be told what to do. They will use the cover cloth of the sick person to go about in the morning, greeting people. When you get back home, you take eighty *kóbò* [10 cents US, in 1988], fold the cloth and give the cloth and the money to some person. The person who was sick will survive the burial of the person who caused the sickness.   (O. Baiyéré)

Similar actions are taken to prevent such misfortunes from affecting an entire household. One man said that in the past, a diviner would advise the head of a house to protect members of his family by sacrificing a particular cloth owned by a family member. The cloth could be given out to a leper, a blind man, or a drummer, or it could be thrown into the bush, so that it would decay (i.e., be taken by a spirit). Just as the cloth would be given, so would protection against disease and death be obtained for his family.

In these cases, the idea behind burning, burying, and giving out cloth is sacrifice as exchange. Something is given so that the afflicting presence—spirit or human—will be placated or subdued.

MEDICINAL CLOTH
AND SOCIAL DOUBLE-BINDS

The tying or knotting of a cloth strip or thread is often associated with the efficacy of a Bùnú incantation or prayer (see Dilley 1986:137). The powers of these words will remain effective until the knot is untied. The idea of the double-bind is somewhat similar to this idea of tying and knotting. A person in a double-bind is like something knotted twice, with allegiances that are both effective and contradictory. Individuals in these ambiguous social positions are frequently mentioned in association with cloth as medicine, used either to harm or to cure.

As the above examples indicate, cloth is often prescribed for reproductive disorders. Because of the positions of women within patrilineages and because of virilocal marriage practices, women often live in households that are not their own but rather those of their husbands. Yet these women retain rights in their own patrilineages and affective ties with these people. Thus they are in the position of the double-bind in that their loyalties are divided and contradictory. Polygynous marriage exacerbates these countervailing tendencies since co-wives tend to be concerned with the health of their own children and their access to their husband's lineage resources, not those of other co-wives. Competition between these women for the attentions and economic largesse of husbands for themselves and their children may result in some women wishing to do their rival co-wives harm.

The position of older postmenopausal women is equally ambiguous. Upon the death of a husband, they do not inherit property and may even be asked by their husband's family to leave their home. The strength of their position depends on their economic acumen and their ties to their children, particularly sons, through whom these women maintain their affinal connections. Yet sons take wives who, though subject to the authority of their husbands' mothers, also may alter mother-son relations. This structural "double-bind" explains, in part, why older women are often the subject of witchcraft accusations.[12] Because children are frequently the focus of rivalry among co-wives and a source of envy for older women worried over their sons' attentions to their wives, childbirth difficulties are often attributed to the malignant intentions of these particular individuals.

The jealousy and insecurity of husbands may also be the source of childbirth difficulties. In Bùnú, as elsewhere, relations between husbands and wives are viewed as problematic ones. The ambivalence felt toward affinal relations in this society is related to local ideas about kin relationships, particularly through patrilineal descent, which continue to be important in defining ties of loyalty. Wives retain membership in their father's lineages, which gives them the option of leaving their husbands and returning to their natal villages. Because husbands need wives who bear children for the continuity of their own patrilineages, they are concerned with controlling the sexuality of these women. Conflict between women and men over the control of sexual relationships and subsequent children is a source of considerable tension in Bùnú villages and may result in individuals taking offensive action.

For example, retaining the placenta after childbirth is said to be caused by three categories of beings—enemies (including co-wives and widows), spirit-doubles, and husbands—as one man explained:

1. If an enemy does not want a safe delivery, he or she will not allow the placenta to come out.
2. If a woman is an ẹlẹ́gbẹ́ [ejínuwọn] and before she has delivered a child, she has promised that she will join her colleagues [fellow spirits], she may deliver but will have a retained placenta [and then die].

3. If a man has a wayward wife who goes about and becomes pregnant by
   another and if the husband is annoyed, there is a way to make a delivery
   difficult and there will be a retained placenta.   (O. Baiyéré)

In the event of retained placenta, a diviner may be consulted. Using
cotton lint and red oil, he invokes an incantation and "calls" the placenta "like a dog." It is said to come out easily thereafter.

The very real dangers of childbirth lead some women to seek additional protection against personal and spiritual exigencies through
the use of cloth. Àrèmú (1982:6) notes that for the Òyó Yorùbá, any
handwoven cloth will serve this purpose: "It is believed that whoever
covers himself [sic] with the *Kíjìpá* [handwoven] cloth is indirectly
protecting himself from the power of evil, illness, disease, misfortunes of accidents, and other calamities and catastrophes."

Cloth used as medicine reflects the difficulties of getting along
with others whose interests are contrary to one's own, yet it points to
the life-and-death necessity to do so for the survival of the community. In Bùnú villages, one of the ways in which the difficulties of interpersonal and social relations are remedied is through consulting
diviners or *babaláwo*. Yet as is implied by the name *babaláwo* (literally,
"father of secrets"), ambiguity and uncertainty surround the motives
of these men, who are in something of a double-bind themselves. For
by knowing curative secrets, they are also suspected of knowing
harmful ones.

FINDING A GOOD BABALÁWO

Bùnú *babaláwo* practice a type of divination in which an oracle or deity, Ifá, is consulted through the casting and subsequent interpre-
tation of four sets of four seed pods, tied together by cord (Obáyemí
1989; cf. Bascom 1984). In Bùnú today, there is usually at least one
babaláwo living in any given village. These men (and occasionally

women) are frequently consulted in cases of illness, their services seen as complementing those of other health professionals, including practitioners of Western medicine in clinics and hospitals. Within Bùnú villages, diviners practice their medical expertise along with others who claim knowledge of traditional medicine, particularly *oniṣẹ́gun*—herbalists (who do not divine) and ritual cult specialists such as *ejínuwọn* women.

Babaláwo, herbalists, and cult specialists are said to share a particular quality, that of extraordinary vision.[13] These individuals, sometimes referred to as *olójúmẹ́rin*, literally, "those with four eyes," are believed to be able to "see" the cause of illness and to prescribe cure. However, their power is viewed with some ambivalence: it is beneficial, but potentially harmful. The ambiguous ethics of their behavior is also related to their position as individuals who are on the periphery of the local political organization of village chiefs.

In Bùnú villages, diviners act as advisors to chiefs yet they do not generally have the wealth or political authority of these men (see Evans-Pritchard 1983:115). In local disputes, the trustworthiness of diviners is suspect, as they may make medicines for both sides (cf. Jackson 1989:54). This distrust is also reflected in the story of the bad *babaláwo* who gave a woman asking for love medicine for her husband poison instead. When the husband subsequently died, the diviner married the woman. This story underscores the belief that not only are some diviners dishonest but that the medicines they prescribe for beneficial purposes may have very different results.

One Bùnú man who had commissioned a type of medicine (*èle*) from a diviner to protect his farm ultimately decided that he could not use it. While it was commissioned as protection, this man considered it too harmful to be used because its red cloth component might cause leprosy, or, as one woman described it, "all the body will be broken" (N. Joseph, Aíyétórò-Kírí-Bùnú). This is why some people say that in using life-threatening medicines such as *èle*, one should also have medicine known as *èrò* (antidote) so as not to be guilty of causing harm in the process of protecting oneself or one's property:

Any *èle* that has no antidote is only used by wicked people. . . . That is why it is necessary that if anybody wants to teach you how to use a particular *èle*, you have to ask what the antidote is. If he is not ready to give you the antidote, the best thing for you to do is abandon the *èle*.
   (J. Ayegboka, Odo-Apè-Bùnú)[14]

Because of the risks associated with such medicines even when used in self-defense, some people have abandoned them entirely, preferring Christian remedies instead. For example, in the past, diviners were consulted, and they made medicine to facilitate difficult deliveries. In the 1990s, in some towns such as Òllè in central Bùnú, some women having childbirth difficulties more often will go to the house of a Christian preacher, relying on the efficacy of prayer rather than on the prescriptions of the local diviner. Others will travel to Dr. Fémi's Clinic, outside of Kàbbà, for medical treatment. In cases which are impervious to prayer and Western medicine, however, many Bùnú villagers continue to consult Ifá diviners and to use cloth as protection from others, hedging their therapeutic bets in the face of uncertain cause.

The uncertainty surrounding the health and wealth of some and the illness and poverty of others is reflected in the suspicions of fellow Bùnú villagers' intentions. Diviners, themselves subject to distrust, attempt to defuse the dangerous social tensions resulting from unequal misfortune. They prescribe remedies to these problems through their special sight, their knowledge of local situations, and the manipulation of material objects, including strings of seed-pods and cloth.

In Bùnú, people use objects such as cloth prescribed by diviners concretely as well as metaphorically to represent the state of social and spiritual relations. Because certain illnesses and reproductive disorders are attributed to the disruption of these relations, cotton cloth and thread—associated with the connection among individuals, spirits, and groups—are often used as remedy in these cases. Specifically, cloth and associated materials may be employed either as protection or sacrifice to counter the effects of harmful medicines employed by others.

These destructive medicines may be used by those wishing to bolster their own good fortune or by those jealous of another's success, though the use of these medicines is sometimes associated with antisocial witchcraft and hence is morally reprehensible. However, those with wealth, fecundity, and long life are also respected because of their achievement. Bùnú villagers' ambiguous attitude toward good fortune is related to the idea of witchcraft as a contradictory force, perceived as both blessing and bane in Bùnú social life. Whether witchcraft is considered good or bad depends, to some extent, on the context of its use (Jackson 1989:93). It fosters the extraordinary success of individuals whose fine houses and educated status may benefit the entire community. Yet the use of harmful medicines is believed to be the cause of illness or death for some community members, sometimes resulting in considerable tension in Bùnú villages—a tension expressed in witchcraft allegations (see chapter 10).

The moral ambiguity associated with illness and health is reflected in the strictures surrounding the use of medicines such as *ogùn sòra* and *èle*. Their use suggests that even those employing medicines with good intentions, i.e., self-protection, can have unintended effects. Only "wicked people" would use *èle* made with red cloth when no antidote was available. And the owners of dangerous *ogùn sòra* medicine, made with white cloth, must take special care not to wish harm on others lest it rebound on themselves.

While cloth is employed as medicine to protect, the ambivalent associations with its use suggest an awareness that unless care is taken, even socially beneficent actions (the protection of children, property, and fertility) may have dire consequences. Conversely, the antisocial use of harmful medicines by individuals (i.e., witchcraft) may have positive social effects (educated children and modern houses) for a community. The use of cloth as medicine in Bùnú suggests that it is not simply a matter of acting either for the social good or for individual self-interest. Rather there is a delicate balance between social and personal concerns that must continually be weighed, for actions in one sphere may have unintended consequences in another.

FOUR

WHY BÙNÚ BRIDES
WEAR BLACK

Aṣọ ni èdìdì ènìyàn,

"cloth is what

binds people."

Yorùbá proverb

Cloth may be used to forge ties of obligation and affection between people as the proverb suggests. It may also be used to sever them:[1]

My own grandmother told me she was going with her cloths [when she died] because her children did not appreciate her. Even before she died, all the cloths that her children would have used were destroyed by termites. If it hadn't been for the termites, she would have told someone to select so-and-so cloths from her box and to bury her with them.
   (O. Ezekiel, Aíyétórò-Kírí-Bùnú)

Yet as Madam Ezekiel, the elderly Bùnú woman who recounted this example of grandmotherly revenge and termite-ridden cloths, observed:

It is better if you have anything against relations to announce it so that matters may be settled and they can inherit the cloth which will make them remember you. Even if a cloth is worn and you would like to throw it away, you should keep a tiny piece to show your children that a [former] relative had this cloth.

Family relations may be difficult to maintain, but the need for economic backing and access to family land and the longing for a sense of social grounding encourage individuals to continue these relationships, despite the knowledge that family members often disappoint. And as Madam Ezekiel later remarked, cutting these relationships by "taking it with you" was ultimately self-defeating. Rather, it is better to air grievances and mend ruptures by giving and receiving cloth.

Younger and older Bùnú women attempt to create a sense of connection and mutual, if unequal, obligation by giving and receiving black marriage cloths. These relationships may be seen concretely by examining the use of black cloth in becoming a Bùnú bride. The social and economic relations and obligations between older and younger women entailed in the exchanges and ritual uses of black cloth are related in turn to beliefs about women, fertility, and spirits. They have also changed in time. Thus it is only through an historical analysis of these relationships—economic, social, and spiritual— that the question of why Bùnú brides wear black can be answered.[2]

Nowadays, black marriage cloths are generally lent by older kinswomen to younger ones since these cloths, with one exception, are no longer being woven and young women no longer know how to weave. Saturated with indigo dye so as to appear black,[3] these cloths represent tremendous amounts of time and labor in their production. The fact that they presently are no longer being made also contributes to their value, as they are irreplaceable. Essential in the performance of Bùnú traditional marriage, which every Bùnú village woman should perform before she dies, the keeping and using of these cloths is a poignant example of how Bùnú village women attempt to maintain intergenerational ties of affection and obligation in the face of social and economic forces (such as migration to urban centers) that undermine them. The continued use of black cloth is also related to an attempt by older, married village women to maintain their authority over younger unmarried ones through control of local economic resources and their knowledge of traditional marriage ritual and midwiving practices. In Bùnú villages, these relations of super- and subordination are reflected in the privileged status of

TABLE 1

THIRTEEN NAMED CLOTHS

IN MARRIAGE BASKET

Cloth name	Description
TOP BASKET	
Àtufù	Predominantly dark blue, with tiny white and red stripes; fringed
Awèrè	Predominantly dark blue, with tiny white stripes
Ojúedewó	Predominantly dark blue, with white checking
(2 types)	Predominantly dark blue, with white, red (silk) stripes
Máabò	Predominantly dark blue with red bands
Òrun patí	Predominantly white, with blue and red edging
Òrun padà	Predominantly white, with tiny red stripes; fringed
Òjá (2)	Red and white sashes
BOTTOM BASKET	
Ojúedewó	Predominantly dark blue with white
(4 types)	Predominantly dark blue with ikat patterning
	Predominantly dark blue with ikat patterning
	Predominantly dark blue with wide red silk stripe

women who have performed traditional marriage and who may wear one specific black marriage cloth, *àdófì*, in public. Women who have not done so are said to have *isò*, "shame," and must not be seen wearing this cloth.[4] Indeed, the production of black marriage cloths themselves served to confirm these relations of authority and subordination (Brett-Smith 1990/91), in which the economics of indigo dyeing played a significant part.

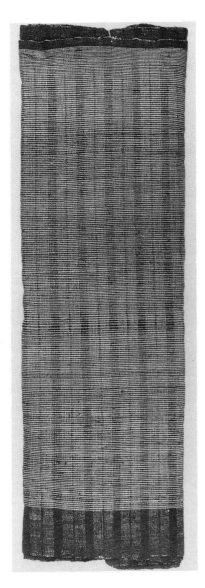

This cloth was bought by members
of the Niger Expedition at Egga
Market in 1843. Its accession card
reads, "Cloth of blue and white
threads in woven. Female dress
used by higher classes. Made by
natives on and behind the
mountain. Abunu, back of
Egga. 3,500 cowries"
British Museum Collection,
AF 1843 A0311, 43 3-11 45.

PRODUCING AND ACQUIRING
BLACK MARRIAGE CLOTHS

Prior to 1950, a group of named, distinctively warp-striped cloths of predominantly black, indigo-dyed, handspun cotton thread were woven in Bùnú for use in traditional marriage (Table 1). Generally these cloths appear not to have been woven for sale in the market, although one cloth collected by the Niger Expedition in 1843 at Egga, attributed to Bùnú weavers, closely resembles the marriage cloth known as *kẹ́tẹ́kènín* (Johnson 1973). Other predominantly indigo-dyed, black cloths—such as the prestigious black-and-white plaid cloth, *ọlọ́ba*, and the blue and black, warp striped cloth, *fágbò*—were woven for nonritual purposes, but generally these cloths were personally woven or commissioned. When they were sold, prices ranged from three to five times as much as prices paid for predominantly white cloths (Table 2). This was because of the expense and labor involved in indigo dyeing as well as the quantity of indigo needed to dye cloth black. Indigo enhanced a cloth's value, much like gold-plating.[5]

INDIGO-DYEING

Indigo-dyeing was a specialized skill practiced by Bùnú women of particular clans. It is not clear whether this craft was restricted to these families (as was the case with such occupations as blacksmithing and brass working [Krapf-Askari 1966b]) or whether they monopolized this market for other reasons (for example, being particularly skillful, having knowledge of special techniques,[6] or having advantageous access to *àlú* indigo vines [*Lonchocarpus cyanescens*]). As distinctive styles of Bùnú cloth design depended on variations of blue-black warp and weft striping, the demand for indigo-dyed yarns was considerable. This demand was reflected in its price.

Knowledge of the indigo-dyeing process was limited to insiders in

TABLE 2

CLOTHS SOLD

BY BÙNÚ WEAVERS

Cloth	Description (no. of pieces)	Price*
Kẹkẹ	White w/blue stripes (2)	3–8 shillings
Ọ̀run	All white (3)	15 shillings
Ojúedewó	Blue shades w/white stripes (2)	8–10 shillings
Àkù	White w/thin blue stripes (2)	5–10 shillings
Fágbò	Dark, medium blue, white stripes (2)	6–10 shillings
Àláàgi	White w/blue stripes (2–3)	3–15 shillings
Arigidi	White w/thin blue stripes (2)	1–2 shillings
Aṣọ ipò	Red wool geometric patterning (1)	3–9 shillings

*Prices are approximate and vary according to number of strips, length of strips, and period sold.

several ways. Ashes were scattered near the dyepots to warn un-welcome others away—these included menstruating women, members of different clans, and strangers to the village. As further protection, the dyepots were also covered, safeguarding them from the looks of such people, who could cause a dyepot to "be spoiled." For example, menstruating women were said to cause a dyebath to spoil (see Byfield 1989) or become red (Fádìpẹ̀ 1970). Postmeno-pausal kinswomen reinforced their control of this craft by asserting that they were least likely to upset the indigo dyepot's precarious chemistry.

Bùnú woman appear to have used techniques in the preparation of indigo dye similar to those of women of other Yorùbá groups (Abíọlá 1980; Barbour and Simmonds 1971; Oyèníyì 1979; Picton and Mack 1979). As one older woman described:

I dyed with indigo (*aró*) at Òkè-Bùkún; the woman who taught me how to
spin taught me how to dye. First you looked for *àlú* and *semse* leaves—but
you wouldn't see these leaves during the dry season. Then they collected
àbètè wood and other types of wood for ash which they put in a basket and
poured water inside, which dripped into a pot. They then put *àlú* and
other leaves in a large pot and soaked them, covered, for five days.
After that, the yarn is dipped three times and by then it will be black.
   (M. Adé, Àpàá-Bùnú)

The dyed indigo yarn could be used in weaving cloth or could be sold
at markets.[7] These cloths and yarns were relatively expensive, judg-
ing from the comment of one weaver who observed that "in those
days, if one sold a cloth for 10 shillings, you were rich."[8] By wearing
and owning black cloths, individuals and their families demonstrated
their wealth. The use of numerous black cloths in the marriage ritual
also reflected the economic and social acumen of a young woman and
her supporters, kin and nonkin alike, to raise the funds required to
obtain them.

WHO MADE

AND WHO GAVE

MARRIAGE CLOTHS

Before 1950, young Bùnú women acquired these cloths in several
ways. They could be woven by the woman herself, commissioned
from other weavers by providing yarn and/or cash, given by an older
woman, or borrowed or rented. Of the fifteen named marriage cloths
obtained in these various ways, one particular cloth, *àdófì*, was personally owned by the bride and most commonly woven by her. Twelve
out of thirty Bùnú women weavers interviewed (whose ages ranged
from around forty-five to over eighty) said that they wove their own
àdófì marriage cloth (Table 3).

   Consisting of two panels, predominantly black with narrow red-

TABLE 3

GETTING AN *ÀDÓFÌ*

MARRIAGE CLOTH

Age	Wove it herself	Wove for another	Mother wove/ bought	Bought herself
60+ (n = 14)*	5	1	4	2
50–59 (n = 14)	7	—	2	5
40–49 (n = 2)†	—	—	—	1
TOTAL	12	1	6	8

*Two women originally from Òwọ̀rọ̀ District not included.
†Data missing on one woman.

and-white warp stripes, this was the sole marriage cloth that was never borrowed. Rather, a cloth was woven by or for each new bride and embroidered with her name. Despite the fact that many young women wove their own *àdófì* cloths, young women were dependent on older women for the indigo-dyed cotton skeins necessary for its production. Older women controlled both the indigo-dyeing process and the proceeds from dyed yarn and cloth sales, derived largely from the labor of these same young women who served them in an apprenticelike capacity. Since a detailed discussion of the relationship of young unmarried girls and older women weavers follows in chapter 7, I will only sketch out this arrangement here, emphasizing the role of young girls and women in indigo dyeing.

Young girls contributed to the indigo-dyeing process in an indirect way. They were primarily responsible for cleaning, ginning, and spinning raw cotton into skeins of natural handspun cotton, which were then dyed by older women. As one woman from northern Bùnú described it:

The junior sister of my father taught me to weave and dye. Any thread that I spun went to this woman who raised me. She would dye it and weave it into cloth which was then sold at the market. . . . Skeins of dark blue yarn were also sold in the market. . . . Anyone who wanted something dyed could bring thread or cloth—the price depended on the type of dye and color. (O. Ezekiel)

Young girls carried finished cloths and dyed skeins to Ódogi and Ag-baja markets where they might spend the profits on materials used in dyeing, such as special types of wood and leaves, including balls of indigo leaves.[9] They also collected indigo and other leaves and grasses locally, then pounded and dried them into balls. Although women attributed their knowledge of preparing indigo dyebaths and dyeing yarn to the older women who raised them, as young girls they learned by observing these processes rather than directly participating in them.

The older women who taught girls to spin, weave, and dye were frequently foster mothers. Girls often had to be forced to clean and spin cotton and it was believed that a girl's mother would be too lenient with her. As young children, therefore, girls were sent to live with foster mothers who gave them instruction, food, and housing in exchange for labor. Many of the women interviewed were raised in this way. When girls were old enough to attend local markets, they would head-load ten to twenty cloths, woven by themselves and the women who raised them. All profits from their sale belonged to the older woman, though this woman might give her "daughter" small gifts. Madam Ezekiel explained: "I might be given five cowries out of her profits, but how would I pay my mother back [except by working] for all that she bought in the market?" Women who were overly harsh or ungenerous ran the risk of young girls running away, either to kin or other patrons: "I had small breasts when I ran away from my foster mother at Òkè-Bùkún who beat me. So I came to my father's house here in Àgbèdè. His wife also knew how to make *aró* and I used to buy cotton and spin it" (M. Adé).

However, young girls often obeyed their mothers, for these women were the most likely sources of the black thread or cloths necessary for a young woman to marry. Gifts of black thread or cloth were the reward for the years of labor that young girls had supplied. They were also reminders of the ties between a young woman and her foster mother and obligations that might be claimed at some future time.

Older women provided marriage cloths directly or indirectly. They donated indigo-dyed thread so that young girls could weave their own, provided funds for commissioning marriage cloths,[10] or lent cloths to (or wove them for) their daughters.

These gifts were also a reward for a young woman's chaste behavior, for foster mothers controlled not only the labor but also the sexuality of the young girls. They were responsible for the virginity of their charges during a time when arranged marriages were common. To insure their interest, a young woman's husband would normally give these women virginity gifts, most often cash or poultry, produce, or livestock. Young women might be given a virginity gift as well but such gifts were optional. This social and economic arrangement in which unmarried women's labor and sexuality were more or less controlled by foster mothers[11] was reflected in restrictions on the use of black marriage cloth, notably *àdófi* cloth. It was only after the performance of traditional marriage that young women were allowed to wear these black cloths publicly. This control of sexuality and black marriage cloths was reinforced by the association of indigo and the color black with fertility, an association repeatedly made in traditional marriage performances. For the wearing of black marriage cloths is closely associated with having children, as the marriage song about the *àdófì* cloth attests:

Àdófì mi fẹ́   Àdófì is what I want,
Aṣọ bá mi gb'ọmọ   The cloth that helps me carry children.

THE MEANING OF

BLACK MARRIAGE CLOTHS

IN TRADITIONAL MARRIAGE

Certain black objects were critical to the performance of Bùnú traditional marriage, in particular the three black calabashes and the blue-black basket containing the black marriage cloths. These calabashes, the basket, and cloths are collectively referred to as the wife's calabash, *igbá obitan*. The large, blue-black, oval-shaped raffia basket (*àbò*) has a smaller round basket inside. Thirteen marriage cloths (*aṣọ obitan*) and a small carved wood box (*àpòtí obitan*) used for storing and mixing camwood are arranged within the baskets. Out of the thirteen cloths stored in the marriage basket, all but three are predominantly blue or blue-black (Table 1).

On the afternoon of the day when the wife is being brought to her husband's house, a kinswoman or friend of the wife will go about the town with the wife's calabash on her head. This display announces the impending move of the bride to her husband's house. On the night when the bride is brought to her husband's house, the wife's calabash accompanies her and stays with her for the next three months until she makes a mock return to her parents' house and the marriage ritual is complete. Unless the new wife is the actual owner,

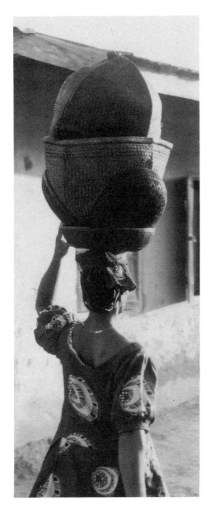

Mrs. Janet Mojúbà taking the wife's calabash and baskets (igbá obitan), *containing thirteen marriage cloths, around the village, to announce the beginning of a traditional marriage performance.*
Àgbède-Bùnú, June 1988.

the calabashes, basket, and marriage cloths will be returned to their owners at this time.

The significance of this journey to and from the husband's house and the black marriage things is related to a particular Bùnú story that tells of a hunter who brings three spirits from the bush to the village to be his wives.

Marriage photograph of Mrs. Gabriel Ọbàlò wearing her àdófì *cloth, by
unknown Nigerian photographer. Note the wife's calabash and basket (*igbá
obitan*) to her right.*
Àpàá-Bùnú, July 1988.

The Hunter
and the Spirit-Wives

One day a hunter found three women in the bush. All three were *ẹbọra* or
nature spirits; one lived in water, another in a palm tree, another in tall
grass. By giving them love medicine, the hunter convinced the three to
become his wives and to accompany him to his house in the town. They
did, bringing all their marriage things. These included the wife's calabash
and basket, which held thirteen marriage cloths, which the spirit-wives
later taught Bùnú women to weave. Just before entering the town, the
three spirit-wives told the hunter their names after warning him that if
he revealed them, they would return from where they came.

Each time one spirit-wife became pregnant, all three wives were
pregnant. Each time one wife wore a marriage cloth, all three wore the
same cloth. They bore the hunter many children, who eventually married

and moved away. In the meantime the hunter's first wife had been trying
to learn the spirit-wives' names. She finally succeeded after obtaining
medicine from a diviner, which she gave to her husband in his beer. She
confronted the spirit-wives with their names and the three spirit-wives
started crying. Wherever their children were, they heard their mothers
crying and immediately returned home. The spirit-wives prepared to
leave the hunter's house and to return to their spirit homes with their
calabashes, baskets, and marriage cloths, with their children following
them. The hunter-husband begged them to stay but they refused. He
asked the king of the village to beg the wives to stay and they refused. One
by one, each wife returned to her home with her children. When the last
wife arrived at her home in the water, the hunter pleaded with her to stay.
She agreed to return if her father permitted it. She and her children
entered the water but did not return. The hunter shot his first wife with
an arrow and vowed never to take a wife again.

Since that time, people have said that you should not reveal secrets to
women. That is why one should take care when drinking millet beer—
someone can die through drink. Because a hunter brought the spirit-
wives, they brought traditional marriage ritual which women continue to
do to this day. The cloths that the spirit-wives wore, those are the cloths
that women today use to perform traditional marriage. This is how
traditional marriage was brought to our town.   J. Olówósaiyé, Àpàá-Bùnú

In their performance of traditional marriage ritual, Bùnú women
play upon ideas of authority, obligation, and control of both individuals and powerful creative forces expressed in this story. In it, the
spirit-wives are said to derive their fertility and knowledge of weaving from their origin in the spirit world. By performing traditional
marriage, earthly wives ritually emulate these spirit-wives, acquiring the knowledge of cloth production and the power of fertility in
the process.[12] While the hunter at the story's end is ultimately unable
to keep the spirit-wives, older women from the husband's family are
successful in begging the new wife, who has returned to her natal
home at the end of three months, to return. Yet despite their success,
there is a certain ambivalence about the spirit world. The spirit
world is the source of the black marriage cloths and extraordinary fe-

Man praying to àbò *marriage basket before commencement of traditional marriage.*
Àkútúpá-Kírí-Bùnú, April 1988.

cundity, but also a dangerous refuge to which women and children might retreat at any time.[13] Older women attempt to control the ambiguities of the spirit world—with its benefits and its dangers—by instructing young women in the proper use of black marriage things in traditional marriage ritual. Despite these precautions, several women described falling ill during their own traditional marriage performance (see chapter 2)—for there are times when the wearing of black is simply too risky.

BLACK CLOTH,
TRADITIONAL MARRIAGE,
AND THE CONTROL OF FERTILITY

During the three-month performance of traditional marriage, Bùnú women wear a series of predominantly black cloths. They wear expensive indigo-dyed cloths to mark their change in status as well as the wealth of their supporters. However, as the story of the hunter and the spirit-wives suggests, these women are also symbolically representing a journey to and from the spirit world, believed to be the source of human fertility. In this ritual, women use black marriage things—cloths, calabashes, and baskets—to represent Bùnú beliefs about women's roles, the spirit world, and children. It is through the ritual reenactment of the journey of the spirit-wives that older Bùnú women who have performed traditional marriage ritually assert authority over younger women whom they control in both economic and domestic domains. Older women use black things in traditional marriage ritual to shape young women into socially responsible beings and symbolically to assert control over their reproductive power.[14]

THE MEANING OF

BLACK THINGS

Black rain clouds portend rain. In regions where rain is scarce or unpredictable, the color black may be associated with dark clouds, heavy with rain, and thus black is an auspicious color (Turner 1967:82, 83).[15] Wives are wrapped with black cloth (aṣọ dúdú), portending pregnancy. Like the black rain clouds, women wrapped in black cloth bring life—in the form of children—to the community.

What significance do Bùnú women attribute to these black calabashes, baskets, and cloths? Madam Margaret Ekúndayọ̀, who acted as a ritual leader during marriages in Àpàá and Àgbẹ̀dẹ in 1987–88, remarked that the wife's calabash, baskets, and cloths are the most important things a wife carries with her to her husband's house. Her explanation of why they were so important, however, was indirect: "The woman who raised the wife gives her the marriage calabash and cloth—they carry the *igbá obitan* around to show all the cloths inside." She seemed to emphasize the financial and personal aspects of

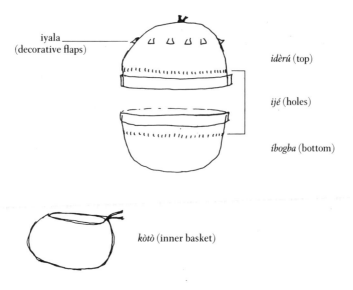

iyala (decorative flaps)

idèrú (top)

ijé (holes)

íbogba (bottom)

kòtò (inner basket)

FIGURE 1: *Drawing of parts of the* àbò *marriage basket.*

their importance, that the wife had amassed sufficient support to perform traditional marriage as evidenced by the many cloths.

However, the blue-black marriage basket, containing the placentalike smaller basket (*kòtò*) with the thirteen "wife's cloths" seated on the three blue-black calabashes, also suggests the image of the pregnant female body. The oval shape of the *àbò* is similar to that of the round, black cook pot, associated by some Yorùbá with the pregnant female body or womb (Buckley 1985; Drewal 1977). When I asked Bùnú women about this association, they were amused and said they had never heard of women's bodies being likened to pots or to the marriage basket. Nonetheless, some association *is* made between the wife's body and her *àbò* basket. If a woman dies during the three-month period after she has gone to her husband's house, it was said

Chief Nathaniel Mojúbà weaving àbò *basket.*
Àpàá-Bùnú, 1988.

that the *àbò* basket and its contents of thirteen cloths will be consumed by termites and disappear.

The idea of cloth as a metaphor for people and particularly for children is commonly held, reflected in the saying *Ọmọ l'aṣọ èdá*, "children are the cloth of people" (Drewal and Drewal 1983:120).[16] The names *Ọmọtoṣọ* ("children are sufficient for cloth") and *Ọmọboniraṣọ* ("children cover more than cloth") also express this association made between people, cloth, and social support. (The latter name implies that children are even more valuable than cloth.) The cloths carried within the marriage basket are like the children the wife hopes to bear who, like cloth, will surround and support her.

The black marriage basket resting on the three calabashes is also similar to the image of the stable black cook pot sitting on the three hearthstones in the Bùnú saying *Àrò mẹ́ta éèyí*, "three hearthstones don't shake." The black pot seated on the three hearthstones (*àrò mẹ́ta*) won't shake, fall down, and break. Thus the black marriage basket filled with cloth, seated on the three "stones," will not shake or spoil, much as the pregnant women's body will not spoil (or miscarry) but will bring forth healthy children.

As with my questions about black pots and the black marriage basket, no one seemed to know why these things should be black. The responses to queries about indigo dyeing, however, suggested an answer. One local *babaláwo*, who was also an herbalist, mentioned the use of indigo dye in indigenous medicines. According to this man, "the eyes of those who dye with indigo don't see all that indigo can be used for" (*Ojú aláró kó kín tó é lè aró*), implying that only those with special vision (supernatural power) can realize its curative potential. Diviners prescribe the water from exhausted indigo dye baths (*omi aró*) to make medicine for skin ailments or other complaints (cf. Buckley 1985:155). They may also take the dregs from the bottom of the dyepot and grind them together with other things to make medicine to counter infertility. After a woman menstruates, the herbalist adds the indigo dregs mixture to ground guinea corn. The woman and man who want a child will eat the corn, and have intercourse, and the woman will become pregnant. Indigo is believed to affect the reproductive capacity of those who come into contact with it (Hoskins 1989:148).

WHEN BLACK IS TOO DANGEROUS TO BE WORN

The effects of indigo on fertility are ambiguous. To wear the black marriage cloth saturated with fertility-enhancing indigo is dangerous to women with reproductive disorders. For example, in a picture of a group of married co-wives in Ọ̀llẹ̀-Bùnú, all but one of the women are wearing *àdófì* marriage cloth. The exception, an *olómi*, "one from water" (known elsewhere in Bùnú as *ejínuwọn*), wears an ordinary wax-print cloth. If she were to wear an *àdófì* cloth, it was said that she "might die and go back to the spirit world" (Ìbéjìgbà 1985:62, 63).

Before a woman performs traditional marriage, a diviner is consulted to determine what special treatment is required by her spirit double. Often, *ejínuwọn* women are told that they are not allowed to carry or come close to the black marriage cloths and the marriage calabash and basket. Rather, they carry a mock wife's calabash without cloths, which consists of light-colored, broken plastic bowls and plates, covered with black-and-white string netting and seated in a single, old, enamel basin. This mock wife's calabash made of broken and dirty things is known as the *àbò yẹyẹ̀*, the ridiculous marriage basket. Women with spirit-doubles must carry the *àbò yẹyẹ̀*, both as a punishment of their worrisome spirit and as a mark of their ambig-

The àbò yẹyè, *wife's ridiculous marriage basket, being prepared for a bride with a spirit double. The women are using broken calabashes, chipped enamelware, and torn plastic to make the basket.*
Àgbẹ̀dẹ-Bùnú, June 1988. Photograph by Sasha Stollman.

uous status in both the human and spirit worlds. It is only after a wife has safely moved to her husband's house, described as "crossing the water," that the real marriage baskets and wife's calabash can be used.

If the black wife's calabash and basket filled with cloth represent the fertile woman's body (and her potential children), which does not shake or spoil (i.e., which is not barren and does not miscarry), the ridiculous marriage basket is its childless-clothless opposite. It is used when fertility is out of control, as when women have children who keep dying and being reborn (or who were themselves such children) or when women cannot get pregnant. These problematic women are endangered by being near the blue-black wife's calabash. To give black things to such women would only complicate the problem, which requires the careful control of fertility, not more of it. Such women should carry the ridiculous marriage basket and they should wear white cloth to placate their spirit-doubles. As one man put it, "You have to do things for them or they will just go back [to the spirit world, die]."

While many women hoped to wear an *àdófì* cloth and to carry the black wife's calabash and basket when coming to their husband's house, many *ejínuwọn* women were told by diviners that they could not take this risk. One woman was furious on learning that she had to wear white and carry the ridiculous marriage basket "after having paid all that money." On the other hand, women who had no history of reproductive problems could carry black things. But even these women were perceived as being in some danger during the three-month interval between moving to their husband's house and the mock-return to their own. During this liminal period, new wives, who are represented as straddling the boundaries of the spirit and earthly domains, are susceptible to the possibility of "going back."

Women who already had shown such a proclivity by frequent illness needed special protection and control, which were evidenced by the use of white and broken things.

These restrictions are related to other, everyday restrictions of young women's labor and sexuality. Young women should not come near indigo dyepots, as they might be menstruating and cause the blue-black dyebath to turn red. There is also the implication that young women should not come near the indigo dyepot as it might endanger their fertility.[17] Older women know how to control the effects of indigo and are also, as postmenstrual women, immune to them. Younger girls should be working for their mothers, without time or thought given to young men. Older women who carefully supervised the labor of their charges also controlled their virginity and, with it, the possibility of their prematurely becoming pregnant. They also participated in arranged marriage plans made by the families of the husband and wife and encouraged young women to accept the choices of their elders.

These relations of authority and control have changed in Bùnú. Older women no longer dye with indigo, Bùnú brides are no longer virgins nor always young, and marriages are no longer arranged. Yet women still perform traditional marriage ritual and use black marriage cloths. Though the association of these cloths with control of sexuality and fertility has diminished, their use as a symbol of local village status and of Bùnú ethnic identity has increased.

WHY WOMEN CONTINUE
TO WEAVE AND WEAR ÀDÓFÌ

Things have changed in Bùnú since the time when young girls spun yarn for their mothers and sold indigo-dyed black cloths at the market. Around the mid-1950s, the economic relationship based on cloth production between older women weavers and young girl apprentices changed as I will discuss in chapter 7. Girls continued to work for their mothers, but they helped in more lucrative occupations (e.g., food processing) that improved transportation had made possible for Bùnú women. Furthermore, women worked to raise the necessary school fees for their daughters' primary school education, made available for girls in Bùnú District at this time. Young girls and women who went to school and afterwards helped on the farm no longer had time to clean and spin cotton for their mothers. Nor was it likely that they wanted to be associated with such old-fashioned practices as spinning. Like handweaving, indigo dyeing was affected by the lack of handspun yarn as well as by the unavailability of materials needed in dyeing. The broken indigo dyepot became a symbol for these economic and social changes.[18]

Several women attributed the shift in relations of authority between older and younger women to schooling and to the decline of the cloth production apprenticeship system (Renne 1990). Others related it to the breakdown in the arranged marriage system, resulting from the introduction of divorce in colonial courts (Renne 1992b). With the possibility that one's prospective virginal wife might disrupt plans of an arranged marriage, men preferred to solidify relations with a prospective spouse through a pregnancy. Thus as one man noted, "No one is paying them to be virgins anymore" (A. Ọbajànọ̀, Àpàá-Bùnú). The authority of older men and women was also affected by educated children moving from villages to urban centers. Local village authority was no longer solely derived from relations of super- and subordination of seniors and juniors. Authority also depended upon the success of educated young people who often took such matters as choosing a spouse into their own hands.

Yet despite these changes in the balance of authority and in the sexual behavior of the young, older villagers were reluctant to sever ties with their children. "We can't reject our children," as one older Àpàá woman observed. Rather, old and young people living in Bùnú District or in urban centers outside continue to use and keep black cloth to express their ties to one another. Black marriage cloths, re-calling past obligations and connections, are still used today but are obtained and valued differently.

OBTAINING MARRIAGE

CLOTHS TODAY

When most Bùnú women were handweavers, young women wove the marriage cloth Àdófì for themselves or were given it by their fos-ter mothers who had woven it. In the 1990s, these cloths are almost always commissioned from one of the few remaining weavers in the village who has made a specialty of weaving àdófì marriage cloths. In Àpàá-Bùnú, this woman was Elizabeth Nua, who bought commer-cially spun yarn and then sold the completed àdófì cloth (in 1988, for 60 náírà, approximately $7.00US). Some recent Bùnú brides com-missioned and paid for àdófì cloths themselves, while others were given cloths as gifts by kinswomen.

Other black marriage cloths have to be borrowed as they are no longer being woven in northern Bùnú or in Bida where they were purchased in the past. Women rely on family connections to obtain these black cloths and marriage things:

My family has the marriage calabashes and baskets that I used. I had to pay 5 náírà for them but if I hadn't been a family member I would have paid twice as much. . . . A woman keeps the igbá ìyàwó—she is the junior sister of my father. Both women and men in a family own it but it is a woman who keeps it and lends it out. (M. Zaccheus)

Kẹ́hìndé and Janet Ògúníbì, performing the third "trip to the market" portion of Bùnú traditional marriage (gbé obitan). *The wife on the right is wearing the marriage cloth* awẹ̀rẹ̀ *as a wrapper, and the wife on the left, the cloth* àtufù, *with* ojúedewó *as shoulder cloths and* ọ̀run padà *cloths on their heads. The cloth tied around the tree is a faded* aṣọ ipò *cloth called* ẹ̀bẹ. *It indicates that the tree is home to an* ẹbọra *spirit.*
Àpàá-Bùnú, January 1988.

Presently much of the cash needed to borrow these marriage things, to commission *àdófì* cloths, and to feed family and friends comes from the earnings of the wife herself. While she is dependent on the older women to lend these things, she is not so dependent on them for cash for these expenditures. In fact, since women may perform tradi-tional marriage long after moving in with their husbands, they often have economic resources of their own. Thus women who perform it when middle-aged or even later may have amassed sufficient funds from trading for its performance.

While associations of women with the spirit world continue to be part of traditional marriage performance, the use of black cloth in controlling young women's fertility is no longer to the point for women who might be grandmothers. Rather, black marriage cloths have taken on other meanings. This change is reflected in a shift in the value of old, indigo-dyed black marriage cloths. Their worth is no longer based on excesses of labor and materials but rather on their irreplaceability and their links with the past. These cloths, which can no longer be woven because of the unavailability of materials and weavers, are invaluable. Because they embody relationships of the past, they legitimate older village women's present claims on and con-nections to their daughters who may be living in urban centers out-side of Bùnú District. A Bùnú daughter should come home to perform traditional marriage.

Even the *àdófì* cloth, which is replaceable, refers to the past. The amount spent for its weaving does not compare with the amount spent on other handwoven and commercial cloths used in traditional marriage. For example, one woman paid 300 náírà ($38US) for an Ebira handwoven wrapper set and 100 náírà ($13US) for a commer-cial wax-print, while spending 60 náírà (around $7US) on her *àdófì* (C. Olútìmáyìn, Àgbẹ̀dẹ-Bùnú). Rather, the value of *àdófì* cloth is based on a different set of criteria. By commissioning a Bùnú woman to weave an *àdófì* cloth on a vertical loom (a technology of the past), Bùnú women remind themselves and others of the spirit-wives who taught their ancestors to weave, and of their mothers who wove in the past.[19] Thus when I asked Elizabeth Nua, the principal weaver in Àpàá, whether this cloth could be replaced by machine-made cloth that imitated its colors and patterning, her response was a blunt "It is not possible."

By keeping black marriage cloth and wearing *àdófì*, Bùnú women attempt to maintain ties with one another and a sense of continuity with the past. As one older Bùnú woman remarked: "If you are really from Bùnú, you must do traditional marriage. It is good to do traditional marriage. There was a woman who did church marriage who still came back to the village to do traditional marriage" (M. Ọmọ́le). Thus despite changing sexual mores, the timing of traditional marriage performance, urban migration, and church marriage, older women still encourage younger Bùnú women to do their traditional marriages. Not only does its performance convey a sense of timelessness in a world of unsettling changes. The exchange of black cloth between older married village women and younger unmarried ones reproduces relations between them which, though difficult to maintain, are too important to sever. As Simmel (1950:395) has observed: "This atmosphere of obligation belongs among those 'microscopic,' but infinitely tough threads which tie one element of society to another. . . . , and thus eventually all of them together in a stable collective life."

Through the keeping and giving of black cloth, Bùnú women attempt to maintain a sense of ordered relationships (e.g., junior-senior, traditionally married–not married) and obligations—with one another, with a particular geographical area, with a particular way of speaking, and with a particular way of knowing the world.

The reasons why Bùnú brides wear black have changed, along with the economic and social conditions that supported the indigo dyeing and the production of black cloth. Formerly, Bùnú brides wore black cloth because of its costliness and association with fertility. Brides today wear it because of its association with the past.

FIVE

THE CLOTHS

OF HUNTERS

AND CHIEFS

The opposition between

men who *have* and

men who *are*

is immemorial.
William James

Cloth plays a pivotal part in the story of a hunter and his spirit-wives recounted in chapter 4. As they leave their spirit homes, each wife makes a point of carrying her marriage cloths with her. After arriving in the village, the wives wear the cloths and have many children and later teach Bùnú women to weave. When they leave the hunter to return to the spirit world, they take these cloths with them. Why is the imagery of cloth so pervasive in this and other Bùnú stories and what is the significance of cloth ownership as expressed in these narratives?

Bùnú stories often revolve around the contradictions of social life—brothers who should love one another but who are in deadly rivalry, kings whose mental acuity is surpassed by subordinates, and children whose affective loyalties to mothers outweigh jural obligations to fathers (Jackson 1982). In order to contemplate these disorderly, unsettling ideas, these stories are often set in a different time—long ago (*àtijọ́*)—and incorporate travel to distant places—the spirit world, the bush, and foreign kingdoms. It is through these stories that the contradictions and the difficulties of charting a moral course in a messy social world are contemplated. Cloth, pervasive in Bùnú social life and in these stories, lends the latter credence by relating the problems of distant times and places to the here and now.

Ideas about political authority and hierarchy in Bùnú society are expressed in stories about hunters and chiefs, whose distinct but related powers are underscored by associations with specific cloths. Hunters wear plain, predominantly off-white cotton shirts, sometimes woven with narrow black-warp stripes, sometimes over-dyed a pale blue. Using powerful medicines, they individually explore the bush, establishing new village sites and overcoming dangerous forces (spirits, wild animals, masquerades) which ultimately benefit society. Kings and chiefs[1] use costly chieftaincy regalia and intricately patterned red cloths, which are displayed at funerals and as part of masquerade costumes. They head kin and village groups, in part through their relations with ancestral spirits, who are associated with physical sites (such as graves and rocks) and represented by masquerades. The dichotomy of the power of hunters—who encounter powerful forces outside of society—and the authority of kings—who control these forces within it—is a common theme in origin myths and stories in several parts of Africa. Hunters are often associated with the founding of kingdoms but rarely rule them because of the more idiosyncratic nature of their power (Boston 1966:125; Turner 1957:32).

While the roles and powers of chiefs and hunters differ, they are also interrelated. In these stories, the power of individualistic hunters who introduce innovations derived from the bush (e.g., weaving and the masquerades) is constrained by material success and political authority of ranked chiefs. The power of these chiefs, in turn, is circumscribed by Ifá diviners—priests who are often hunters—with powers of divine communication, who must be consulted before action may be taken. Cloth is an appropriate medium for expressing the opposed but interrelated qualities of hunters and chiefs, for it visually expresses through color and patterning the nature of their respective claims to power. Further, the impermanence of cloth also suggests the finiteness of these claims, which may only be overcome by constantly attending to their reproduction through time.

The telling of stories and the ownership of cloth may be seen as part of the construction of the present through the reproduction of the past.[2] This construction has political, social, and economic consequences for different groups of individuals because the past is used to assert and legitimate present-day claims about the roles of women and men and of hunters and chiefs in Bùnú society. Further, the stories themselves suggest that the reproduction of social roles and relationships of authority is related to assertions about who can own, produce, and keep cloth. These ideas are explored in the following three Bùnú stories, told by men. In them, relations of authority between husbands and wives, chiefs and hunters, and junior and senior brothers are established through the exchange of cloth.

STORIES AND CLOTHS
OF HUNTERS AND KINGS

Two of the principal themes in the story of the hunter and the spirit-wives are the loyalty of wives and the rivalry between co-wives. In Bùnú, women move to their husbands' houses after marriage but retain rights and responsibilities in their natal homes. This structural tension may be exacerbated by the machinations of a senior co-wife who attempts to make younger wives leave. In the story of the hunter and the spirit wives recounted in chapter 4, the marriage cloths brought by the spirit-wives from their natal homes express the idea of enduring ties with kin as opposed to those with often difficult married relations. The hunter is unable to keep the spirit wives from leaving, and they depart, taking their marriage cloths and children

with them. Yet in other Bùnú stories, wives return to kings and
chiefs who make extensive gifts of cloth. In the following story about
a mute wife,[3] the implications of the control of cloth and wives are
examined. Further, the story suggests how the control of material resources such as cloth is part of a process whereby the political authority of kings and chiefs is maintained.

The Mute Wife

A man had two wives. The senior wife (*iyálé*), who was pregnant, went to
the farm to get firewood. On the road she saw a single grain of guinea
corn. As she bent to pick it up, the child in her stomach said, "If you pick
up the guinea corn, from the day that you give birth to me, I will not talk."
So the woman went on, still thinking of the guinea corn. She stopped and
slowly walked backward, thinking her child would not realize what she
was doing. She quickly picked up the guinea corn and ate it. But the child
had seen everything. When the woman gave birth to a baby girl, the child
did not talk or cry because she was mute (*adìdò*). She grew and played with
others yet she did not speak.

One day when the king went walking through the town, he saw a group
of children playing. He saw a small, light-complexioned girl and asked,
"Who is the mother of that child?" The king said he wanted to marry the
child. Everyone was surprised that he wanted to marry a mute girl but
he insisted. He walked to her parents' house, carrying the child on his
shoulders. When he got there, he put the child down and gave her some
money. When he returned to his house, he prepared different cloths and
sent them to the girl. He did this every year until she was old enough to
come to his house as a wife.

When the day came for her to marry, they brought her to the king's
house and sang and danced for her for seven days, but she did not talk
because she was mute. The second day after the marriage, the husband
entered her room. Soon he was staying with her every day, much to the
discontent of the other wives.

The king's other wives, led by his senior wife, decided to discourage the
king's affection for his new wife, first by killing a ram by her door and
blaming the mute wife. Since she could not speak, she could not deny it.

Despite doing this, the king continued to stay with his new wife. The
wives continued their plan but were still unsuccessful. Finally the senior

wife killed her own child, the king's first-born son, and put the body by the door.

Three days later the king announced to the townspeople that he was sending the mute wife away to be killed by his aide-de-camp, Dandoko. Dandoko took the wife away but as he was about to kill her, she held up her hand and pointed three fingers to her stomach. Dandoko made ready to kill her again and she did the same thing. The third time, as he went to kill her, he realized the meaning of the three fingers that the woman used to touch her stomach: she was three months pregnant. He took her secretly to his mother's house.

The mute wife gave birth in his mother's house and whenever the child would cry she would sing a song, recounting the treachery of her co-wives. The child would stop crying. One day a man from the town traveling along the road overheard the child crying and the mother singing. He returned to town and told the king. The king knelt down and thanked him before going to Dandoko's house.

When he arrived at Dandoko's house, he knelt before him. After Dandoko had told him what had happened, the king wanted to take the mute wife back. He sent someone to beg Dandoko's mother and after the messenger explained things, she said, "I think the mute woman is the king's wife." So they sent someone to ask the mute wife if she would return to the king's house. She agreed. The messenger returned to the king and he was very happy.

He prepared for her return. They took many types of cloth and started putting them on the road from the king's to Dandoko's house. The king sent the mute wife royal slippers and cloths for herself and the child to wear. On the day that the wife came, the people following her were like a river of water. When she was almost at the house, the king brought out an ancient chieftaincy stool and placed it on the spread cloths. When the king's co-wives saw the mute wife, they were very surprised.

The mute wife knelt before the king and as she did so, the child began to cry. She took the child from her back and when she began singing, the child stopped. Everyone knew the meaning of the song. The mute wife told the king that she did not blame him as it was the fault of the senior wife whose head she asked for. The king called Dandoko who took the senior wife away, returning with her head.

Since then, we have learned that evil intentions toward others may come back on us. And since then, the child in the stomach no longer speaks as before, when the unborn child would talk with its mother wherever they went.   (Baba Àbú, Aíyétórò-Kírí-Bùnú)

The most obvious theme of this story is the deadly rivalry for domestic authority between the senior wife and the king, though this is unknown to him until the story's end.[4] Other more subversive topics are explored, such as the contrast between the dangerous unreliability of kin—reflected by the mute wife's mother, whose cupidity results in her daughter's condition—and the help of strangers (nonkin) such as Dandoko's mother, who harbors the mute wife. The story also considers the consequences of the judgment of the king's adjutant, Dandoko, who disobeys the king's orders and refrains from killing the mute wife. This upset of protocol is dramatically represented by the socially superior king kneeling to his subordinate. Finally, the story also suggests the dangers of uncontrolled emotions. The king's infatuation with the mute wife led to his ignoring social conventions and not visiting his other wives, the cause of his problems.

Yet despite the king's bad judgment, he regains the mute wife, who acquires speech by the story's end. The frequent references to the king's gifts of cloth suggest how this turn of events is possible. The king, on seeing the mute wife as a young girl, gives her annual gifts of cloth, thus establishing his suit as her future husband. Such annual gifts were part of the former practice of arranged marriage in Bùnú. When the mute wife finally returns to his house, it is with an extravagant display of cloth. Cloths are used to cover the road to the king's house, the mute wife and her child are given royal cloths and slippers to wear, and she is seated on a chieftaincy stool which rests on cloth. Unlike the hunter who has no cloth, the king is forgiven his mistakes and the mute bride returns.

This contrast between kings with cloths and hunters without them is explored in the following story. In this story, the linking of political authority with the keeping of cloth is even more clearly defined.

How the Masquerades
Were Brought to Bùnú

A hunter went to the bush but he didn't see animals to kill so he returned
to his house and called his wife. He asked her to make three steamed
cornmeal cakes that he would take when going to the bush. "On the third
day, if I have finished eating my corn-cakes and I don't see any meat to kill,
I will come back to the house."

As he was going, going, going, he got to a clearing. He climbed to the
top of a tree with his bow and arrow and waited. Soon a wind began to
blow, "fú fú fú fú," and he saw the bush spirit, Àgbó. Àgbó looked up at
the top of this tree and seeing the hunter, told him that he wouldn't see
animals to kill that day but that something else was coming. "As I'm talking to you now, . . . you will see goodluck today. But it is not an animal
you will carry to the house today. . . . What you will see today, when you
reach home, take it to the house of the king of the town straight away. You
cannot keep it in your house, it cannot accommodate it. But you are the
owner. Go and beg the king to keep it in his house. Now wait for the rest
of them," and Àgbó went into the bush.

Shortly after, another wind began to blow, "*fú fú fú,*" and the hunter
saw something red and long crawling along the ground toward him. He
saw the masquerade they call Iyelúgbó, followed by others, Òùna, Nároko,
and Egàbọm. When they arrived, the hunter called them and asked if they
had seen their master Àgbó sitting nearby. They went to meet Àgbó.
Others came including *imọ̀lẹ̀* and *òfósì* cult women.[5]

Then another wind blew up, like the first, "*fú fú fú fú.*" The hunter
looked and saw Ọpaláno, the powerful bush deity with one leg, one hand,
and one eye.[6] Ọpaláno said, "I am the owner of all these people and have
brought them today. You have been a hunter for a long time but have
nothing to show for it. You only have one shirt, one cloth, and one cap.
But you have become a rich man today. . . ."

So the hunter took the masquerades and the *òfósì* and *imọ̀lẹ̀* women
with him to his house. He did not see Ọpaláno again. As they came to his
house, the villagers asked, "What kind of things are these?" Some people
ran away. As he approached his house, his wife hid inside. The hunter
told her to come out and to bring water. The hunter took the water and
poured it on the ground. Then he gave water to the *imọ̀lẹ̀* and the *òfósì*
women, Àgbó, and the masquerades—they all poured it on the ground.

The hunter then went to the king's house. He said, "My own house is
too small. You are the king. You are the one who has a house that can
accommodate these people. Take them."

This is how he gave them to the king of the town. The hunter was the owner of Àgbó, òfósì, imọ̀lẹ̀, and all the masquerades before he took them to the king.   (Chief Tolúfá Moses)

This story examines the nature of power and authority in Bùnú society by attributing the discovery of the masquerades to a hunter, who then gives them to the king. Here the hunter's power is clearly attributed to his relationship with supernatural beings in the bush, rather than on his material wealth. The hunter, the original owner by virtue of discovery, gives the masquerades (whose costumes are constructed of red funeral cloth) to the king, who has a house big enough and, by implication, political power sufficient to keep them.

Keeping things such as the masquerades and quantities of other cloths is important as they may be given in exchange for political support.[7] The legitimation of political authority based on the ownership of cloth and related items of regalia is explored in the following story.

Àjọ̀n and the
King's New Clothes

This story explains why King Asèje
began the annual celebrations
to commemorate the death
of his wife Àjọ̀n, which continue
to this day in Kírí.

Asèje was a trader who used to go to Idah [in Igalaland]. When he got to Idah, he saw the king holding a whisk, wearing a red cap (*odi*), and tying the cloth strip, *àkì*. He was wearing the robe *ibòrí* and was holding the *ẹ̀dà olúkó* fan. King Asèje admired the way that the king of Idah was wearing all these things as he sat on his throne. Afterwards, he bought things to trade and returned to his home.

When he got to the house, he went to meet his senior brother. He told his brother about the town of Idah where he went to trade and how the king was dressed. He asked his brother to give him money so that he could buy his brother things like the king of Idah had worn. His brother agreed to give him the money to buy things when he traveled to Idah again.

So when King Asèje was going to return to Idah, he collected the money
from his older brother and began his journey, taking along his wife and
child. When they got there, he sold all his market goods. He then went to
buy all the things they are now using for the chieftaincy title of king [in
Kírí]. He bought a red cap, a red cloth strip, a fly-whisk, a fan, a drum,
and so on. When he had finished buying them, he packed them together.
The wife carried some, the son carried some, and King Asèje himself
carried some. They returned to their home at Òkè-Kírí though his senior
brother was living at Bakin [both in northern Bùnú].

After they got to Òkè-Kírí and rested a while, King Asèje called his wife
Àjọn. He told her that he wanted her to deliver a message to his brother,
that he wanted to bring the things he had bought.

But his wife was surprised and said, "How will you go and give them to
him?" They didn't speak. After a while the husband again told his wife
that he wanted to give the things to his brother. The wife said that he
should let her think about it.

Three days after they had returned from Idah, King Asèje called his
wife again. "As my elder brother sent me to buy these things for him, it
is good to take them to him."

His wife answered, "If you want to do things for someone, it is good to
do things for yourself first. My husband, it is good to do for yourself first."
She then asked, "Where are the trousers?"

Her husband showed her and the wife told him to wear them. She then
asked him to put on the shirt and then the red cap. She asked for the red
head tie and the husband brought it. She tied it around his head. She
then asked him to hold the fan. She asked him where the drum was and
he showed her. So the wife, Àjọn, called the child that went with them
to beat the drum. When she heard the sound of the drum, she started
to shout, "Wílírírí!"

When the wife made this sound, the rest of the village heard it and
looked at them. When people at Àkútúpá heard it, they looked to see
where the noise was coming from. As they climbed Òkè-Kírí hill, they
saw something red on the hill, the cloth that King Asèje was wearing.
When they finished climbing, they found King Asèje seated on his
throne, dressed as king.

Everybody sat down and they started beating the drum. All the townspeople near Òkè-Kírí started climbing the hill to see them. Later, as the
people from Bakin came from their farms, they were surprised to hear the
noise of the drums. They climbed the hill to see what was causing the
noise. When they got to Òkè-Kírí, they met King Asèje sitting on a throne.
Then they left the people on the hill to tell the elder brother of King Asèje

at Bakin what they had seen. The money he had given his younger brother to buy things at Idah, his brother had used for himself. Now he was sitting on the throne like a king.

The senior brother was very surprised and said, "Is that what they were doing? Good. He is my junior brother so I cannot do anything against him. But from now on, he must never come to Bakin to meet me here. And I myself will not go to Òkè-Kírí before I die."

This is why the king of Kírí doesn't go to Bakin to this day. Later, every town started to have its own king and each family started to have its own king. But later it was only Olú-Kírí that remained. That is why they only have Olú-Kírí now.   (Chief Tolúfá Moses)

Unlike the senior wife in the story of the mute wife who sought to undermine her husband's authority, the wife Àjòn made her husband a king by insisting that he keep the king's regalia which he had purchased at Idah. This story explores several themes. It contrasts the loyalty of the wife with the disloyalty of her husband, the younger brother. It considers the problems of political leadership, particularly when a junior brother surpasses an elder in ingenuity and wealth. It also suggests that the clothes make the king, despite junior ranking, underscoring the way that cloth is used in asserting the legitimacy of political claims.

THE HIERARCHY OF KINGS, CHIEFS, AND HUNTERS

These three stories examine the importance of cloth wealth in the constitution and maintenance of a system of local political authority based on a hierarchy of chiefs (Murra 1962; Weiner 1985). In Bùnú, ascendance to the highest ranked positions is based on rotation and ascription, rather than on membership in royal lineages as is the case in other parts of Yorubaland. While political authority is diffused among different clans, lineages, and individuals, the keeping of regalia and red cloths owned by former chiefs and kings strengthens the claims of these groups and individuals. Further, the political hier-

Chief Zachias Olú wearing hunter's shirt (àwǫdę) woven for him by his mother. He is also wearing a head-lamp used for night hunting. Àpàá-Bùnú, November 1987.

archy of chiefs and kings that exists in Bùnú is visually marked by the use at funerals of patterned, red cloths, which are themselves ranked (see chapter 6).

While hunters control forces in the bush, chiefs and kings have their own special powers to legitimate their control within the village. Kings and chiefs use their material resources to acquire and keep things and thus assert the legitimacy of their own claims. These different but related claims of supernatural power and sanction are reflected in the types of cloths associated with hunters and kings.

THE POWERS AND CLOTHS
OF HUNTERS

Knowledge of supernatural medicine and incantations characterizes the special powers of hunters, who may use them to mesmerize dangerous animals in the bush and transport themselves great distances to escape harm. Medicine for performing these feats is kept in the pouches of white-and-black-striped hunters' shirts. There are several named patterns of the predominantly white cloths with intermittent black stripes that are used in making these shirts, including the cloths called *kẹkẹ* and *àláàgi*.

The white-and-black-striped *kẹkẹ* cloth was one of the most common trade cloths formerly produced by Bùnú weavers. It was also one of the least expensive cloths—its price approximately one-third that of comparably sized black cloths. In hunters' shirts, two separately woven panels are joined, with the lower front seams left open to form a pouch. Hunter's shirts of *kẹkẹ* cloth continue to be woven and worn because of their durability and association with the power of hunters, which is represented by medicinal pouches.

Aside from their ubiquity, cheapness, and durability, *kẹkẹ* cloths used in hunters' shirts have other connotations. While hunters tend to hunt alone, they belong to a village hunters' association (*egbẹ́ ọdẹ*). There are various restrictions on members' behavior and the association does have a head, but in general there is no ranking of hunters as there is of chiefs. Likewise, the *kẹkẹ* and other cloths used by hunters are not ranked. In fact, in relation to other cloths, *kẹkẹ* and *àláàgi* are among the least valued cloths in Bùnú. What seems to be suggested by hunters' use of such cloth is not only the nonhierarchical nature of their organization but also a playing down of material wealth and an emphasis on the wealth of spiritual power. The deity Ọpalánọ observes the material poverty of the hunter, "You only have one shirt, one cloth, and one cap." But when Ọpalánọ gives the masquerades to the hunter, telling him that they will make him "rich," it is not so much in the material sense but in the sense of his special abilities associated with power from the bush. Indeed, the phrase "one shirt, one cloth, and one cap" may refer to the phrase "one arm, one leg, and one eye," which is used to describe the unilateral deity Ọpalánọ, who is the original owner of the masquerades.

The material poverty of those who wear *kẹkẹ* cloths, in contrast to the material wealth of kings and chiefs who own cloths sufficient to cover roads for great distances, is expressed in one northern Bùnú (Kírí) song. Inexpensive cloths such as *kẹkẹ* used in hunters' shirts are contrasted with the costly red funeral cloths associated with kings:

Íghónyín ghonyìn ólú t'asọ	These are the king cloths
Ọ̀ghọn fàlẹ̀	There is *ifàlẹ̀*
Ọ̀ghọn àbatá	There is *àbatá*
Ọ̀ghọn apọ́núpọ́nyìn	There is *apọ́núpọ́nyìn*
Olú t'asọ	King cloths
Íghónyín ghonyìn árú t'asọ	These are the slave cloths
Ọ̀ghọn kẹkẹ	There is *kẹkẹ*
Ọ̀ghọn àláàgi	There is *àláàgi*
Ọ̀ghọn arigidi	There is *arigidi*
Árú t'asọ	Slave cloths

(Sung by Baba Alárọ́, Gìrò-Kírí-Bùnú)

The commissioned red funeral cloths, generally referred to as *asọ ipò*—of which three are specifically named here, *ifàlẹ̀*, *àbatá*, and *apọ́núpọ́nyìn*—are only displayed at the second burials of kings and chiefs (Renne 1992a). However, inexpensive named cloths such as *kẹkẹ*, *àláàgi*, and *arigidi* used by hunters can be bought and sold indiscriminantly and are likened to slaves.

Hunters are able to bring supernatural forces to society but their powers are constrained in the village by their lack of material resources. The noninstitutional powers of hunters, conceptualized as derived from the spirit world outside of the village, are visually differentiated by means of cloth from the political status of titled chiefs. The ranked authority of kings and chiefs, shown in the ornate patterning of chiefs' red funeral and masquerade cloths, contrasts with the nonhierarchical power of hunters, reflected in the plainness of the white or pale blue, black-striped shirts.

CHIEFS, KINGS, AND RANKED RED CLOTH

If the plainness of white-and-black-striped *keke* cloths is related to the nonranked status and the supernatural powers of hunters, what are the implications of patterned red cloths for the special powers and claims made by chiefs?

In two of the stories, the imagery of "something red" seen in the distance is evoked. The power of attraction associated with the color red was remarked on by one Bùnú diviner who observed that red cloth was used to alert people to hidden animal traps in the bush. He also noted that red cloth, a principal ingredient in some types of medicine, is believed to protect farms from theft by the threat of leprosy (Z. Olú). These qualities of red cloth—distinctiveness and threatening power—are also associated with titled chiefs. These men distinguish themselves by paying progressively larger sums to acquire progressively higher-ranked chieftaincy titles. Since only a few attain these titles, this accomplishment is attributed to extraordinary powers, implicitly suggesting sorcery. In the past, for example, such chiefs were thought to control rain (Niven 1982), evidence of their supernatural power. Men who wear long red caps, marking their status as high chiefs, are respected because of their achievement but also are feared because of the power they wield.

The stories examine this dual aspect of political authority, in part, through references to red cloth. The respected achievement and material wealth of chiefs who serve their kin group and the community are marked by red things. These include regalia obtained outside and a series of patterned red cloths that are expensive in materials and extremely labor intensive in production. However, the extraordinary personal power that makes the ownership of such things possible also threatens the unity of kin groups and communities. Conflicts between junior and senior brothers may result in the splitting and weakening of lineages and villages. In these stories, these disputes take the form of quarrels over the ownership of regalia and red cloths.[8]

Cloth marks the material success of kings and chiefs in several stories. In the story explaining the origin of the masquerades, only the king has the material wherewithal to house the red cloth masquerades adequately. In the story of the king's wife, Àjọ̀n, the second brother's successful trading activities alert him to the possibilities of acquiring the clothing and paraphernalia used by the king of Idah. Through the acuity of his wife, the second brother keeps these things for himself and thus becomes a king.

The story of Àjọ̀n emphasizes an important element in the constitution of authority of Bùnú kings and chiefs. Like hunters, an aspect of their power is associated with forces outside the local community. Unlike hunters, however, these forces were not related to those of dangerous bush spirits but to those of powerful neighboring kingdoms. The red caps, the red robes, the special slippers worn by Bùnú kings come from their association with powerful kingdoms (Igala, Nupe, Hausa) outside of Bùnú. Even the red thread used in the local weaving of funeral and masquerade cloths came from European red cloth imported via the kingdoms of Benin, Idah, and the Sokoto Emirate (Renne 1992a:66). The use of these foreign cloths and things not only implies powers similar to those of the kings who use them elsewhere. Within Bùnú, the difficulties of obtaining red cloths and things also distinguish those who can from those who cannot, thus enhancing the status of the former.[9]

The acquisition and ownership of these cloths by particular lineages or clans differentiate these groups and (implicitly) rank them. Thus, in the past, families preparing for the second funerals of prestigious relations such as titled chiefs might go into debt, sell off slaves, or pawn children to acquire the necessary red funeral cloths (Èbájẹ́mítọ́ 1985:38). Failure to do so would not only be humiliating as a breech of filial respect for a kinsman and future ancestor, but would also mark a decline in status of surviving kin group members.

Similarly, the *egúngún* masquerades, the embodiment of ancestral spirits, kept by chiefs of different lineages or clans in Bùnú distinguish these groups and enhance their positions. Their ownership reflects both the material wherewithal to keep and maintain the masquerades and the legitimating aura of past ancestors who acquired them. The ability of chiefs to sacrifice to and intercede with ancestral spirits, represented by masquerades, is used to support present-day leadership and kin group claims.

Yet there is danger associated with the use of red cloth. The masquerades, while owned by chiefs, ultimately represent uncontrollable spirits which may behave in unpredictable ways. Two Bùnú stories in which the problems of sibling rivalry are examined in terms of cloth ownership consider further dangers associated with these valued red cloths. In the story of Àjọ̀n, the claims of a junior brother to the highest chieftaincy title, *olú* or king, are based on his keeping the chieftaincy cloths and things purchased in Idah. When his senior brother hears of this usurpation of cloth and chieftaincy position, he severs ties with his brother and their respective villages where there can be only one king. In a related story (see page 218, note 8), three brothers each acquire particular chieftaincy cloths, which results in the two elder brothers drowning the youngest, who had managed to obtain king's cloth. While the status of families is enhanced by ownership and display of red cloths and regalia, the individual achievement that such ownership represents may also constitute danger for the continuity and unity of kin groups.

Bùnú kings' and chiefs' spiritual authority comes from their identification with ancestral spirits of their kin group. Some kings and chiefs are believed to embody *ẹbọra* nature spirits as well (Krapf-Askari 1966a:4). Their authority is also enhanced by their custodianship of masquerades and by their candidacy as future ancestors, by virtue of their earthly accomplishments. Yet despite their individual accomplishments, they are dependent on kin and others to help in masquerade performance and to make them, upon their deaths, into ancestors with sumptuous displays of red cloth. This dependency contrasts with the spiritual powers of hunters whose individual successes in the bush are unhampered by kin and community. In these stories, the chiefs and hunters are associated with particular types of cloth that demonstrate their respective ascendancy in village and bush. Cloth is also used metaphorically to explore the ironies of the interplay between "socialistic adaptation to society and individual departure from its demands" (Simmel 1971:294). For the red funeral cloth, masquerades, and regalia distinguish but also circumscribe the behavior of individual kings and chiefs who are constrained by social expectation. The poverty and unranked status of hunters who wear plain cloth shirts warrant no such expectations and thus allow for idiosyncratic behavior, since their power is conceptualized as derived from outside of society.

The three stories might have been analyzed differently, laying stress
on the moral ambiguities of particular aspects of social life that
these, and other folk tales, contemplate (Beidelman 1986; Jackson
1982). The analysis pursued here focuses instead on the ways in
which they explore the nature of political authority through representations of hunters, chiefs, and cloth. The fact that cloth should
be such a dominant metaphor in these stories is significant. Because
of the pervasiveness of cloth in Bùnú society—as a symbol of continuity between domains, as a source of cure and harm, of wealth and
fertility—this should not be surprising. These stories emphasize the
importance of cloth, particularly the red funeral cloths and things
such as the red chieftaincy caps, in establishing and maintaining relations of hierarchy and political authority in Bùnú society. Handwoven cloths, like the stories that comment on them, are valued as
things of the past that are drawn upon to legitimate present-day
claims and beliefs. Thus, in the commemorative celebration of Àjọn,
which continues to be observed in northern Bùnú (Kírí), the
present-day Olú-Kírí (the king of Kírí) wears regalia identical to that
described in the story. Similarly, the ownership of red funeral cloths,
masquerades, and regalia plays an important part in substantiating
present-day political concerns.[10]

In focusing on the ways in which these stories reflect on the
powers of hunters and kings and their use of cloth, the implications
of the fact that cloth in Bùnú was primarily produced by women have
not been considered here. Yet the stories suggest that this fact was of
some importance. The spirit-wives' production and control of black
marriage cloths and the hunter's inability to keep these women contrast with the king's ability to regain the mute wife through the con-

trol of massive quantities of cloth. Further, the story of Àjọ̀n suggests one way by which chiefs and kings amassed cloth independently of Bùnú women weavers, that is, through the importation of cloth by trade. In the next chapter, the relationship of gender, cloth production, and political authority are examined more closely, as another solution to the control of chieftaincy cloth is explored.

SIX

WHAT

BÙNÚ MEN

WOVE

There was no high scaffolding,

no scarlet cloth . . .

Conrad, Lord Jim

Unlike the plain cloth shirts worn by hunters, the five patterned, red, handwoven cloths known generally as *aṣọ ipò* used by men who are chiefs contribute to the exercise of political authority in Bùnú. These cloths—whose red color associates them with death but also marks the achievement and dangerous power of those who control them—are displayed in the funerals of chiefs and used in masquerade performances, reinforcing a particular form of political organization based on the successive ranking of titled chiefs. Woven in strips which are used singly or joined together to make larger cloths, their red geometric patterning and carpetlike thickness distinguish them from all other Bùnú cloths. These cloths continue to be kept for use in important rituals associated with high-ranking chiefs despite the fact that they are no longer woven. That the use (and, formerly, production) of these cloths would have important political consequences should not be surprising. The control of both ritual performance and the production of ritual objects is an important source of power in many African societies (Fraser and Cole 1972).

The use of red cloths in chieftaincy rituals was and continues to be restricted. Formerly their production, with one exception, was not. In the past, Bùnú women wove all but one type of cloth on the broad, vertical looms used by women throughout Nigeria. There was only one cloth they did not weave, the red *aṣọ ipò* cloths used in the funerals of kings.

Village men were, and continue to be, predominantly farmers and hunters. In the past, they also occasionally wove,[1] but only the five red *aṣọ ipò* cloths associated with chieftaincy. However, unlike most male weavers throughout West Africa who wove on narrow, multi-heddle, horizontal looms—including Yorùbá weavers to the west and Nupe weavers to the north (Lamb and Holmes 1980; Sieber 1972)—Bùnú men wove cloth on the same vertical looms used by Bùnú women. How can Bùnú men's use of the "women's loom" be explained and why did they only weave the red cloths associated with chieftaincy? These questions may be addressed through an examination of beliefs about women's and men's roles in the production of cloth and about the reproduction of children and ancestors.

Traditionally, Bùnú as well as other Yorùbá groups (Buckley 1985; Ìdòwú 1962) held beliefs about the cyclical nature of the world in which death is perceived as a stage in the transformation of human beings into ancestral spirits and childbirth as the rebirth of ancestral spirits in human beings. Men control processes of ancestral transformation while women are largely responsible for practices associated with bringing children into the world.[2] This view is held by many Bùnú villagers, although conversion to Christianity has altered this perspective of creation for some.

These representations of women's and men's distinctive relationships to the spirit world and their different regenerative powers are reflected in cloth use and production. The close connection of women with the spirit world, from which the ability to conceive children and to weave cloth are believed to derive, is expressed in several ways (see chapter 4). For example, should a woman die (i.e., return to the spirit world) before finishing a cloth, the cloth, like an unborn child, will be buried ("taken") with her. Men's regenerative power vis-à-vis the spirit world is reflected in their ability to "make" and depict ancestors, through the use in funerals and in masquerade performances of red *aṣọ ipò* cloths. These symbolic representations expressed in terms of cloth are not insignificant. As in the comparison of the powers of hunters and chiefs, symbols such as cloth underwrite ideas about the nature of authority and, in this case, gender, and thus have political ramifications.

Through an examination of these symbolic representations, a possible explanation of why Bùnú men wove only red chieftaincy cloths on looms used by women may be found. In rituals demonstrating male chiefs' ability to communicate with and create ancestors, it is possible that men sought to control the production of relevant cloths (see Ben-Amos 1978:51). I suggest that in seeking to emphasize their own creative power, men played upon images of reproduction associated with women—the weaving of cloth on broad vertical looms—while at the same time distinguishing their own reproductive capacities by weaving only red cloth associated with the rebirth of ancestors. This emphasis was carried further in the prohibitions surrounding the weaving of one *aṣọ ipò* cloth, known as *apọ́núpọ́nyìn*. Only certain men, because of their superior mastery of spiritual forces, were said to be able to weave this dangerous cloth. While both women and men could weave all other types of red *aṣọ ipò* cloth, the fact that only men could weave the most potent of these red cloths used in the burial of kings reinforced ideas about a hierarchy of male and female titled chiefs, headed by men.

Weiner (1987) has examined the ways in which cultural meanings associated with reproduction of children and the production of cloth have important implications for the extent of power exercised by women and men in the Trobriand and Polynesian societies. In Bùnú, gender-specific representations of cloth production and of human

and ancestral reproduction authorize those who control these processes, affecting beliefs about the respective power of women and
men. Thus, assertions about who can and cannot weave particular
cloths are not disinterested but rather suggest that such claims may
be continually redefined in small but significant ways.

BELIEFS ABOUT BIRTH
AND REBIRTH IN BÙNÚ

Male chiefs express their authority, in part, by communicating with
ancestral spirits through blood sacrifices that they alone can make.
This special relationship with the world of ancestral spirits is also
reflected in their control of second-burial ritual, which marks the
transformation of deceased kinsmen into living ancestors. Likewise,
the appearances at funerals of masquerades, which are believed to
embody ancestral spirits, are orchestrated by village chiefs. Red aṣọ
ipò cloths, formerly buried with the corpse in the performance of
second-burial ritual and a necessary element in masquerade costumes, are instrumental in this regenerative process whereby humans are reborn as ancestors.[3]

The connection between masquerades, ancestral rebirth, and red
cloth is evocatively portrayed in performance preparations made for
the masquerade known as Òùna, as described by one Bùnú man:

In the past, there was something at Òùna's back which made it look as if it
were a mother backing a child. It was prepared with a whole human being
[often the corpse of a slave]. Whoever put the masquerade cloth on during
any ceremony must not see that thing. He would stand while somebody
would put it on his back like backing a child. . . . The whole thing is
always inside the masquerade cloth

Presently, a she-goat is substituted for Òùna's human load. However,
the imagery remains the same: the masquerade Òùna, carrying on its
back not a child but a dead body, with its spirit presumably going to

Young Bùnú mother carrying child with handwoven baby tie, ọ̀já, probably the product of Ebira weavers. The mother and child are holding sprigs of tree leaves, part of the ritual cleansing of the town performed during Àjọ̀n celebrations. Aíyétórò-Kírí-Bùnú, March 1988.

the spirit world. This image mirrors a mother backing her newborn baby, whose spirit has recently come from the spirit world. In their performance of traditional marriage ritual, women represent their close relationship with the spirit world and fertility. These images of the backing of bodies associated with spirits recently arrived or departed emphasize traditional Bùnú beliefs about the cyclical nature of creation.

In northern Bùnú, women and men also portray ideas about the recycling of spirits through the performance of a special ritual referred to as *ó mú ni mọ pákó*,[4] during which the ancestral spirit reborn in a child is identified. Prior to the performance of this ritual, a small white cloth with tiny red-and-blue warp stripes called *òrun padà* is woven in one day by a kinswoman of the child (see chapter 2). On the eve of the *pákó* performance, a woman who is sponsoring the ritual would be accompanied by other women who have done this ritual. They go silently at midnight to the house of an Ifá diviner. The woman sponsor gives him four bits of wood, four stones, or four cowries after secretly naming each bit for one of the child's grandparents. The diviner selects one of the bits, thereby identifying the spirit of the particular grandparent (or other deceased ascendant relative) reborn in the child.[5]

The woman sponsor then returns home before sunrise, carrying the things she had brought to the diviner in a wife's calabash placed on top of a marriage cloth on her head, and followed by the other women.[6] These women should not talk on the way to and from the diviner's house, nor should moonlight be allowed to enter the house through windows; only the light of a palm oil lamp (as used in *ejínu-wọn* ritual) can be used. The use of marriage things, the speech and lighting prohibitions, the period of time, all suggest separation from the human world and crossing into that of the spirits. Upon returning to the child's house, they inform the father of his child's ancestral identity.

The *òrun pàdà* cloth itself is not brought to the diviner but rather is left in the house after having been soaked in a mixture of camwood and water. Yet it is nonetheless part of the identification process. One man said that if it was not woven in the prescribed one day's time, the cloth would not "speak," i.e., reveal the child's spirit identity. After the women's return, this cloth is given to the child who wears it until it eventually shreds and disappears.

In this instance, women and men collaborate in communicating with the spirit world. Women weave cloth and carry things as if performing traditional marriage ritual, and male Ifá diviners communicate with the spirit world in order to learn of the child's predecessor. Similarly, male diviners may help women midwives during difficult childbirth deliveries. In rituals associated with red *aṣọ ipò* cloth, however, men's and women's associations with the spirit world are presented in a somewhat different way, reflecting a different perspective on the respective ritual participation and political authority of men and women.

AṢỌ IPÒ CLOTH

The term *aṣọ ipò*—*aṣọ*, cloth; *ipò*, red cloth (literally, "cloth from red cloth")—refers to a group of five predominantly red cloths woven on vertical, single-heddle, nontreadle looms by the Bùnú Yorùbá women and men. Relatively narrow (8-inch) strips of cloth were produced by a technique that combined a warp-faced plain weave foundation with supplementary weft patterning in a soumak weave variation (Renne 1992a:67). These strips were sewn together to make the thick, red cloths which are unmistakable in their overall geometric patterning and carpetlike thickness.[7]

The red wool yarn used in producing the characteristic patterning of these cloths was not indigenous to Bùnú. Rather, weavers obtained their red wool yarn from various sources, which included unravelling red wool from red hospital blankets bought in Okene during the colonial period. Earlier, red cloth was obtained either via the trans-Saharan trade or through European coastal trade with Benin and the Delta States.[8] In any event, the imported red cloth used to weave aṣọ ipò would have been extremely expensive, which made these cloths available only to those with great wealth. Thus they were appropriate objects to be used in the burials of wealthy, high-ranking, titled chiefs.

Like chiefs who have titles of various grades, the five aṣọ ipò cloths are ranked. They are distinguished according to size, which varies according to the number of cloth strips, the price, and the associated spiritual attributes. The small ẹbẹ cloth, consisting of a single, short strip (8 inches by 50 inches) woven on the day of the funeral, was displayed at all funerals for titled chiefs, as was the cloth ifàlẹ̀ (54 inches by 70 inches), made of seven long strips sewn together. Two other cloths—ọ̀já, a very long single strip (98 inches or more) and àbatá (83 inches by 78 inches), a large cloth made of eleven strips—would be shown at the funerals of chiefs with high-ranking titles. These "rules" were enforced by a council of village chiefs, men who controlled the use of particular cloths and also collected fees for their display, based on a sliding scale (Èbájẹ́mítọ́ 1985). These four cloths, red only on one side and white on the other, were woven by both women and men on looms that were usually kept in compound courtyards or in houses. There were no special restrictions on who could weave these cloths nor was the process hidden in any way.

The production and use of the fifth cloth, apọ́núpọ́nyìn, was restricted, however. While I have been unsuccessful in my attempts to

Vertical single-heddle loom set up to weave the aṣọ ipò *cloth,* ọ̀já.
Àkútúpá-Kírí-Bùnú, March 1988.

see this cloth, I was told that it was woven in one wide piece on a women's loom and that it was red on both sides. It could not be woven by women but had to be woven in the bush by men. Further, it was only displayed at the funeral of the king and then buried with him.

RED CLOTH
AND BÙNÚ FUNERALS

Aṣọ ipò cloths were formerly displayed and then buried in the grave at the time of second-burial ceremonies. Unfortunately, there are few written descriptions of Bùnú burial practices. One of the earliest comes from an 1878 journal entry of the CMS catechist Obadiah Thomas.[9] Thomas was visiting the old site of Àpàá, then located in central Bùnú. His plans were disrupted by the death of an important official's kinswoman:

A relative of the Mayaki in one of the farm villages, her remains were only brought here for interment. . . . The corpse [is] to be preserved for a fortnight before interment. It is the custom of the Bùnú tribe in general to preserve by drying the remains of a deceased person for several months or years prior to interment.   (O. Thomas 1878, CMS)

While this description does not include any references to cloth, it suggests the extensive cultural elaboration that ensued after an individual's death. These activities reflect the idea that biological death was just the beginning of a complicated process that included drying and culminating months to years later in the burial of the corpse. This transitional interval, often perceived as the time it took the spirit of the deceased to leave the world of humans for that of the ancestors, is an important part of second-burial practice (Hertz 1960). During this period, cloth used in the final burial rites is often accumulated or produced.

A description of the actual use of red funeral cloths in the second burial of a high-ranking chief was given by a colonial official in the 1930s:

On the day following the death, or on the same day if the death has taken place in the early hours, . . . the body is washed and dressed in fine clothes, capped and shod and is placed in a sitting position in a chair. . . . In the evening the body is buried, clothed as it is, inside the room in which it has been seated . . .

On the following day . . . the approximate date of the final burial ceremony is announced—usually in three months' time. During the period, the relations get together the means to buy the burial cloth, an ox, gunpowder, [etc.] . . . The burial cloths (usually woven by the Bunus) vary in price according to the means of the relatives and the status of the deceased, the cheapest burial cloth "*Egenja*" [Bùnú, *ẹbẹ*] costing about 15/- and rising in value to about £5 for "*Baleton*" [*àbatá*] or more for the most expensive. . . .

On the day appointed the ox is killed at the door of the chief of the town and, with presents of money, is divided among the members of the *Orota* [second highest ranking of chiefs].

The relations return home and place the burial cloth together with three gowns on the roof of the room where the body has been buried. . . . On the following morning three to five of the old women of the house walk around the town with the burial cloth carried on their heads for all the world to see and they are followed by male and female relations. . . . About an hour later the party returns. The burial cloth is rolled up and put on the shoulders of men and women who dance and play with it for a short time. The shaft of the grave is opened, the cloth is put inside and the grave finally closed in the presence of male relations and the Ofosi [members of a women's secret cult associated with chieftaincy]; the women stay outside and weep.   (Harris 1931, NAK)

This extended description is fascinating because of its detailed attention to funeral cloth use. Although the burial described above was performed for a titled chief (*orótà*) of the neighboring O-kun Yorùbá group, the Owé Yorùbá, who also use *aṣọ ipò* in funerals, the details are similar to Bùnú practices (Ẹ̀bájẹ́mítọ́ 1985). It differs significantly from that of the earlier Bùnú burial, probably less because of different Owé cultural practices and more because colonial officials had prohibited the long-term drying and display of corpses for sanitary reasons. Further, it suggests how the rolls of bulky *aṣọ ipò* cloth, "put on the shoulders of men and women who dance and play with it for a short time," were used as a substitute for the preserved corpse which formerly would have been interred at the same time as the cloth.

Presently, this substitution has been taken a step further now that the second "burial" no longer entails burying cloth or corpse. Because red funeral cloths are no longer buried, "a surrogate had to be used. In [the case that] the dead relation was a male a he-goat had to be slaughtered or [a bull] depending on the wealth of the [descendants]. If . . . the dead person was . . . female, a she-goat or cow would be slaughtered on the grave. It was the blood sprinkled on the grave that would represent the cloth that was not buried" (Èbájẹ́mítọ́ 1985:38). Implicit in the sacrifice of animals was the wealth of the patrons who could afford such expenditures, the visual relationship of the redness of sacrificial blood and of *aṣọ ipò* cloth, and the precolonial practice of burying human sacrifices along with cloth during the second-burial rituals of important chiefs and kings.

In addition to not burying these cloths, a further adaptation has been made in the way that cloths are displayed at the second-burial performances. While displayed at the house of the deceased, they are no longer placed on the roof, as the thatching has been replaced by iron sheeting (see Picton and Mack 1979:10). Thus, in a recent second-burial celebration in Àpàá (in 1987), three red funeral cloths—*òjá, ifàlè,* and *àbatá*—were hung from a pole in front of the deceased man's house. The cloths had been borrowed from members of another lineage, having been kept by the male head of this family. On the afternoon when these cloths were displayed, masquerades came out. The first masquerade, Egún Oku, prayed for the cloths

while members of a special women's cult (*òfósì*) praised the cloths,
comparing their greatness to the vastness of the Niger River, also
known as Ohíminì in Bùnú, singing: "Ohíminì, *aṣọ kàn lòkájo* [one
cloth from Àpàá], Ohíminì."

FUNERALS, MASQUERADES,
AND THE ANCESTORS

The use of red funeral cloth in the performance of second-burial ritual is reinforced by the appearance of red-clothed masquerades at
these events. These Àpàá masquerades and another set of masquerades from southern Bùnú, which make even more extensive use of
aṣọ ipò cloth in their dress, represent generalized ancestral spirits.
This differs from other parts of Yorubaland where masquerades may
represent individual ancestors and where particular masquerades
may be owned by royal lineages (Morton-Williams 1960:37). The
generalized aspect of Bùnú masquerades reflects the relative dif-
fuseness of its political organization, in which the highest chieftaincy offices are rotated among three family groups and where the
nomination of candidates is determined by ability, rather than by
royal lineages. Nonetheless, some masquerades are said to have been
introduced by the ancestors (named or unnamed) of particular families. Such masquerades are thereafter owned by descendants who
may enhance their local political status and authority through masquerade performances.

The southern Bùnú villages of Àgbèḍè and Àpàá represent two
separate masquerade traditions. The former is related to the masquerade complex found among other confluence area groups (e.g.,
the Ebira) and consists of five named masquerades—Nároko, Egàbọm, Òùna, Olúkókó, and Iyelúgbó—which are danced biannually.
The latter, related to northern Bùnú (Kírí) masking traditions, consists of four masquerades—Egún Oku, Gbángele, Ogbin, and Ìró—

Egún Oku, the masquerade that prays, accepting payment for predicting the customer's future during funeral observances for Chief David Láráiyetàn. Small pieces of red aṣọ ipò cloth are incorporated in the headdress. Àpàá-Bùnú, December 1987.

*Bùnú masquerade performance showing seated (l–r): Nároko, Òùna, Olúkókó,
and Egàbọm. All but Òùna incorporate aṣọ ipò cloth in their costumes.
The young men are wearing a variety of Western-style clothing, including
a Bob Marley tee-shirt by the man at the far right.
Àgbèdè-Bùnú, March 1988.*

that come out during second-burial performances. Dressed in the
red funeral cloth that associates them with ancestral spirits and their
authority, one or more of these masquerades may appear suddenly
during periods of duress (drought, epidemics, and violent disputes),
admonishing villagers and predicting their future. Whenever masquerades appear, however, they are always in the company of chiefs
and, indeed, only men who have taken a chieftaincy title are allowed
to dance them. In Àpàá, these restrictions are taken further in the
case of the masquerade Ìró, which should not be seen by women at
all.[10]

Ìró is unusual in Bùnú where all other masquerades may be seen
by women. Nonetheless, as elsewhere in Nigeria, Bùnú masquer-

ades reflect an attempt to distinguish the reproductive powers of women and men. As Morton-Williams has observed for the Ọ̀yọ́ Yorùbá, "Men may have *egúngún* which guarantee them social immortality. Women do not. Ordinarily, women . . . [have] children" (1960:37). This distinction between men's and women's regenerative roles also supports men's authority over particular actions of women. In Bùnú, women are restricted in their reproduction and depiction of ancestors-masquerades and in their access to them.

Women's movements may also be circumscribed by ancestral indictment acted out by masquerades. When one woman who had traveled returned to Àgbèdè to find that her husband had died, one masquerade prevented her from reentering the village. Her traveling during her husband's illness implied that her trading activities took precedence over his health. On other occasions as well, women's travel and trading were blamed by men chiefs for local misfortunes. These restrictions on the movements and powers of women, which the red-clothed masquerades enforce, represent men chiefs' attempts to assert their own authority and to circumscribe that of women.[11] Similarly, restrictions on the weaving of certain red cloths by women limit their participation in the making of chiefs, further enhancing the political authority of kings.

GENDER, CLOTH, AND POWER

The one cloth that women could not weave was the most highly valued *aṣọ ipò* cloth, used only in the burials of kings. It was called *apọ́núpọ́nyìn* (literally, "oneside, otherside"), referring to the complete covering of the white cotton warp on both sides with red yarn. Only those men who had the supernatural power to "see both sides" could weave it, i.e., men "with four eyes" (*olójúmẹ́rin*; see chapter 3). Such power was needed to counter the deadly character of this cloth, which was sometimes referred to as *aṣọ burúkú* (bad or evil cloth).

This cloth could not be woven in the village because it was dangerous and because women were not allowed to view the weaving process. Several people said that when this cloth was displayed, it moaned or hummed, calling for blood. If a sacrifice was not forthcoming, a person in the house or associated with the cloth would die. One man who formerly wove it described weaving it in a special place in the bush, outside the village. A goat would be sacrificed every day before weaving began. Otherwise, he said, the weaver's blood would dry up in his veins (O. Olúkòtán, Àpàá-Bùnú).

Apónúpónyìn cloth was displayed only at the second burial of the highest chief, the *olú*, and thus it was rarely woven. It was also never kept. More recently, when all *asọ ipò* cloths have become scarce and are no longer buried, *apónúpónyìn* cloth cannot be kept because of the dangers associated with storing it. One woman said that this cloth could cause a house to burn down. To overcome these difficulties, I was told that nowadays when a king dies, two *àbatá* cloths will be sewn together, back to back, to display in its place (A. Tèmítáyọ̀, Aíyétórò-Kírí-Bùnú). Although Bùnú kings are now Christians (and *apónúpónyìn* cloths are no longer woven), their extraordinary power, which enables them to communicate with the ancestors through sacrifice, continues to be celebrated with cloth, red on both sides, when they die.

WHEN WOMEN CAN USE

RED FUNERAL CLOTH

Women neither make blood sacrifices nor weave *apónúpónyìn* cloth. However, there are occasions when women can use this and other *asọ ipò* cloths, though only in the context of chieftaincy. In precolonial Bùnú, as in many parts of southern Nigeria, there were men and women chiefs who led their respective village male and female contingents. In Kírí (northern Bùnú), the highest-ranking woman chief, the *èjìgí*, by virtue of her wealth and with the approval of village women, was named their leader. When this woman died, men chiefs allowed for the display of *apónúpónyìn* cloth during her second burial (B. Olórunípa, Ìgbo-Bùnú).

In central and southern Bùnú, a titled woman chief of a lower rank, the *iyedé*, would have the other *aṣọ ipò* cloths displayed for her. Now that these titles are no longer taken by women, older important women may be honored with the display of red funeral cloth by a more circuitous route. Their families will prepare for a second burial in the name of a long-deceased male chief and then will include the name of the woman as well (J. Olówósaiyé).

Thus the use of *aṣọ ipò* cloth continues to be closely associated with titled chiefs. In the event that these chiefs are women, or important women "standing" or, perhaps I should say, buried with chiefs, they would have been older, postmenopausal women.

By culturally embellishing death in a particular way, men emphasize their own reproductive capacities—their capacity to culturally produce ancestors through their control of second-burial rituals and masquerade performances. Through their ability to control this aspect of a cycle of birth and rebirth, their authority as chiefs is enhanced. Indeed, women of child-bearing age are portrayed by men as vulnerable and flighty—as less in control of the spiritual power that allows them to bring children into the world of humans—which is reflected in restriction on their use of red cloth.

WOMEN WHO SHOULD

NOT WEAR RED

Women who are mothers, and their children, should not wear red cloth. One traditional healer said that to be safe, women and children should wear white (Z. Olú). This, he said, was because all women and children were vulnerable to their spirits, *ejínuwọn* or *olómi*, which come "from water," in other words, the spirit world. Women and children were vulnerable to these spirits, which could cause them to "go back," or die, at any time.

Women performing the traditional marriage ritual wear indigo-dyed, blue-black or white cloths, with perhaps narrow red stripes, but never cloth that is predominantly red. Women who have been sickly or have trouble bearing children wear white cloth during part of the ritual (Àrèmú 1982). These marriage cloths and white cloths are both associated with the spirit world. Both types are woven exclusively by women. Indeed, the rituals with which these cloths are closely associated, traditional marriage and the *ejínuwọn* spirit-possession cult, are performed to promote the birth of children and protect mothers and children from disease and death. Women's procreative power, perceived as deriving from their spirit world connections, are ritually managed by older women marriage specialists and spirit cult leaders.

Women control the birth process, at times with the aid of men diviners, unless there are complications, at which point women may be taken to clinics and hospitals in Kàbbà. Although not ritually embellished the way that the making of ancestors is, the biological fact of giving birth is culturally elaborated in various ways, transforming the newborn spirit-child into a social human being. Immediately after birth, the child is sprinkled with cold water and then washed with black soap to remove all remnants of its former existence in the womb. In some parts of Bùnú, a small sacrifice is also made to the child's nature spirit (*àlùjọnú*) residing in nearby streams or bush. After a child's birth in Àpàá, for example, an older woman midwife carried three bits each of red camwood, black soap, and white shea butter on a leaf and threw them into the bush.

While no particular cloth is prescribed for a newborn child, an Ifá diviner might be consulted to discover whether the child's spirit has any special requirements. One woman noted that though any type of cloth could be used, the child should be carried with cloth on a woman's back before being laid on a bed.[12] The use of cloth to "back" children emphasizes their continued fetal-like dependence, as when they were carried in their mothers' wombs, and their continuing vulnerability to spirit world forces. Although men may hold infant children, they never "back" them.

After eight days, a child is given a Bùnú name and sometimes a Christian name. The latter may be given during christening ceremonies later in church. No particular cloth is worn, though a child might be wrapped in a cloth identical to that worn by its father and mother (aṣọ ẹbí, family cloth). However, in one small traditional naming ceremony that I witnessed in Àpàá, the mother wore her àdófì marriage cloth. As the mother and child emerged from the cooking-house, water was poured on the roof with a calabash, the water falling on mother and child. These two references to traditional marriage practice—the wearing of the àdófì cloth and the pouring of water on the roof—are reenacted to refer to the spiritual connections of women and children.

Women's reproductive capacity, represented by their ability to weave and to bear children through their ties with the spirit world, is the basis of their power. It was through their success in these activities that they were formerly able to become chiefs themselves and to participate directly in local political affairs. These activities thus implicitly, and at times explicitly, challenged the political authority of men chiefs.

Although men cannot alter the biological fact that women give birth to children, men can enhance their position as chiefs by making cloths used in the rebirth and depiction of ancestors. By restricting the weaving of certain chieftaincy cloths to men, they downplay the reproductive powers of women in the making of ancestors, while stressing their own. Further, women are portrayed as vulnerable to the powerful forces represented by red cloth and should weave and wear white instead.[13] In the town of Ọ̀llẹ̀ in central Bùnú, I was told that the red cloth, *àbatá*, the cloth after *apọ́núpọ́nyìn* in the hierarchy of *aṣọ ipò* cloths, could not be woven by women. I was told this nowhere else in Bùnú. It suggests a process by which, had the weaving of *aṣọ ipò* continued, the weaving of other red cloths might eventually have been limited to men.

MAKING WOMEN'S THINGS

INTO THINGS OF MEN

Even though *aṣọ ipò* is no longer woven, Bùnú women today continue to weave cloths used by men in chieftaincy rituals and in hunting. These cloths are altered in various ways to make them into things of men.

The *àkì* cloth tied around the heads of high-ranking chiefs and kings is the same *àkì* cloth, woven in one day, used by *ejínuwọn* women, though it is slightly altered. When used in *ejínuwọn* spirit possession the cloth is white; when worn by kings, the cloth has been dyed red with camwood. Similarly, the red funeral cloth woven by women is later doctored with medicines to alter its character before it is made into masquerade costumes by men.

Medicines are also used to change the hunter's shirts woven by women. Indeed, these medicines warrant the prohibition that a wife must not touch her husband's shirt for fear of contaminating this medicine. Even when women have their own hunter's shirts (see chapter 2), the shirts incorporate medicine in a way distinctive from that of men. Women's shirts have medicine attached externally to the back and front, while men's shirts contain medicine with a larger pouch in front. As with other Bùnú cloths, this differentiation of men's and women's hunters' shirts is not insignificant but rather reflects beliefs about their different powers. This medicine, hidden in pouches that suggest the "deep" medicinal knowledge of hunters who are often Ifá diviners and traditional healers, is being contrasted with women's medicinal knowledge, which is perceived as limited and superficial.

AṢỌ IPÒ, GENDER, AND
POLITICAL HIERARCHY

There is no single reason why Bùnú men only wove one type of red cloth, known as *aṣọ ipò*, but rather a more complex explanation having to do with political hierarchy, beliefs in ancestral spirits, and ideas and assertions about the respective powers of women and men.

To say that there were political, religious, and social reasons for men's weaving red cloth on vertical looms associated with women does not deny that there may have been other reasons as well. It may have been simply more practical for men to weave on looms that were already available. Further, the weaving of *aṣọ ipò* cloth provided Bùnú women and men with the opportunity of accumulating considerable wealth from its sale.[14] Because it was in constant demand for funerals and because of the high price it commanded, *aṣọ ipò* weaving, along with brasswork (Krapf-Askari 1966b), was one of the most remunerative of all craft specializations in Bùnú. One Bùnú man suggested that men took up weaving *aṣọ ipò* for economic reasons alone (E. Àyìnmódè, Ọllẹ̀-Bùnú). However, men did not weave other types of cloth woven by women, which though not as remunerative nonetheless enabled astute women to finance the taking of chieftaincy titles. Indeed, textile production was the source of older Bùnú women's considerable economic independence in the precolonial and early colonial periods. While economic opportunity was probably a factor in men's weaving of *aṣọ ipò* cloth, the importance of red cloth in representing ideas about political authority, gender roles, and regenerative powers suggests that these factors were of comparable importance.

Bùnú women's and men's claims to political authority and power rest on their assertions of particular connections with the spirit world. Bùnú women and men support their claims through their actions at rituals of birth and death, their production of associated cloths, their economic acumen, and their roles in establishing kinship connections. Their actions and claims are distinctive but not necessarily conflicting. That women and men weave, that they have independent sources of income, that men perform rituals of death and women perform rituals of birth, and that strong ties with bilateral kin are maintained—all are factors which have contributed to the considerable complementarity of political power of Bùnú men and women. This complementarity and mutual support are evident in the story of Queen Àjọ̀n (recounted in chapter 5), who was commemorated by her husband for her instrumental part in making him a king.

Yet concurrent with this complementarity was a historical process whereby men asserted control over the production of the funeral cloth of kings. Restrictions on this cloth's production reflect a tendency toward the centralization of power related to the strengthening of the authority of kings.[15] This centralization tends to diminish the role of others, be they women or priests (Hocart 1970a), in the political process.

Nowadays, *aṣọ ipò* cloths are no longer woven by either women or men, but rather are kept by men family heads who continue to use them in masquerade and second-burial performances. Bùnú women no longer weave *aṣọ ipò* cloths, they no longer take chieftaincy titles, and their local political power is diminished, largely as a result of colonial political and economic policies and missionary teachings. While Bùnú women's local political participation has been undermined, Bùnú chiefs have won a Pyrrhic victory. For the political authority of men village chiefs has been circumscribed as well, earlier in the century by officials of the colonial state and after 1960 by local government, state, national, and military officials who are backed by the authority of the State of Nigeria.

This centralization of political authority is not unrelated to the decline of handwoven cloth production and cotton cultivation in Bùnú, which is examined in the following two chapters. By focusing on changes in cloth and cotton production in Bùnú, we can more clearly see the responses of rural women and men to economic, political, and social changes advocated by colonial government officials and by missionaries.

THE DECLINE
OF HANDWEAVING
IN BÙNÚ

**In making cloth she showed so
great a bent she bettered those
of Ypres and Ghent.**
Chaucer, Canterbury Tales

Assistant Resident H. B. James, in describing the state of hand-weaving in a 1914 Assessment Report of Bùnú District, wrote that "most of the thousand odd looms are idle, and it is only weaving of cloth for ceremonial purposes which provides any employment for them. . . . Already, as an industry, weaving has been killed by competition with European cotton goods" (James 1914, NAK). Yet only two years earlier, the German explorer-archaeologist Leo Frobenius (1913:415) had visited the Nupe market at Bida and had noticed "the [women] dealers with great bales of home-spuns [who] come daily in from the Bùnú district in the South, an outlying province of the Yoruban territory." How can this discrepancy be explained? And what part did Bùnú women weavers play in encouraging an assistant resident's fantasy about "idle looms" and in hampering British efforts to replace locally produced cloths with their own?

James's statement represents the wishful thinking of a British colonial officer, perhaps helped along by misunderstanding and by Bùnú women who sought to misrepresent the extent of their economic activity to a stranger. Its imagery projects the idealized final stage of a colonial policy referred to as "cotton imperialism" (Johnson

1974:182). Under this plan, high-ranking colonial officials promoted the growing of cotton by Africans, which was to be sold to British cotton firms that in turn planned to sell finished Manchester textiles to Africans.

Ironically, it was only after the departure of the British—Nigeria became an independent state in 1960—that most Bùnú women abandoned handweaving finally. In this chapter I consider the related questions of why Bùnú weavers continued to weave during the colonial period and why they gave up handweaving when they did. For the timing of their decision did not rest on the simplistic economic formula expressed by Assistant Resident James, who assumed that competition from cheaper Manchester textiles would run the less efficiently produced and thus more costly handwoven textiles out of the market. Rather, their decisions were based on an assessment of the changes in social and economic relations between older and younger women, the availability of and access to raw materials, and opportunities of alternative employment opening up to Bùnú villagers as a result of improved roads and motor transport. An examination of the interrelated social, economic, and political factors on which Bùnú women based their decisions to abandon handweaving reveals the responses of a group of rural women to policies of the colonial state. Rather than passive victims whose "industry . . . [was] killed by competition with European cotton goods," Bùnú women had their own stratagems for adopting, and adapting to, colonial policies, including whether or not they continued to weave.[1]

CLOTH PRODUCTION
AND BRITISH COLONIAL RULE

The decisions of Bùnú women concerning handweaving were, nonetheless, related to decisions made by British colonial officials. By considering aspects of the political economy of colonial northern Nigeria as well as the administrative particularities of Bùnú District, we may better understand the context of Bùnú village women's economic options and decisions.

In 1900 when the Protectorate of Northern Nigeria was established (Niven 1926:300–301), colonial officials justified their actions to Parliament and the British public on the basis of economics. They argued that the colonial presence would make available both large quantities of raw cotton for British textile firms and markets for their finished products (Johnson 1974:182). These great benefits would be attained at relatively little expense through the institution of a policy known as Indirect Rule, advocated by the Protectorate's first governor, Sir Frederick Lugard. According to this policy, British intervention and administrative costs were kept to a minimum by utilizing local political rulers to implement British policies. Elsewhere referred to as "governing 'on the cheap' " (Beidelman 1983:97), this contradictory policy depended on the cooperation of indigenous "traditional rulers" whose political authority was nonetheless circumscribed by the British.

In areas such as Bùnú District that were marginal to British economic and political interests, the influx of British personnel and funds was very indirect indeed. Thus colonial policies, which initially sought to discourage handweaving while encouraging cotton production, were impractical to implement under the constraints of Indirect Rule, particularly in Bùnú District where colonial officers were rarely present. Further, by fostering a political program of customary rulers legitimated by traditional practices that included the use of handwoven cloth, colonial officials indirectly promoted handweaving. They also sanctioned women's cloth production by sending handwoven cloths to provincial exhibitions.[2]

One Kàbbà district officer summed up the colonial policy of "benign neglect" largely practiced in Bùnú: "Their chief desire is to be allowed to continue their farming and weaving in peace, with as little administrative disturbance as possible" (Squibbs 1935, NAK). This policy had its benefits as Bùnú residents were not subject to drastic taxation or to forced labor schemes applied by European colonial officials in other parts of Africa. However, it also meant that road- and school-building programs came much later to Bùnú District than to other areas of Nigeria. Bùnú village women's economic opportunities were limited, especially compared to what was available to women weavers in more geographically advantaged areas.

Thus the Bùnú material on cloth production supports, with some important exceptions, Johnson's 1978 analysis of why handwoven textile production has continued in Nigeria, despite the influx of less costly mill-woven imports. According to her argument, handweaving continues among those who have not been able to find more remunerative employment (1978:267). Bùnú village women,[3] questioned about their decisions to stop weaving, often gave reasons related to the availability of more lucrative, less laborious occupations. They noted that improved transportation allowed them to trade in farm produce at local markets. They also saw that the introduction of primary schools in Bùnú had not only restricted access to child labor, leading to the scarcity of cotton handspun yarn, but had led to the possibility of more highly paid, white-collar employment for their daughters as well.

Nonetheless, a few older women in most Bùnú villages continue to weave because of demand for particular types of cloth associated with Bùnú ritual practices and religious beliefs. By maintaining these traditions, Bùnú villagers make a moral virtue of political and geographic isolation compared to neighboring groups who have abandoned these practices. A purely economic explanation of continued cloth production fails to grasp the importance of social and ideological factors associated with certain types of cloth and cloth production.[4]

THE HANDWEAVING INDUSTRY IN BÙNÚ

Until the mid-1960s, handweaving was considered *the* primary form of women's work—women did not actively participate in agriculture.[5] Most if not all of the women in Bùnú over forty years of age have worked as spinners and weavers and while most are no longer weaving, they remember much about their former occupation. Women spoke about their training as spinners and weavers, the types of cloths woven and sold, trade patterns and markets, cloth prices, and the uses of proceeds of sales. The picture that developed was one of a well-defined sexual division of labor, women weaving and men farming, each with their own separate and independent economic means.

WEAVERS' TRAINING IN BÙNÚ VILLAGES

Thirty Bùnú women, ranging from approximately forty-five to eighty years of age,[6] were questioned about their experiences as handweavers. Of them, only seven were taught to weave and spin by their biological mothers. It was commonly felt that mothers would not be sufficiently strict with their daughters, so that daughters were often given to senior wives of their fathers or to grandmothers for instruction. Young girls four to five years of age were first given cotton bolls (*òwú*), which were to be picked for dirt. Soon after, they were taught the process of seed removal, using an *apákó* (wood block) and *ọmobọ* (iron rod). The cotton lint was then

The late Madam Ọbàlò preparing and spinning cotton. Demonstration of the
igọnrun, *used for fluffing cotton fibers after the seeds have been removed. The*
ọmobọ *and* apákó, *the iron rod and wood block used for removing cotton seeds,*
can be seen at the lower left.
Àpàá-Bùnú, *January 1988.*

Spinning cotton—the bowl on her right contains ash to keep her fingers dry while spinning.

"fluffed" using an *igonrun* (which looks like an archer's bow) in preparation for spinning. After the girl had learned these preliminary tasks, she was given a small practice spindle to learn spinning. Thereafter she was expected to spin for her mother (either biological or foster). Cotton preparation and spinning was the work of these young girls from morning to evening, during the dry and rainy seasons. Children who refused to work were chided with the question, "If you don't do it, how will you eat?" (C. Ọbajànọ̀, Àpàá-Bùnú). Many informants admitted that they had to be forced to spin and some were beaten.

By approximately their twelfth year, girls would be taught to warp looms and weave simple cloth. One woman described how the first cloth woven would be thrown on a crossroads in the bush as a sacrifice for the future life and financial success of the weaver. Afterwards, when weaving began on a newly prepared loom, a prayer would be invoked in memory of the woman who taught the girl to weave. The four corners of the loom would be touched with the weaving sword while the weaver says, "I honor [the one who taught me] and God (*Mojúbà [person's name] àti Qlórun*)."

Girls would continue to spin and weave for their mothers, helping to take cloth to market to sell, in return for the time and expense these older women had taken in raising them (see chapter 4). Proceeds from cloth sales were returned to their mothers, who might give their daughters cloths and gifts in preparation for marriage. After moving to their husband's house and giving birth to a first child, young women began to weave for themselves, keeping the profits from their sales. Giving birth defined adult status for Bùnú women and it was at this time that many former weavers said that they had quit weaving in the 1950s and 1960s.

BÙNÚ CLOTHS

WOVEN FOR SALE

Bùnú women named several different types of cloths distinguished by warp- and weft-striping, colors, and number of pieces, which were woven specifically for sale (Appendix 1). Generally, wider cloths made with three or more indigo-dyed panels were more expensive. While it is difficult to assess from oral information the amounts paid for these varieties of cloths, the less expensive cloths were competitively priced with some imported cloth, which varied in price and quality as well. Two women weaving in the 1950s said that they sold white and blue striped *kẹkẹ* cloths at the market at Lokoja for six to seven shillings a pair, while paying six shillings for two yards of waxprint (*ànkàrà*) imported cloth.[7] Several Bùnú women mentioned buying *ànkàrà* cloth at large markets with cash earnings from their own cloth sales, though food purchases were mentioned more often. In relatively isolated, inland areas such as Bùnú District, the price advantage of imported cloths was off-set by increased transportation costs. Thus while Bùnú women did buy imported textiles for special occasions from itinerant Ijẹṣà cloth traders (Peel 1983:154), imported cloth did not replace local cloth.

One particularly inexpensive cloth, called *arigidi*, was woven not for Bùnú consumption but strictly for sale at the large Igbo market at Onitsha. This cloth consisted of two very narrow, loosely woven, handspun cotton strips and was said to be used by Igbo tapsters and fishermen as loincloths, as towels, and as chair slings.[8] Bùnú women would carry it to local markets at Ódogi and Kàbbà, or cloth traders from Kàbbà would come to Bùnú villages to buy *arigidi* cloth. One such trader, Àjìgí, was remembered by many women in Bùnú villages. Presently living in Kàbbà, he described the former *arigidi* trade:

I went to the Bùnú villages of Àgbẹ̀dẹ, Àpàá, Agbadù, Odo-Apẹ̀, Afotu, Aiyegúnle, Akerin, Adira-Tẹ̀dó, Aiyede, Ọ̀llẹ̀, Abihi, and Òkè-Bùkún. I went to Àgbẹ̀dẹ and Àpàá and came back that day. I used to pay two shillings for two pieces [a pair] of *arigidi*. If the women saw me they would go and bring me *arigidi* and I would pay them immediately. Sometimes I would advance money so when I returned they would give me *arigidi*. I started buying *arigidi* cloth after the Omi Mímọ́ movement [in 1930]. When I first bought it, I paid one shilling for two pieces.
    I also used to buy *arigidi* in Ódogi Market for two shillings when it was good. When I had collected it, I would enter a motor going to Lokoja (for five shillings) and then take a ferry to Onitsha. At Onitsha, I would sell the cloth to an Igbo trader, making a profit of three pence, depending. I used to do this every three months.
    I also would buy *kẹkẹ* and *àrìkúkù* [two types of blue and white cloth] from weavers in Bùnú for three shillings and sell it at Onitsha. At Onitsha, I would buy *aṣọ òyìnbó* [white people's cloth, usually imported wax print cloth], eight yards for three pounds. I would sell it in Bùnú for four pounds.[9]

Arigidi cloth production must have been considerable because Kàbbà District Officer H. S. Bridel devoted a section to the sale of *arigidi* in the 1929 annual district assessment report:

The average women (about 70% of the adult population actually practice weaving) will weave four Arigidi cloths a month and sell them for 1/- to 1/6 each; the profit, the cost of cotton being deducted, is from 3d to 5d according to the size. For two months of the year, November and December, no work is done owing to the scarcity of cotton. The average income is therefore 13/4d a year.   (1929, NAK)

Women may have intentionally underestimated the amount of *arigidi* cloth that they wove in a month, as Bridel's figure of four cloth pairs a month seems low. It is difficult to estimate how many cloths on average were woven monthly, though it was likely that it was two to four times the amount that Bridel estimated.[10] Bridel's estimates are intriguing as they suggest that the gap between women's and men's earnings was quite small. Taking these income estimates on their face, women weavers earned approximately three-fourths the amounts earned by men.

Bridel's information on weavers was of interest to colonial officials for tax purposes. Officials were also interested in indigenous cloth production because of colonial policies that encouraged the growing of cotton and sales of British manufactured cloth. There was competition between the local handweavers and the British Cotton Growing Association (BCGA) for locally grown cotton, local weavers buying up the best cotton at higher prices, sometimes up to four times the prices offered by BCGA brokers (James 1928, NAI). According to the 1927 Kàbbà Province Annual Report: "Both in Igbirra and Kàbbà Divisions considerable quantities of cotton is used locally in the manufacture of the so-called Kano cloth, which is then taken to Kano and Lagos, etc. for sale. It is only the surplus cotton which is offered to the British Cotton Growing Association" (Sciortino 1927, NAI).

Competition for cloth markets, on the other hand, was less acute during the 1920s when sales of both local and imported cloth increased, due to increased availability of cash and to improved roads and motor and rail transport. People were buying British manufactured cloth, though in limited quantities as it was not much less expensive than locally handwoven cloth and was less durable. However, the market crash of 1929 reversed this trend. Resident Officer H. B. James observed in the 1930 Kàbbà Province Annual Report that

the drop in prices of manufactured goods had not stimulated their sale and very little is done in such lines in comparison with other years. Agents of firms attribute this to money being scarce . . . but the real reason is connected with a policy of retaliation which is being consistently pursued. . . . What did affect them was the drop in prices paid for produce and there will be a meagre market for manufactured goods until these rise again.   (1930, NAI)

It is difficult to assess whether Resident Officer James's suspicion of retaliation was correct. Clearly, the low prices paid for local produce meant that even prosperous Bùnú villagers had less money to spend on imported cloth. It was also possible that villagers resented the wide fluctuations in prices paid for commodities such as cotton which British officials encouraged them to grow. Thus, by 1933, the author of the Kàbbà Province Annual Report noted that "everyone is well fed and well-dressed—not so noticeably in Manchester cottons . . . but in the excellent locally woven cloth which is being produced in increasing quantity" (Rosedale 1933, NAI).

Cloth imports from Britain actually remained approximately the same in the period from 1891 to 1938 (Johnson 1974:187). While the processing and weaving of locally grown cotton continued into the 1940s and early 1950s, colonial officials ceased to promote it as they had earlier. As other economic opportunities became available to Bùnú women in the postwar period, the purchase of imported manufactured cloth, particularly inexpensive Indian and Japanese textiles, increased. Some Bùnú women continued to weave *arigidi* cloth until shortly before the Nigerian civil war (1967–70) when trade between the Igbo and the northeast Yorùbá halted. Demand for and production of this cloth did not begin again after the war and for many Bùnú women interviewed, it was the last cloth they wove.

The *aṣọ ipò* cloth used in Bùnú funeral ritual and in masquerade costumes also had a specialized market trajectory. Woven by commission for Bùnú customers, it was woven for sale to Ìjùmú and Owé Yorùbá people, and to the Ebira people at Okene. Families of important chiefs who had recently died would purchase these cloths, which were used in funeral ritual. *Aṣọ ipò* cloth strips were taken to Okene and Kàbbà where they were sold privately, taken to specific compounds rather than to the market. Bùnú women from Ìsàdó-Kírí in northern Bùnú walked south toward Kàbbà, stopping at Ọllẹ̀ and Gbeleko and reaching Okene in about four days.[11] While both women and men wove these cloths (as discussed in chapter 6), women marketed them.

MARKETS AND THE CLOTH TRADE

Most Bùnú women not only wove but also walked long distances to sell their cloth at several markets, including those at Kàbbà and Okene in the south, Agbaja and Lokoja to the east, and Abúgi and Bida to the north.[12] For women living in old Àpàá in northern Bùnú, it took four to seven days to make the round trip to Lokoja, with stops at Jakùra and Agbaja. Weavers from Àgbẹ̀dẹ in southern Bùnú would

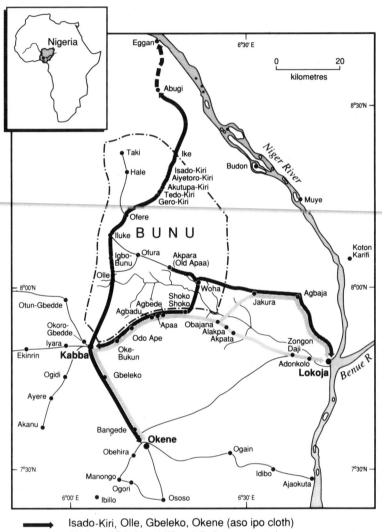

Map of Bùnú District, indicating former market routes of Bùnú weavers.

take three to four days round trip, stopping at Àkpàtà and Sángo before arriving at Lokoja. The experiences of these Bùnú women traders were probably similar to those of Ìjèbu women cloth traders from southern Yorubaland described by novelist Wọlé Ṣóyínká: "They frequently arrived late at night like a weatherbeaten caravan, heavy-laden baskets and fibre sacks on their heads. They were filled with smoked meats, woven cloths and local ointments" (1988:128).

In the early 1930s, women's marketing was made easier by the introduction of motor transport, which made possible a return trip from Kàbbà to Lokoja in one day. Improved transportation had a profound effect on the economic choices available to women, and District Officer Bridel noted that women "bless their [motor vehicles'] coming" (1929, NAK). Because they were no longer limited to amounts they could head-load and could make more trips to markets, they could increase the quantities and types of goods they traded.

Prior to the introduction of motor transport, Bùnú women described collecting bundles of ten cloths woven by themselves and other women which they head-loaded to various destinations. Women did not pay those who carried cloths, but rather took turns carrying for one another. Proceeds from sales belonged to married women responsible for weaving these cloths. While husbands might be given food prepared from their wives' purchases or might be given loans, these women's earnings belonged to them alone. The economic independence of Bùnú women and men was emphasized by the fact that women could purchase cotton grown by their husbands or purchase it in local markets. This exchange of cotton for cash gave the women what was in effect "clear title" to the proceeds of cotton cloth sales. One woman mentioned that her husband might give her cotton without charge, but would expect her to weave something for him (M. Ọmọ́le). Women wove some cloths for domestic use, particularly the older informants who were weaving before machine-woven cloth was widely available. When weaving for members of their families, they did not expect payment if thread was brought to them for weaving. Many mentioned weaving cloths not sold in markets, such as the prestigious ọlọ́ba cloth, baby ties (ọ̀já), and marriage cloths, most of which had to be commissioned or be woven by oneself. However, all women stated that they wove cloth principally for sale in local and long-distance markets.

COTTON PRICES, CLOTH PRODUCTION, AND TAXATION

After British administration of the area began in 1900, officials eventually realized that handweaving was the major industry in the area. Based on the assessment of women's and men's incomes from weaving and agricultural sales, respectively, individuals rather than households were taxed in Bùnú. Women paid three shillings, men six shillings annually in taxes. It is unclear whether the taxation of women was introduced to discourage cloth production, as earlier toll taxes had been instituted to do (Johnson 1974: 182–183). In their early efforts to discourage local cloth production while encouraging cotton-growing and the sales of imported Manchester textiles, British colonial officials and cotton brokers had interests contrary to those of Bùnú women. The institution of "head taxes" for women, however, insured that they would continue to weave because Bùnú village women had few other options for raising cash.

The nongraduated head tax, without "deductions for dependents," was extremely difficult for many women to pay. Women used most of their cloth earnings to purchase foodstuffs such as pepper, fish, and red oil as well as medicine, cloth, and later schoolbooks for their children. One Bùnú woman described having to work very hard in order to collect the necessary three shillings for taxes. "If you didn't pay it, they would take you away" (R. Mọni). While Bùnú (and Kàbbà) women did not openly rebel against paying the three-shilling head tax as women did elsewhere in Nigeria (Van Allen 1976), there was probably considerable complaint.[13] Bùnú women continued to pay three shillings in tax until the mid-1940s.

While direct interaction between Bùnú village women and British district officials was limited, colonial policies nonetheless affected decisions that Bùnú women made for themselves and their daughters about the occupation of weaving. There were important changes in relations of production resulting from girls' primary education and the institution of court-divorces. These changes affected older women's access to and use of the labor of young girls, which ultimately led to most women abandoning handweaving altogether.

WHY HANDWEAVING
DECLINED IN BÙNÚ

In 1880, Pythias James Williams of the CMS Mission Station at nearby Gbebe wrote that "the women [are occupied] spinning and weaving coarse native cloths and the little children in cleaning cotton with their little fingers" (1880, CMS).

Women weavers depended on these children, specifically young girls, to prepare the cotton and then spin it. The expansion of primary education throughout Nigeria after World War II cut off this supply of child labor. In Bùnú, girls began attending primary school in the mid-1950s (J. Baiyésheá, Àgbèdẹ-Bùnú). School attendance not only reduced the time available for cotton preparation and spinning but also led some people to associate handspinning with "unenlightened" behavior. Consequently most Bùnú women born after 1950 do not know how to spin. When young girls were sent to school in other towns under their families' sponsorship, their mothers' access to and control of their labor was limited. Their control over their daughters was limited in other ways as well.

Most of the women over sixty years old were betrothed as small girls; their parents chose their husbands for them. According to one informant, "One accepts one's parents decision in those days—one doesn't reject it" (I. Ọbájáfà, Àpàá-Bùnú). By 1933, however, with the institution of divorce, the situation had changed. District Officer W. O. P. Rosedale wrote:

Actions involving the payment or return of brideprice are many, the principal cause being undoubtably the practice of early betrothal of girls before they are of an age to appreciate it and often without their knowledge. These young girls are fast asserting themselves in this manner of demanding a say in the choice of a husband. (1933, NAI)

Changes in marriage practices and the increase in educational opportunities meant a loosening of control of mothers over their daughters. But even this process was not a simple one. Many parents still influenced their daughters' choice of marriage partner, if not by arranged marriage, then by other means. Young girls were dependent on their families for sponsorship at school. Thus older women still had considerable influence over their young women's labor. It appears from interviews of Bùnú women in their late twenties that it was their mothers, not rebellious daughters, who determined whether the girls learned to spin or not. Some of these girls instead helped in farming, sold prepared foodstuffs, or were sent to other towns for schooling. When they were away from the watchful eye of the mother who raised them, they had relative freedom. One woman put it eloquently: "During my own time, when I was young, you had to stay with your mother in the house. She will give you cotton to spin—you have to stay with her. This school—when she [the girl] is in form 2 or 3, she will start having breasts and she is in school [far away] at Odo-Apè and will you know what she is doing?" (M. Ekúndayò).

Social change, particularly the introduction of divorce laws and education for girls, affected a whole production complex which included child apprentices, fostering, and arranged marriage. These changes seriously affected the availability of handspun cotton and consequently handwoven cloth.

CHANGES IN DEMAND

The decline in handspinning and availability of handspun cloth was compounded by a decline in the demand for cloth handwoven from handspun thread when fashion taste shifted toward lighter weight cloths (described in chapter 9). Several women now in their fifties reported that they abandoned weaving for other occupations, particularly farming and trading in agricultural products, which they sold at Lokoja market. Women's profits from the sales of the produce they raised, like sales from the cloths they had sold earlier, were their own. Many of these women did not teach their daughters to spin and weave, but rather encouraged them to go to school.

Lack of child labor and the resulting scarcity of handspun yarn, changing fashion tastes for lightweight cloth, increased earnings from the sales of agricultural produce in large markets, and decline in demand for *arigidi* cloth, all contributed to the decision of many women to abandon handweaving for other occupations. This would have been from the mid-1950s to the mid-1960s, the latter period marking the decline in demand for *arigidi* cloth.

DECLINE OF *AṢỌ IPÒ* WEAVING

Bùnú women and men also stopped weaving the red-patterned *aṣọ ipò* cloth in the early 1960s, again because of the difficulties of obtaining yarn and labor. However, there were other factors, particularly the special religious associations and material requirements of these cloths. The red wool from unravelled hospital blankets required for weaving *aṣọ ipò* cloth became increasingly difficult to obtain. Red wool hospital blankets, formerly available at markets at Okene, Kàbbà, and Ódogi, became scarce in the 1940s as colonial officials attempted to substitute locally produced, red cotton blankets, probably due to the pressures of World War II.[14]

Aside from the difficulties of obtaining raw materials, a decline in the use of *aṣọ ipò* was related, in part, to widespread conversion to Christianity in Kàbbà and surrounding areas in the 1930s. *Aṣọ ipò* cloth was associated with "pagan beliefs" and traditional burial practices which some Christians, on moral grounds, no longer observed.

Similarly, the shift to Muslim funeral observances (with the use of white cloth) on the part of major *aṣọ ipò* consumers, the Ebira of Okene, also affected demand for this cloth. However, these ideological concerns had political and economic dimensions as well. According to both Bùnú and Ebira informants, the former king of the Ebira, Atta Alhaji Ibrahim, forbade his subjects to buy *aṣọ ipò* on the grounds that the Bùnú people and their cloths were causing undue death among the Ebira.[15] It is unlikely that Bùnú weavers had such decisive powers of life or death over their Ebira customers. Rather they had a particular economic monopoly which Atta Ibrahim effectively broke by insisting that henceforth the Ebira people use an Ebira-woven white cloth (*itaogede*) for burials.

The escalating cost of *aṣọ ipò* resulting from the increasing cost of materials and labor exacerbated the decline in demand for *aṣọ ipò*, even among people such as the Owé and Ìjùmú Yorùbá who still use such cloths for funerals. Money spent on costly cloths that would have been buried is now spent on education, houses, and cars. Today Bùnú keep and reuse old *aṣọ ipò* cloths rather than bury them.

Mrs. Elizabeth Nua, the principal weaver in the village of Àpàá-Bùnú,
weaving a commissioned marriage cloth, àdófì, *on a vertical single-heddle*
loom.
Àpàá-Bùnú, February 1988.

CLOTHS THAT ARE
STILL WOVEN

Despite the difficulty of obtaining materials and the expense of finished cloths, a limited amount of handwoven cloth continues to be
woven by Bùnú women. Presently, handwoven cloths are obtained by
commission only, usually from the one or two active weavers in a village. Only three types of cloth are typically still woven: marriage
cloths, particularly *àdófì* cloth, hunters' shirts, and white cloth. Demand for these cloths continues because the spiritual beliefs associated with white cloth, hunters, and wives are still strong in Bùnú.

White cloth remains important in solving a range of spiritual and
medical problems. Hunters, associated with the ancestral founding

of many Bùnú villages, wear shirts imbedded with medicinal substances which allow them to overcome dangerous bush spirits. And
it is traditional, not church, marriage, with its symbolic represen-
tation of spirit-wives, that continues to be celebrated in towns and
villages in Bùnú. Thus a decline in the weaving of one group of
cloths—those woven for commercial markets—does not automati-
cally mean the demise of all handweaving. While the many types of
commercial cloths are no longer produced, "ancestral" and "spirit"
cloths associated with traditional beliefs still maintained continue to
be woven.

The production of handwoven cloth *has* declined in Bùnú though not
in the ways that early colonial officials predicted. The reason for its
decline was not simply the influx of cheaper imported textiles but
largely rested on Bùnú women's opportunities and decisions to take
up more remunerative occupations. The Bùnú cloth industry was
also affected by changes in marriage patterns and in Western-style
education. Young girls who had formerly worked for their mothers
until marriage by the mid-1950s began attending school. Thus,
handspun cotton thread became increasingly difficult to obtain. Indeed, this and the decreasing demand for *arigidi* cloth by Igbo buyers
were oft-cited reasons given by women, too old to take up other occupations, for explaining why they no longer wove.

There was also a shift in fashion taste for lighter weight cloths,
which led to a decline in demand for cloths woven with heavy handspun cotton. Why didn't Bùnú weavers adopt the use of lightweight,
machine-spun thread, as did neighboring Ebira women weavers to
the east in Okene or men weavers in Ìlọrin? Handwoven cloth produced in Okene and Ìlọrin is very popular in Nigeria today. Clearly,
Okene's proximity to Lokoja market made access to machine-spun
yarns easier, while Bùnú District was relatively remote and trans-

portation costs were high. Equally important, however, was the fact that the capital needed to invest in quantities of machine-spun yarn was simply unavailable to Bùnú weavers who had formerly relied on inexpensive cotton yarn handspun by young girls. Further, there was no lack of available farmland in Bùnú, unlike the situation in Ebiraland. Thus farming and produce sales were probably seen as more viable economic alternatives, particularly in light of improved transport, which meant access to larger markets.

Older Bùnú women informants had little nostalgia for the former cloth trade. One woman stated that she hoped they would never see those days again, that they had suffered much from the arduous trips carrying cloth to Lokoja (R. Moni). Hence mothers would not necessarily encourage their daughters to spin and weave, particularly if the institutions that had socially bolstered such behavior had been weakened.

In light of these comments about the sufferings of women engaged in producing and trading handwoven cloth, perhaps the question is not why did handweaving decline, but rather why did it continue at all as other economic options became available? The weaving of certain cloths continued in Bùnú because of their association with religious beliefs and ritual practices. However, it was demand for Bùnú handwoven cloth that explains its continued large-scale production during the colonial period, despite colonial policies and the presence of Manchester imports. Demand in Kano, Lagos, Onitsha, and local markets continued for Bùnú handspun, handwoven, indigo-dyed blue-black and white striped cotton cloth, which had a considerable "brand-name" following because of its durability. Further, low prices paid by British firms for commodities such as cotton and palm kernels affected people's attitudes about buying imported cloth, as much as these low prices reduced their ability to do so. For "the noticeable return to use of native cloth in preference to the imported article," reported by a Kàbbà district officer in 1932 (Payne 1932, NAI), suggests that demand for handwoven cloth may have continued despite the actions of British colonial officials and trading firm personnel as well as because of people's reduced incomes.

The contradictions of British colonial policies regarding cotton production and cloth imports undermined colonial efforts to get Bùnú villagers to buy British. Because of the political and economic strictures of Indirect Rule, colonial officials supported a range of traditional rulers and customs, of which handwoven cloth production and use was part. At the same time, they fostered a policy of cotton production which, if it had been successful, would have meant the demise of the handweaving industry altogether. The contradictory attitudes of individual district officers toward women weavers and the inconsistencies of Indirect Rule provided Bùnú women with a gray area within which to manage their affairs as best they could. Thus, Bùnú weavers sought to minimize the disadvantages of colonial domination—e.g., head taxes—while maximizing the benefits of the colonial system—e.g., increased transport and trade—within their particular world.

Ironically, when many village women eventually did stop weaving, they began farming just as British colonial officials had hoped. They did not raise cotton, however, but concentrated on food crops instead. Based on a complex of social, economic, and political factors, Bùnú women's decision to stop weaving was, to some extent, a matter of their own choosing.

EIGHT

COTTON,

CONVERSION,

AND SOCIAL CHANGE

**It appears as if the way God
made everything in this world is
like a book which is divided into
chapters. When God brings one
time, He allows us to use the
season, after which he closes it
and opens another chapter which
is another season.**
Mrs. Comfort Ògúníbì, Àpàá-Bùnú

The decline of handweaving by Bùnú women and of cotton production by Bùnú men are related phenomena. Fewer women wove cloth
commercially during the 1960s and men grew less and less cotton.
Yet cotton production, like handweaving, had formerly been widespread in the area, evidenced by the accounts of several travelers and
missionaries during the nineteenth century (Baikie 1856; Lander
and Lander 1832; Schon and Crowther 1970; J. Thomas 1858–75,
CMS).[1] However, unlike the case of Bùnú women's handweaving,
missionaries and colonial officials alike went to considerable lengths
to encourage cotton production. Their perception of the benefits
of cotton for Bùnú farmers reflected their own particular ideological perspectives which served to motivate and justify their actions. Bùnú farmers, on the other hand, perceived cotton differently.

For them, it was a commodity to be grown if demand and price warranted it.

In this chapter, I focus on cotton production in Bùnú, examining the mix of conflicting and overlapping material and ideological concerns of Church Missionary Society missionaries, British colonial officials, and Bùnú villagers, which affected their actions. By considering these concerns from the perspective of one particular thing, cotton, I emphasize the importance of material objects as vehicles for perceiving new ideas about social relations and practices. Things may convey a sense of continuity through their association with the past, but may also be the focus of images of the future, underwriting processes of social change.

Bùnú villagers were not opposed to change categorically. In the 1930s, they converted in large numbers to Christianity, around the same time as they abandoned cotton production for the export market.[2] However, it was the Book and literacy, not cotton, that were perceived as the source of innovation. Bùnú villagers became Christians, in part, to take advantage of the material benefits associated with mission schools and reading. Equally important was their belief in a new spiritual order that offered hope in a world which seemed out of control. Thus their conversion had both economic and ideological dimensions. Unlike early CMS missionaries and British colonial officials who ideologically related cotton-growing to salvation and progress, respectively, Bùnú farmers made no such connections. In "playing their hand" amidst a range of opposing choices, Bùnú villagers had their own reasons for the timing and manner in which they responded to changes that affected their lives. While not all hands were equal nor were all successful in the playing, Bùnú villagers' various decisions reflected an assessment of their own particular situation, however limited their choices as small farmers might have been.

———

At its founding, the Church Missionary Society combined a program of antislavery activism and evangelism with cotton production. The responses of Bùnú villagers to early CMS efforts are seen through the eyes of one catechist, James Thomas, a Bùnú man trained by the society, who worked at the Niger Mission at Gbebe from approximately 1860 to 1880.

In the following pages, I examine British colonial cotton policies in Kàbbà Division from approximately 1900 to 1940 and the ways in which their images of cotton growing served to justify, both ideologically and economically, their presence in Nigeria. Their views are reflected in Kàbbà Division Reports of the period, from which the responses of Bùnú farmers to colonial cotton-growing schemes during this period may also be gleaned.[3]

While Bùnú farmers no longer grow cotton today, it continues to be perceived not in terms of change and the future but, like hand-woven cloth, in terms of the past. Thus, during the ritual "trip to the farm" during chieftaincy installation, men symbolically plant three cotton, guinea corn, and maize seeds, along with three coins, to represent the basis of their wealth in the past. How Bùnú villagers have negotiated their future as well as their past is reflected in their perception of ideas embodied in things.

COTTON PRODUCTION
AND THE INTRODUCTION
OF CHRISTIANITY

Processed and woven into cloth, cotton had certain spiritual associations in traditional Bùnú religious belief. This is particularly true of the white cloths used by *ejínuwọn* women and in divination and with those used in sacrifices (*aṣọ ẹbọra*, spirit cloth; see chap. 2). Cotton thread and lint as well as the seeds themselves are also used medicinally, sometimes as curatives for spiritually attributed complaints. The white cloth, ọrun padà, is associated with beliefs about the cyclical nature of the cosmos, whereby the spirits of deceased ancestors are reborn in bodies of their descendants.

These indigenous associations of cloth with spirit overlap in several ways with Christian conceptions of white cloth. The association of whiteness with the extraordinary is evident in this passage from the Gospel according to Matthew: "An angel of the Lord descended from heaven; his face shone like lightning; his garments were as white as snow" (28:2,3). Further, water—described as white according to Bùnú color classification—plays an important role in Christian ideas about spiritual rebirth. These overlapping ideas about water, whiteness, and rebirth were played upon by Christian evangelists in the Omi Mímọ́ (Holy Water) revivals of the 1930s in southern Nigeria.

In the novel The Interpreters, Ṣóyínká (1965:167–68) dramatically depicts an experience of rebirth, drawing upon images of whiteness and not water but cotton:

Yea though I walk through the valley of the shadow of death. . . . It was in that valley that I felt the hand of God. I dreamt that I was walking through a field of cotton, cotton wool which was just floating up from the pods. But there was no sound, all round me were cotton pods bursting softly, at my feet a carpet of cotton, in the air, in the sky, bursting pods that made no sound. The cotton wool pressed out gently like small pillows with the wool coming out when your head presses it. Everything was white. After a while I began to be frightened and I began to shout, calling on the cotton farmers to come and show me the way out.

Ṣóyínká alludes here not only to whiteness—associated with "another world" in Yorùbá and European religious thought—but also to the role of cotton in the early endeavors the Church Missionary Society in Nigeria.

The Church Missionary Society, one of the principal mission groups working in Nigeria, was founded in London in 1799 (Àjàyí 1965:8). As the principal Church of England missionary body, its members played an important part in the passage of the Slavery Prohibition Bill in 1834, because they saw the abolition of slavery as essential to the success of their evangelism. In 1839, *African Slave Trade and Its Remedy* was published by a British evangelist and antislavery leader, Thomas Buxton. This book influenced both the formulation and application of CMS goals in Africa. Buxton advocated the development of commercial enterprises—primarily cotton production—which would serve as substitutes for the slave trade: "I now come to the article which demands the largest share of our attention, viz. cotton; because it requires little capital, yields a steady return, is in vast demand in Europe, and grows naturally in the soil of Africa" (Buxton 1967:332). He went on to claim that cotton production had dividends for Europeans as well:

If Africa, when delivered from that evil which withers her produce, and paralyzes her industry, can be made to supply us with the commodity which we so much need, she, in her turn, will be the customer of Europe to the same vast extent, for the manufactured goods which Europe produces.   (p. 335)

As a step in the transformation from slavery to commerce, the CMS established a mission school at Freetown, Sierra Leone, which was viewed as a base for expansion into the interior of West Africa. In 1857, a Niger Mission station was founded at Gbebe (near Lokoja and Bùnú) in Nigeria, under the leadership of Bishop Samuel Crowther. Station personnel consisted largely of freed slaves, many of Yorùbá origins, who had been trained at CMS schools in Sierra

Leone. One man who worked at the Niger Mission at Gbebe was James Thomas. Born in northern Bùnú at Ikùdon, Thomas returned twenty-five years later to "go up the Niger and preach the gospel to my country people in my own Language."[4]

JAMES THOMAS AND THE CMS
IN NINETEENTH-CENTURY BÙNÚ

In the nineteenth century, Bùnú villagers were subject to slave raids by Nupe horsemen and to kidnapping by rival villagers (Squibbs 1935, NAK; Ọbáyẹmí 1978a). Stories about these raids are bitterly recalled by many older Bùnú women and men: "When the Nupe came, they would survey the whole place and knew the loop-holes—they knew where people farmed. They would hide and then come out and capture them . . . and take them to a distant village" (O. Ọbárokàn).

James Thomas was kidnapped from his father's village in 1834, brought down the Niger, and sold as a slave in Aboh. Soon after being put aboard a slave vessel at Bonny, Thomas was freed by the British and taken to Freetown, Sierra Leone, where he received an education under CMS sponsorship. In 1857, he was asked to make preparations to join the Niger Mission.[5] Thomas left Sierra Leone with his wife and three children on February 13, 1858, and landed at Fernando Po, off the Nigerian coast, on February 25, 1858. The family then traveled up the Niger River, reaching Gbebe on September 3, 1858. His journals, along with those of his son, Obadiah, cover a period from 1858 until 1878, providing perhaps the earliest and most extensive written documentation of Bùnú society.

James and Obadiah Thomas worked as catechists under Bishop Samuel Àjàyí Crowther, who was responsible for establishing and maintaining the CMS Niger missions stations. Bishop Crowther, who was himself captured as a slave in 1821, concurred with the mix-

ture of evangelism and enterprise fostered by the early CMS leadership. Indeed, one of the first pieces of equipment taken by
steamship up the Niger River to Gbebe was a cotton gin (Àjàyí
1965:209). Crowther emphasized education and encouraged cotton
growing in the area surrounding the CMS station at Gbebe (near Lokoja) as part of the conversion process. His approach is exemplified
by the following excerpt from the CMS Proceedings of 1863–65
(1863:70):

While Mr. Crowther was at Gbebe, one of the messengers of the great
[Nupe] King Massaba, being about to return to his master, Mr. Crowther
took him around the Mission premises, and showed him the school room,
and then the cotton gins, and the press, and the bales of cotton which are
thus prepared. "I asked him," says Mr. Crowther, "to deliver this message
to his king, " . . . there, pointing to the schoolroom, we teach the
Christian religion; pointing to the cotton gin, I said this is our gun; and to
the clean cotton puffing out of it, that is our powder . . ."

Crowther saw conversion as a gradual process which was most effective when explained in terms of the experience of the people whom
he sought to convert. James Thomas described an impromptu sermon given by Crowther in 1867, and, here again, cotton serves as primary metaphor in Crowther's vision:

The Bishop spoke to them by parable and said that the trousers he put on
. . . [were] made of sheep's ears [wool]. If now he was about to teach them
[how to make them] and [then] they knew it [and] by themselves [could]
make it—and sell it—for themselves . . . [will they] make him come and
pay them [after what he has taught them]? They all answered together no,
no.
    Again he asked them that always each of you went to the country
fashion makers [Ifá diviners]. After the man made Ifas for you, after the
man finish it—will the man pay you [afterwards]? They all answered again
no, no.
    So the Bishop told them that they are rich off [in ways] that they do not
know. . . . He told them that [the] cotton white man made clothes with,
white man has to buy [it] from far country. But you have ground here to

work for yourselves and will sell it [at] a good price [this] cotton to the
white man. So God blessed you for many things of which you know not.
After this [the] poor people said the Lord is God, the Lord is God.
   (1867, CMS)

Crowther supported sending older men like Thomas from Sierra
Leone, who perhaps were imperfectly literate in English but who
"command[ed] more respect with chiefs than young, inexperienced,
college-trained men" (cited in Àjàyí 1965:222). Further, James
Thomas, because of his prior connections in Bùnú as the son of a
chief and a relative of the Ọbádòfin of Àpàá, easily established relations with leading members of Bùnú society.

   Thomas traveled through Bùnú twice, visiting his home village at
Ikùdon (Íke) and passing through Ọwọ́rọ̀-Bùnú villages and Àpàá
(Àpàrá) on his way. There he noted that "most of the [population] are
farmers and some are traders. They export cotton, Beniseed, ginger,
etc. etc." (J. Thomas, 1875b, CMS). What did Bùnú villagers make
of Thomas's and Crowther's efforts to encourage them to grow cotton
and to convert them to Christianity?

   At Àpàá, local leaders were anxious to establish a school as well as
promote cotton trade. The Mayaki (the Nupe appointee and de facto
head of northern Bùnú) promised Thomas land, materials, and labor
to build a CMS school and chapel in 1863. Thomas insisted that
plans wait until Crowther gave permission.[6] Later, in 1874, the Mayaki visited Thomas in Lokoja where he reminded him of his promise
to start a school and chapel in Àpàá. He also told Thomas that "he
would be very glad also if the merchants would join the missionaries
when coming" (J. Thomas 1874, CMS). Clearly, the ideas of reading
and cotton production, if not conversion, were viewed as beneficial
changes by the Mayaki, a major political figure in Bùnú at that time.[7]

   Bùnú villagers and their leaders, some of whom knew Thomas
from the past, were an enthusiastic audience for his proposals and

preaching.[8] Yet Thomas mentioned neither the baptism of Bùnú villagers nor cotton being brought to Lokoja for processing. For despite his efforts, the political situation in Bùnú was not conducive to the sorts of changes that Thomas and the CMS advocated at that time.

Many Bùnú villagers participated in and benefited financially from slave-raiding, which continued during this period. Thomas's uncle, for example, offered to bring two slaves to redeem him in 1859 (J. Thomas 1859, CMS). According to one older man from northern Bùnú, many Bùnú chiefs colluded with Nupe slave takers:

This practice [of sending slaves to Nupe overlords] was not easy to stop for us, because at that time [the Nupe] devised a method of paying our chiefs every month on the basis of their success in persuading villagers to contribute people. It was not easy to stop because by stopping this practice, the chiefs would not have their monthly salary. If that happened, where would they get money to eat? (T. Moses)

Further, the CMS was unable to establish an industrial institution at the Kippo Hill Station to process cotton (J. Thomas 1875b, CMS), which, in any event, would have been impossible to safely transport from the surrounding areas because of continued raiding.[9] Thus the association of cotton processing, Bible reading, and Christian conversion which Thomas and the CMS sought to promote never materialized in Bùnú. Bùnú farmers continued to grow cotton, but it was used by local weavers.

Thomas was successful, however, in establishing churches and schools outside of Bùnú, at nearby Lokoja and at Gbebe, where Bùnú migrants gathered to avoid the dangers of slave raids and to trade. At Lokoja in 1871, "a chief of the Bùnú tribe, who a year or two before had placed himself and 300 of his people under instruction, was baptized together with some forty of his tribe. His successor followed his example and became a Christian, and the chapel in which the members of the tribe gathered for worship had to be enlarged three times in rapid succession" (CMS 1909:56). Thomas's work in Lokoja was reflected in the later successes of other Bùnú men who were trained as CMS evangelists and readers at Lokoja. These men combined prayer and education in establishing CMS churches and schools in many towns and villages in Bùnú District.[10]

By the 1890s, earlier CMS interest in promoting cotton production and processing at Lokoja declined, in part because of doctrinal disputes within the CMS and also because the project linking cotton with conversion had failed. With the British annexation of the Protectorate of Northern Nigeria in 1900,[11] the perception of cotton shifted from one of salvation from slavery to one of salvation from economic backwardness, the latter theme promoted by British colonial officials.

THE COLONIAL PRESENCE
AND THE BRITISH COTTON
GROWING ASSOCIATION

Aiyé péjó	The world is complete
Nígbàtí òyìnbó dé	The day the white man came
Aiyé péjó	The world is complete (Bùnú song)

This song sums up the initial attitude of Bùnú villagers toward the British annexation of northern Nigeria and the defeat of the Nupe. "After that," as one man explained, "children could sleep on the farm alone—there no longer was fear." However, as the same man observed, "[we] started working for the white man too. When the white man came [to our village], we would have to carry him to the next village. After some time, the people started wanting to be independent of the white man too" (O. Ọbárokàn).

Colonial officials were interested in converting Nigerians, not so much to Christianity, but to their own ideas about commerce and progress. Trade and road-building as well as the production of cotton were viewed as keys for entering the world market and hence were, albeit belatedly, to the benefit of British society. As one district officer wrote: "The Kàbbà Division needs good roads to encourage Trade and to bring methods of civilization to the more backward of the people" (Cator 1917, NAK). The promotion of cotton-growing schemes and the establishment of ginneries by the BCGA were part of their perception of commercial progress.[12]

Farmers in Bùnú District and Kàbbà Division apparently initially shared this perception of cotton's economic benefits.[13] Several Bùnú farmers who had formerly raised cotton said that they viewed British policies on cotton exports as an additional economic opportunity. Their early support is evidenced in production figures from the 1920s. During this decade, the amounts of cotton brought to BCGA buying stations at Okene and Kàbbà increased (Table 4). In Kàbbà, this may have been in part due to the efforts of District Officer J. F. J. Fitzpatrick who observed: "It was of primary importance that, with the growing of cotton at its present stage in this Division, nothing should be done to lessen the confidence of the native grower" (1920, NAK). After the 1929 market crash, however, prices paid by the BCGA plummeted. In the following years, while most Bùnú farmers continued to grow cotton, they sold it to their wives and at local markets where prices paid per pound were consistently better. According to a district officer writing in 1929: "At the current price the average farmer is unwilling to dispose of his crop to the Association as he is able to make more money by the weaving of cloth or by its sale in the local markets where the price is higher" (Bridel 1929, NAK). Another district officer noted in 1931 that "the bottom dropped out of the commodity market" (James 1931, NAI), and by 1932, cotton was again "almost entirely absorbed in the local manufacture of cloth as the export price is considered uneconomic" (Payne 1932, NAI).

TABLE 4

COTTON QUANTITIES AND

PRICES FOR KÀBBÀ DIVISION,

1909–30

Year	Quantities (lbs.)			Price (per lb.)	
	KÀBBÀ	OKENE	BOTH	BCGA	OTHER
1909	N.A.	N.A.	N.A.	7⁄10d	
1910	—	—	—	—a	
1911	—	—	—	—	
1912	—	12,000	—	—	
1913	—	60,000	—	—	
1914	—	58,000	—	—	
1915	—	112,735		3⁄4d–1d	
1916	—	—	113,127		
1917	—	—	—	—	
1918	—	—	—	—	
1919	—	—	103,836	—	
1920	205,368	409,485	614,853	—	
1921	—	—	831,000	3 1⁄4d	
1922	—	—	—	—	
1923	—	—	—	1 1⁄4d	2db
1924	—	—	258,533	—	
1925	24,482	—	—	1 3⁄4d	
1926	71,919	433,847	505,766	1 3⁄8→1 1⁄4dc	
1927	—	501,679	—	3⁄4d→1 5⁄8d	
1928	—	265,945	—	1 3⁄4→1 1⁄2d	
1929	—	241,332d	—	1 5⁄8d	2 1⁄2de
1930	—	903,924d	—	1 1⁄2→3⁄4d	3df

aNo quantities or prices given but note that "cotton suffered a big decrease" (Ley Greaves 1910, NAK).

bPrice paid by trading firm, John Holt and Co.

cArrow indicates change in price during the year.

dQuantities estimated from number of bales reported, at 1,428 lbs/bale.

ePrice paid for lowest grade of cotton in local markets.

fAverage price paid for cotton in local markets.

By 1937, "the price offered by firms is so low that the people prefer to sell it in the local markets or to use it for weaving. I understand that it is now unsaleable in any quantity and there is now talk of burning it" (Rosedale, 1937, NAI).

While the colonial government imagined cotton production as the means for improving Bùnú farmers' lives and as an economic incentive for political support in England, the low prices paid by BCGA buyers led Bùnú farmers to bring only surplus cotton to its buying stations at Kàbbà and Okene. Thus despite the numerous cotton-growing projects and government and BCGA "propaganda in favour of cotton growing" (Duggan 1922:206) in the early decades of the century, the image of cotton as economic panacea was abandoned in Kàbbà Division after 1930.

Even during the first three decades of the twentieth century when cotton was promoted, Bùnú farmers were largely left to make their own decisions regarding cotton production, unlike cotton farmers elsewhere in colonial Africa.[14] In northern Nigeria, for example, cotton farmers were given cash advances by BCGA agents in order to obligate them to grow cotton (Shenton and Lennihan 1981). In other parts of Africa, farmers were forced to raise cotton (Bassett 1988; Isaacman et al. 1980). However, in Nigeria, as one colonial official put it, "It is not the policy of the Government to force natives to plant cotton" (Goldsmith 1912, NAK). Such a policy certainly would have contradicted the image of "cotton-growing as beneficial self-improvement" that colonial officials sought to project. On the other hand, taxation was seen as a legitimate means of meeting these ends. As was the case in Bùnú women's handwoven cloth production (see chapter 7), the imposition of head taxes actually undermined British hopes to increase cotton exports from Kàbbà Division. Farmers had the option of obtaining cash through the sale of food crops (Ánjórìn 1966:3), which gave much higher returns.[15] For example, estimates of the income from crops raised on one acre of land in Kàbbà District in 1929 ranged from 4 pounds, 12 shillings for yams, to 1 pound, 4 shillings for beans, to 9 shillings, 7 pence for cotton[16] (Bridel 1929, NAK).

The optimistic image of increasing cotton production, evidenced in Kàbbà Division annual reports in the first three decades of the century, disappeared from these reports after 1930. For Bùnú farmers, the drought of 1927 and subsequent food shortages, the sharp drop in prices paid for commodities such as cotton,[17] the lack of cash, influenza outbreaks, and locust attacks—all contributed to their sense of disorder during this period. In the early 1930s, many Bùnú villagers converted to Christianity, in the wake of the Omi Mímọ́ (Holy Water) revival movement that began in 1930 (Peel 1968:91). And it was in the Book, not in cotton, that Bùnú villagers perceived their salvation lay.

CHRISTIAN CONVERSION AND
ENLIGHTENMENT IN BÙNÚ

The evangelist preacher Reverend J. O. Babalọlá, who led the Omi Mímọ́ revival in 1930–32, attributed these disasters to God's disapproval of "heathen" practices. During revival gatherings, he encouraged people to abandon their old beliefs and accept the teachings of Christ, found in the Bible, as the new basis of belief and practice. By obtaining the holy water (*omi mímọ́* or *omi ìyè*) sanctified by the prayers of Babalọlá, people attempted to make sense of a world in which, despite the British policy of "Indirect Rule" (see chapter 7), the bases of authority were changing. Many Bùnú people traveled to Kàbbà in 1932 to take part in the Omi Mímọ́ revival services held there:

There was the belief that he [Babalọlá] healed different kinds of disease so we all had to trek to Kàbbà from Àpàá, there were no vehicles then. We left at 5 am and arrived around 2 pm. They had started a CMS chapel at Old Àpàá by then but the òfósì cult women and the witches would disturb the people in church. So we went to Babalolá to seek relief from the disease that had broken out.   (R. Moni)

While their participation in Omi Mímó revivals predisposed many Bùnú villagers to become church members, it was the activities of early CMS lay teachers and evangelists from Lokoja (or their students) who taught Bible reading who consequently gave material form to their beliefs.

CHURCHES ESTABLISHED
IN BÙNÚ

The road linking Kàbbà with Lokoja skirts the southern border of Bùnú District. Built in the 1920s to facilitate the transport of cotton from Kàbbà to Lokoja, this road was later used by Bùnú men trained as CMS lay teachers, returning home to their villages. As they traveled on this road, they introduced Christian ideas and practices, for the most part represented concretely by the Bible, to Bùnú villagers along the way.

The Bible played a prominent role not only in CMS doctrine but also in the perception of Christianity by Bùnú villagers. James Thomas described the initial uncertainty felt by villagers in the mid–nineteenth century toward this book:

The headman named Anzio told me that they still fear me he said because [of] the Bible I opened before them. They never had seen it before.
 (1859a, CMS)

Still [the] King and his people surrounded me daily with wonder, looking upon the Bible in my hand.   (1863b, CMS)

In his meeting with the Mayaki of Àpàá in 1878, James Thomas's son Obadiah recorded an example of mutual cultural misunderstanding, which centered on the Bible:

During the long address I showed him my Bible—telling him, that as the colour of the wrapper is black, so is the heart of man made black by sin. . . . I also told him whosoever King or chief [who] receives the Bible shall surely be blessed—telling him also that it is the secret of England's greatness. At the close he begged me to make a book which I understood to [mean] protective charms. I then seized the opportunity of addressing him at length on the folly of confiding in charms. . . .   (1878, CMS)

The imagery of power associated with the Bible ("the source of England's greatness") and the reading of gospel suggested by Obadiah Thomas was later taken up by Bùnú CMS evangelists and lay teachers from Lokoja. These men established chapels in villages along the Kàbbà-Lokoja road, including the school at Odó-Àpẹ, which provided training for the future CMS lay teachers and pastors of central and northern Bùnú.[18] Other Bùnú men were taught by Samuel Àgùdà, who traveled throughout Bùnú teaching the Christian gospels and Bible reading. In 1944, Àgùdà's student, Michael Baiyéshéá, along with Isaiah Olútìmáyìn, founded a church and later instituted reading classes at Àgbẹ̀dẹ-Bùnú. By 1960, Christian chapels, some which also ran schools, were started in most Bùnú villages. They linked Christian faith with the Bible, with reading, and with moral and material progress, the latter referred to as ọ̀làjú, often translated as "civilization." The literal translation of ọ̀làjú, "opening the eyes," underscores its connection with sight and reading. In Bùnú, literacy was associated with new ways of both seeing (reading) and of conceptualizing knowledge.[19] Thus, during one Bùnú marriage performance, women sang:

T'ẹ́ bá fẹ́ m'odì   If you want to know
orin wa   the meaning of our song
Ke mú ìwé, ke mú báírò   Take your book and pen

Compared with the rich associations made with the Bible and with reading, Bùnú farmers' perception of cotton-growing was rather one-dimensional. Nor was any particular moral or spiritual quality attributed to cotton, in contrast to the yam, a principal and much-loved foodstuff, which was celebrated in an annual festival.[20] Compared to yams, cotton was regarded as a crop of secondary importance.

Bùnú men grew cotton for sale, either to one's kinswomen or wives or through local markets for cash. The decidedly free-market response of Bùnú farmers to cotton-growing led them to sell their cotton to the highest bidder. If there was no demand or if a proposed price was uneconomical, they stopped growing it. This was what happened during the 1960s, when Bùnú women stopped weaving for commercial purposes. Until this time, cotton continued to be grown on a small scale in Bùnú in much the same way as it had been grown in the past.

According to older Bùnú men, no special preparations were made for planting cotton, although certain procedures were followed for improving cotton harvests.[21] Land was first cleared and then hoed before cotton seeds were planted in June, after the rainy season was well under way. Cotton was interplanted with yams or planted alone in mounds. Two types of cotton were grown in Bùnú, one known as *ẹlẹpọ̀n*, which was reddish-brown, and the other called *kẹsẹ*, which was white. In the past, all men who farmed raised some cotton, but both men and women harvested the ripe bolls approximately six months later. After picking the cotton, some farmers left the stalks in the ground in order to obtain a second year's growth, although it was more common to uproot the stalks and replant the following year (A. Ọbajànọ̀).

During the 1930s, a seed distribution program was begun to in-

Man cultivating his farm with a hoe.
Àpàá-Bùnú, 1988.

troduce American cotton seed (Allen variety) to Bùnú farmers (Miscellaneous files, 1929–39, NAK). Bags of seed were distributed to villages along the main road on Native Authority trucks from Kàbbà. However, there was no system for buying cotton or for transporting harvested cotton to ginneries. As no one returned to purchase cotton from Bùnú farmers, "we did not have much interest in growing it," one farmer from central Bùnú explained (E. Ọbalúhà, Ọ̀llẹ̀-Bùnú). In fact, after government officials unloaded the requisite number of bags of cotton seed in his village, some would come to collect their share of seed to plant while others used their share to cook in cotton seed soup.[22] Thus, while this program continued until the 1960s, it had little impact on Bùnú cotton production because farmers had no means of transporting cotton to market and preferred to grow other more lucrative crops on the same land.

When asked why they stopped growing cotton, older Bùnú men responded that people stopped buying it:

I stopped growing cotton because it was no longer selling well. Again, many people especially women do not know how to spin like before. Before it was cotton that we used to weave *kíjìpá* that we used as cloth, but now that cloths are imported and people started buying the *aṣọ òyìnbó* (machine-woven cloth), people growing cotton stopped growing it.
   (M. Owónaiyé, Ọ̀llẹ̀-Bùnú)

Several men mentioned that in the 1980s, government officials from the Nigerian Ministry of Agriculture encouraged farmers to grow cotton. One man said that they have not done so yet, largely because of the excellent returns they have recently received for cassava (A. Ọbajànọ̀). Once again, officials of the state along with commercial textile manufacturers (this time, both Nigerian) are encouraging small-scale farmers to embark on the commercial production of cotton. Yet unless cotton is perceived as economically viable, perhaps supported with state or corporate subsidies (Bassett 1988:283), Bùnú farmers are likely to respond as they have in the past.

Church Missionary Society missionaries' and British colonial officials' perception of the benefits of growing cotton ultimately failed because of the particularities of Bùnú history and place. In the nineteenth century, the CMS clergy from the Niger Mission did not have the political backing to counter the economics of slavery in Bùnú. In the twentieth century, British colonial officials who had the political wherewithal had little economic interest in developing relatively isolated areas such as Bùnú. These factors, as well as the actions and options of villagers, help to explain why Bùnú cotton farmers' experiences differed from those of small farmers elsewhere in Nigeria and Africa where colonial officials also promoted cotton production.

Bùnú villagers, who initially welcomed the CMS catechist James Thomas and British colonial officials—with their various cotton-growing schemes—imagined at first that cotton would materially help them. When it did not, they abandoned it as a vehicle of change in favor of the Bible and literacy. Yet Bùnú villagers' response to the Bible and what it represented—Christianity, literacy, ọ̀làjú—was neither simultaneous nor monolithic. Several Bùnú villagers described the hostility of some toward those—often younger men—who advocated this change in belief: "My husband started the CMS church in Àpàá. He had opposition! . . . It was like fighting a war. Even his mother didn't want him and the villagers kept reporting on him. . . . Some said that people will be too civilized, that they will go anywhere, so they didn't want them to be educated, to be too wise" (M. Ikúsemí, Àpàá-Bùnú).

The Bible became the symbol of a new way of acquiring knowledge used by some Bùnú villagers to assert new claims, while others worked to protect old ones. Not everyone benefited from the changes introduced by the British and by Bible literacy taught by CMS evangelists and teachers. Older men whose local authority rested on carefully guarded ritual knowledge, for example, were threatened by younger men whose Christian training encouraged them to disparage these rituals. Indeed, the Bible and literacy have contributed to a sense of discontinuity in the ways that authority and social relations are constituted in Bùnú villages. Now, local histories are recounted in privately published books, funeral and marriage exchanges are recorded in booklets, and divorce summonses are issued by the local court. These changes, attributed to books and schooling, are not universally viewed as beneficial, but are seen as the source of present-day problems by some (Peel 1978).

Nor was the image of cotton uniformly viewed as a vehicle for change by all CMS missionaries or by British colonial officials. Tensions and competing interests among various factions within the CMS leadership led some to emphasize education and cotton production as a remedy for slavery, while others decried this emphasis on material concerns as too worldly. Similarly, differences in the backgrounds and interests of members of the British colonial community in Nigeria were reflected in their attitudes toward cotton-growing. While many British colonial officials in Kàbbà Division supported cotton-growing policies, some sided with Bùnú farmers in their decision to stop selling to BCGA agents because of the low prices paid.

Thus, Bùnú villagers, missionaries, and colonial officials used things—cotton and books—to assert their ideas about the future and to support their past and present positions. In Bùnú, cotton was perceived, at least momentarily, as a common symbol for an improved

future, both moral and economic, among parties with rather dispa-
rate concerns. That it was ultimately unable to sustain the weight of
these associations was a result of the economic inappropriateness of
this perception. Rather than the expansion of cotton production en-
visioned by missionaries and colonial officials, Bùnú villagers have
perceived progress and change through its demise.

NINE

EVERYDAY FASHION
IN BÙNÚ

Fashion always occupies the

dividing-line between the past

and future, and consequently

conveys a stronger feeling of the

present. . . .

Simmel

If *ọ̀làjú* (civilization, enlightenment) was associated with education, "the Book," and Christianity by Bùnú villagers, the change in the perception of knowledge and spiritual matters was manifested in a bodily fashion as well. During the 1930s and 1940s, Bùnú villagers began buying imported cloth, generically known as *aṣọ òyìnbó* (literally, white people's cloth), from itinerant Ijẹṣà Yorùbá cloth traders and from urban markets. Gradually replacing their own handwoven cloth (*kíjìpá*), which they previously wore as everyday dress, with these cloths, they instituted new fashions, including the wearing of wrappers (*ìró*) with separate blouselike tops (*bùbá*) and brassieres (*kọ́múṣẹ́tì*) for women and tailored shirts (*àwù*) and trousers (*ṣòkòtò*) for men. When asked why they changed to these new cloth and dress styles, many people said that it was because of *ọ̀làjú*. Through their use of these cloths and, later, ready-made clothing, they expressed their identification with a wider, "civilized" world and their approval of changes introduced by missionaries and colonial officials.

Yet at the same time villagers acknowledge this broader identity as progressive advocates of *ọ̀làjú*, they also attempt to maintain a local identity as Bùnú people. By keeping and using traditional marriage and funeral cloths—perceived as God-given and hence immutable—Bùnú villagers express a certain ambivalence about the "civilizing" changes that have altered their lives. As one man put it, "Civilization has two sides—one bad, one good." One is civilized when one goes out in the world and comes back, bringing progress to one's home village. "That is *òlàjú*. But there are some who will want to destroy their town or village—that is *ojú àlà habù*, lack of civilization" (G. Ọbàlò, Àpàá-Bùnú). Having gone out into the world, one should not destroy one's town through neglect, by abandoning its inhabitants and festivals. The desire for a wider social identity as Nigerians should be tempered by the maintenance of tradition (*ìgbà*), marking a distinctive cultural past:

Anything that has to do with culture or tradition has to be guarded jealously. Like traditional marriage or the masquerades, they are parts of our culture. Nothing should be able to change them. . . . So despite the fact that *òlàjú* has come, the cloths used for celebrating these things must not change.   (G. Ọbàlò)

In earlier chapters, I focused on this "jealous guarding" of handwoven cloths used on specific occasions to conserve a unique Bùnú identity. This chapter considers their opposite—the mass-produced, machine-woven cloths sewn into tailored ensembles, tee-shirts, blue jeans, etc., that constitute everyday fashion in Bùnú villages today. These cloths and styles link their wearers with fashion trends in distant Nigerian towns and cities. The shift in everyday dress from that made of locally handwoven cloth (*kíjìpá* or *aṣọ ofì*) to clothing of foreigners' machine-woven cloth (*aṣọ òyìnbó*) reflects Bùnú villagers' sense of a wider, more worldly identity. Yet it is in the oscillation between these two tendencies—the need to maintain things associated with a particularistic, inalienable past and the need to identify with a more general, impersonal present—that the meaning of cloth in Bùnú society may best be understood.

Tailor's price list for sewing European and Yorùbá-style clothing.
Aíyétórò-Kírí-Bùnú, July 1990.

THE INTRODUCTION OF *AṢỌ*

OYÌNBÓ IN BÙNÚ

While it is difficult to say when the first *aṣọ òyìnbó* cloth made its appearance in Bùnú, the introduction of these new cloths came primarily via two routes. First, there were the women traders, Bùnú and non-Bùnú alike, who walked to markets at Lokoja where imported *aṣọ òyìnbó* cloth was available from agents of firms such as John Holt and United Africa Company (UAC). Second and more importantly, during the 1930s there were the itinerant cloth traders, mainly from Iléṣa, known as the *òṣọmààló* ("I will squat down until I'm paid"), who brought imported machine-woven cloth from cities in the south to sell to Bùnú villagers on credit. These men occupied a temporary marketing gap in the distribution of machine-woven cloth which was later filled when better roads and motor transport gave villagers easier access to large urban markets.

It was villagers' exposure to these traders, as well as experiences outside of Bùnú, that brought changes in everyday fashions to Bùnú. Prior to the wearing of wrapper and blouse of *aṣọ òyìnbó* cloth—currently thought of as traditional Yorùbá dress—women wore a single wrapper of handwoven cloth securely tied over the breasts. One Bùnú woman described the effects of seeing the new style of women's dress while working at a construction site at Kàbbà: "I first saw a woman with *ìró* and *bùbá* at Kàbbà. . . . I was surprised when I first saw the woman and I was also fascinated so that I had to find the money to buy something like that for myself" (C. Ògúníbì). Several other women mentioned having similar experiences and individually decided to buy the new cloths. However, according to one Àpàá man, "the time when [widespread] changes started to be noticed in the wearing of cloth was when people started to send their children to school" in the late 1940s and 1950s (P. Ikúéndayọ̀, Àpàá-Bùnú).

SCHOOL AND UNIFORMS

Students initially wore uniforms made of *kíjìpá* handwoven by their mothers. In 1939, for example, such uniforms were being worn by students at the CMS school in Kàbbà, as evidenced by a government educational officer's comment about "the smart uniform[s] of locally woven cloth" (Clark 1939, NAK). These uniforms made of handwoven cloth were soon to be replaced during the 1940s and early 1950s with those made with machine-woven cloth.[1]

In southern Bùnú, a small school associated with the CMS church was established at Odo-Apè.[2] One Bùnú woman who lived near the school described what students wore, probably in the early 1940s:

*Woman shelling ẹ̀gúsí melon seeds, wearing commercially woven "lace"
cotton outfit of wrapper skirt (ìró), blouse (bùbá), and headtie (gèlè).
Àpàá-Bùnú, 1988.*

The time that school started, there were not more than 10 pupils then with only one teacher. There was no specific type of uniform for the pupils then. It was later they started to use a type of locally woven cloth called *kẹkẹ wẹrẹ*.

After that they changed to a type of white cloth that was of the imported type. It was the teachers who told the pupils to change from *kẹkẹ wẹrẹ* cloth. . . . The only reason was that because both young and old people alike were wearing it, in order to differentiate the pupils, the teachers announced that there was the need to change from the use of handwoven *kẹkẹ wẹrẹ*.   (E. Nua)

Another woman suggested that students were told to stop wearing striped handwoven *kẹkẹ wẹrẹ* cloth because prisoners wore it. It is more likely that these teachers sought to emphasize their students' Western education through distinctive European-style dress.

Indeed, school uniforms were an important part of the colonial education system, in which British colonial officials introduced ideas about orderly behavior, routine, and cleanliness. Wearing uniforms made of neatly pressed imported cloth was part of this process. Students were learning new ideas through reading but also, as Mauss (1973) suggested in his essay on body techniques, through bodily comportment and dress.[3]

The new imported cloths used in making school uniforms were often purchased from *òṣọmàààló* cloth traders:

The name of the cloth I bought from the *òṣọmàààló* cloth traders was called *fẹrósí*. It looked like handwoven cloth (*kíjìpá*). We men used it in those days to make trousers. When you had a son in school, you could buy that *fẹrósí* to make pants, then you could look for other cloth to make a shirt.   (G. Ọbàlò)

Purchased machine-woven cloths would then be cut and sewn in prescribed styles by male tailors. Another fashion innovation included the use of iron buttons, purchased from Kàbbà, which were sewn across the shoulder of schoolboys' uniforms. One can imagine students' pride in wearing tailored uniforms of imported cloth, for as one woman put it, wearing this cloth "made us feel more important."

THE *ÒṢOMÀÀLÓ*—

CLOTH TRADERS WHO

STOOPED TO COLLECT

During the 1930s and 1940s, male cloth traders known as *òṣomààló* came from the area around Iléṣa to the southwest bringing machine-woven cloths with names such as *dínrìn*, *àpatúpa*, *àtòrìnbàdàn*, and *olórí*[4] to sell in Bùnú villages. Cloth was paid for in installments, with an initial amount followed by one or two smaller payments at intervals several months later. The name *òṣomààló* refers to one of the traders' collection tactics: squatting in front of a debtor's house until they were paid.

Information from Bùnú villagers complements what Peel (1983) has written of *òṣomààló* traders interviewed in 1974 at Iléṣa. Peel puts the beginning of the *òṣomààló* trade around 1910, a date corroborated by Bùnú villagers' memory of *òṣomààló* as coming prior to the influenza epidemic of 1918 but after the appearance of the British— around 1900 in the Kàbbà area. *Òṣomààló* traders were most active during the twenties and thirties, spreading out to sell cloth in the savannah area around Ìlọrin and moving east toward Bida. Identified by their Ijẹṣà dialect and facial marks, they came to Bùnú on a regular basis probably somewhat later in the 1930s, as earlier established markets became saturated with newly aspiring *òṣomààló* traders.[5] Initially these cloth traders came on foot, though later they used bicycles. Bùnú villagers said that when motor vehicles became common in the area, the *òṣomààló* traders stopped coming, probably in the early to mid-1950s.

Bùnú informants generally confirmed what has been written of the *òṣọmààló* (Peel 1983:152–59), though viewing them from a different perspective. For Bùnú villagers, these men were a source of excitement and novelty, even while they could be harsh in their collection methods. When an *òṣọmààló* trader would appear in a village, word would go round that he had arrived ("*Òṣọmààló ti dé o!*"). He would then proceed to lay out his cloths in front of the king's house for display to curious villagers who would make their selections.

While anticipating their visits, villagers nonetheless referred to *òṣọmààló* behind their backs as *olútinpá*, a derogatory term that meant "those who get things by using force." "We used to call them *òṣọmààló* in their presence, but the name *olútinpá* was what we called them when they were not there," one woman observed. People also called them *fọ́páwọ̀n* ("they measure with a stick"), though this term was not insulting and simply referred to a measurement system different from that used with handwoven cloth.[6]

The *òṣọmààló*'s reputation in Bùnú for "getting things by force" derived from some of their debt-collection methods. Bùnú villagers, like the Ijẹ̀sà traders (see Peel 1983:155), have their own versions of these stories. One man's description was typical:

Whoever could not pay—*ise dé e* [trouble has landed]. If the debtor was a woman, if the *òṣọmààló* came and met her cooking food, he would scatter the fire underneath the pot or sometimes would pour water on the fire, then sitting down with the debtor until the money was paid.
  (O. Ọlọ́runtóba, Àpàá-Bùnú)

Sometimes the village chief would be asked to intervene or more drastic strategies were employed:

The *òṣọmààló* even used to gather tin cans and other things like snail shells that would make noise. They would tie them around the waist of the debtor and then would make them dance around. Whoever saw such persons would feel moved and if they were in a position to help, would pay the debt to prevent further embarrassment. (D. Ọbadémowó, Àpàá-Bùnú)

Despite these humiliations and the knowledge that the cloths sold by the òṣọmàlò were more expensive than comparable cloths sold at Lokoja Market, Bùnú villagers continued to buy cloth from them because, as one woman put it:

If we decided not to buy from them, there was no other place where we could easily get cloth to buy. As a result of that, we did not quarrel with them. If we paid them, they would come next time. And even if we did not pay all we owed them, we could beg them and then they would still sell cloth to us. (G. Baiyésheá, Àgbèdẹ-Bùnú)

WHY AṢỌ ÒYÌNBÓ
WAS IN DEMAND

Bùnú villagers preferred machine-woven imported cloth to their own handwoven *kíjìpá* cloth for both practical and social reasons. *Aṣọ òyìnbó* made of finely spun cotton was lighter in weight, more comfortable to wear, and easier to tie and tailor than the thicker *kíjìpá* cloth. Because it was lighter weight, it was also easier to wash[7] and dried more quickly. Several people associated *kíjìpá* with dirt and insects, mentioning that lice would hide in among the threads of coarse, handwoven cloths.

The social reasons for using imported cloth were equally persuasive. Some people changed because they saw other, important people—including teachers, clergy, and colonial employees—wearing it. As more people began to wear *aṣọ òyìnbó* cloth, *kíjìpá* cloth came to be associated with poverty and backwardness. One man remarked, "We can say that it is because of shame that nobody wants to wear it like before." Shame (*ìtìjú*, literally, "closing one's eyes") in this case implies unenlightened, uncivilized behavior, the opposite

Commercially woven aṣọ òyìnbó *cloth put out to dry.*
Àpàá-Bùnú, *December 1991.*

of ọ̀làjú. The wearing of tailored fashions made from machine-woven cloth became an integral part of "civilized" behavior.

One not so obvious outcome of this shift in everyday fashion from handwoven to machine-woven cloth was a virtual revolution in undergarment wear. Lightweight, machine-woven cloth was used to make a range of underwear—from knickers (*drósì*) to brassieres (*kó-músẹ́tì*)—replacing older types of underwear constructed of handwoven cloth. While some undergarments are still hand-tailored from machine-woven cloth, presently most Bùnú villagers buy ready-made underwear (underpants, singlets, brassieres, and slips) from local markets and shops in larger towns.

Again, the reasons cited for this switch were comfort and social acceptability. The acceptance of *kó̩músẹ́tì* (literally, "come sit here," referring to placement of the breasts) reflects these dual concerns. Following a trajectory similar to that of blouses and wrappers made of machine-woven cloth, women saw others wearing brassieres, admired them, and purchased or made them for themselves.

Several women mentioned that by wearing brassieres they could run without discomfort. Brassieres also kept one's chest from becoming flat "like a man's." While one woman mentioned that "it was said that it would not be proper to leave one's breasts dangling (*jàlà jàlà*)," no one mentioned shame of exposed breasts as the reason for this change. Rather, it was the social stigma of not keeping up with fashion that seemed to generate Bùnú women's demand for brassieres. This is supported by one woman's remark that "those of us whose breasts had not developed used to pray to God to make our breasts develop quickly so that we could start to wear *kọ́músẹ̀tì*," i.e., be fashionable.

Aside from brassieres in machine-woven cloth, imported cloth also replaced handwoven *kíjìpá* cloth in the making of women's traditional underskirt, the *tobì*. Men's underwear changed as well, from *àsòsò* (a pantlike loincloth[8] made of handwoven cloth strips) to tailored knickers known as *drósì*, made initially from old salt bags and later from imported, manufactured cloth.

The fact that these undergarments were generally concealed does not deny their contribution to a sense of being fashionable, "up-to-date," and "civilized." Indeed, one woman described the impression that could be made when fashionable underwear was revealed through the intentional readjustment of a wrapper: "Those who were wealthy enough could use buttons to decorate the *tobì* skirt. If you had an underskirt decorated with buttons, you could pull off your wrapper deliberately for others to see that you were wearing a skirt decorated with buttons" (C. Ògúníbì). A small zippered pouch, still popular today, was often added to the *tobì* underskirt, which allowed market women to keep money more conveniently.

Men's everyday dress changed as well, from the *àwù* (shirt) and

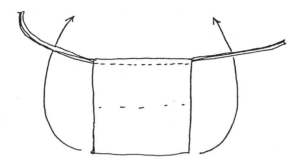

FIGURE 2: Àsòsò, *traditional Bùnú undergarment made from handwoven cloth.*

àsòsò (loincloth) constructed of handwoven *kíjìpá* to the tailored shirt and trousers made of imported cloth. As everyday dress for farmwork, machine-woven cloth was actually less durable than handwoven cloth and for this reason some people objected to its use. However, as fewer and fewer women spun or wove cotton cloth, handwoven cloth was difficult to get and men substituted wornout machine-woven cloth when going to the farm.

ON FASHION, CHANGE, AND THE PAST

Bùnú villagers no longer wear handwoven cloth on an everyday basis as in the past. Rather, they are wearing outfits made from machine-woven cloth with names like Babangida, Barry Wonder, and Enyín Awólòwò ("the teeth of Awólòwò"),[9] making reference to contemporary Nigerian national figures. They may even go international, sporting secondhand tee-shirts advertising American ophthalmologists ("Call Innovation Vision") or universities ("Sea Myrtle University—No Classes, No Exams, No Sweat").

On entering a Bùnú village on any given day, the visitor will have no sense of locally distinctive dress. Men wear pants or jeans with ready-made shirts, women dress in cotton-print wrappers with blouses or tee-shirts, and children wear secondhand clothing (asọ àtutà) in various stages of repair. Although not attired in the latest up-to-date Lagos fashions, villagers are nonetheless dressing "in the present," implicitly expressing a contrast with the past.

Simmel's (1971) insight about fashion as "a heightened present" and as a break with the past—the "old-fashioned"—is reflected in Bùnú villagers' acceptance of machine-woven, tailored clothing. By wearing such everyday fashions as tee-shirts and jeans, one is associated with ọlàjú, with progress, and with civilized and sophisticated behavior rather than with a parochial past.

Yet respect for the past is part of the Bùnú conception of progress and of civilized behavior. This came out in an interview with a Bùnú woman. She had just explained that handwoven kíjìpá cloth was no longer woven because of ọlàjú, civilization. My Owé Yorùbá research assistant from Kàbbà then asked, somewhat facetiously, whether Bùnú women's continued use of another handwoven cloth—the marriage cloth, àdófì—was a result of ọlàjú. "Yes," the woman said. "It is associated with traditional marriage." "But it is not used in Kàbbà," my research assistant replied, implying that it wasn't so civilized because urban Kàbbà people didn't use it. "Well, if that is the case," the Bùnú woman responded, somewhat huffily, "it means that *their* own traditional marriage at

Kàbbà is different from *ours*." Or as one Bùnú man put it, their "way of civilization is not the proper way."

In Kàbbà, as in other large towns and cities in Nigeria, enlightened, "civilized" behavior means actively abandoning many aspects of the past. The Owé Yorùbá living in and around Kàbbà are neighbors of the Bùnú yet have their own distinct history. As residents of the largest town in the area, the Owé have benefited economically from colonial and postcolonial developments, including the building of a treasury, a general hospital, and paved roads.

In the past, Owé Yorùbá women—like Bùnú women—wove and had specific, named cloths reserved for traditional marriage performance. However, none of these cloths has been preserved. Rather, when traditional marriage is performed in Kàbbà today, handwoven cloths from Ìlọrin, and sometimes Okene, are bought and made into wedding attire. Their traditional marriage cloths of the past have been abandoned.

Their own "way of civilization," then, differs from that of Bùnú villagers, whose experience as residents of a geographically isolated and largely undeveloped district has led them to evaluate "civilization" somewhat differently. While the Bùnú generally associate "civilized" behavior with the present, this behavior should be tempered with respect for the past, which includes the preservation of certain handwoven cloths. Their appreciation of this particular interplay of past and present was expressed in several astute observations about cloth and change.

People emphasized that not all kinds of handwoven cloth needed to be preserved. Some types of handwoven cloths, such as those woven in quantity for sale, were easily abandoned. As one man explained, "*Kíjìpá* was easy for us to change because it was something we made with our hands," alluding to the secular, mass-produced aspect of their production. But other handwoven cloths—such as traditional marriage cloths said originally to have been woven by spirits and used in rituals perceived as sacred, God-given essentials of Bùnú identity—should not be given up: "Things like *aṣọ obitan* (marriage cloth), civilization cannot change it, because it is the type of cloth that has been used '*latayé-bayé*'—from the beginning of the traditional marriage ceremony. Therefore it has to remain like that. It is *igbà*—tradition" (D. Kọ́láwọlé).

Several older women and men mentioned this fundamental quality of traditional marriage and of masquerade performances—that civilization could not change them. Yet, at the same time that the woman quoted above was asserting that handwoven marriage cloths could not change, she acknowledged that there *have* been changes in the use of marriage cloth: "I must tell you that it is because of civilization that we are using [machine-woven] *àñkàrà* cloth as some of the cloth used in traditional marriage. But this *àñkàrà* cannot replace traditional marriage cloth" (D. Kọ́láwọlé). At one level—an ideal, official level—people maintain that tradition remains unchanged, while at another, practical level people realize that traditional performances of ritual are not the same. These changes are graphically perceived in terms of cloth use. The old, indigo-dyed, handwoven marriage cloths are no longer being woven. While some of these cloths are being kept for use in traditional marriage, they are also being supplemented with new machine-woven cloths which may eventually supersede the older cloths.

It is not just anthropologists whose "longing for meaning frequently assumes the form of a nostalgia for the traditional" (Jackson 1989:127). Some Bùnú villagers adamantly insist that tradition (*igbà*) is something that cannot change. Other, perhaps braver, individuals

admit that, indeed, change—no matter how unsettling of assumed
meanings of existence and established social relations—is occur-
ring:

> The masquerade festival and the traditional marriage ceremony are things
> we inherited from our forefathers. But I want you to realize that there are
> changes. For example, what forty people were doing before, now not more
> than five people can be found practicing it. Is that not a change? Changes
> are coming to it. It is true we do not abandon it completely, but people
> practicing such things today are not as many as before.   (C. Ògúníbì)

TO SHOW ỌLÁJÚ

Through cloth, Bùnú villagers conceptualize the present as well as
the past. There are cloths that may be easily abandoned and replaced, situating their wearers in the ever-changing present. And
there are cloths that should be preserved, identifying their wearers
with a timeless past.

The fact that the machine-woven cloths that constitute everyday
fashion in Bùnú are soon outmoded and devoid of ritual importance
does not mean that these cloths are insignificant. Indeed, their widespread acceptance by Bùnú villagers, unremarkable perhaps because
of the familiarity of machine-woven cloth, marks a profound shift in
Bùnú identity and social relations. Through changes in everyday
fashion from clothing made of locally handwoven to foreign machine-
woven cloth, Bùnú villagers distance themselves from the past and
accentuate the present. Changes in related processes such as the tai-
loring, measuring, fastening, and washing of these cloths contribute
to this sense of difference as well.

By wearing clothing made of machine-woven cloth, Bùnú villagers
are showing ọlàjú, sophisticated and "civilized" behavior as Nigerians and as citizens of the world. Yet at the same time, by keeping particular handwoven cloths, they are attempting to preserve a

distinctive Bùnú identity, an identity which the wearing of such worldly fashions threatens to efface.[10]

It is perhaps this conundrum that lies at the heart of Bùnú villagers' somewhat contradictory definition of ọ̀làjú as enlightened progress—implicitly dismissive of the past—which must nonetheless include respect for traditions of the past. This formulation of ọ̀làjú is particularly cogent for older Bùnú villagers whose authority over the young has been undermined by easy mobility, cash, and changes in social mores. As the custodians of tradition, older people have an interest in its continuation, in part because it serves as a source of authority over the young. Thus, it should not be surprising that not all Bùnú women and men, especially the young, share this sense of ọ̀làjú. For them, as for my research assistant from Kàbbà, "civilized" behavior largely means the rejection of traditions of the past. Because of this, "people practicing such [traditional] things today are not as many as before," as the woman quoted above observed.

On the one hand, these "conflicting notions of custom . . . expose custom as an aspect of authority" (Cohen and Odhiambo 1989:131). On the other hand, many Bùnú villagers, including young men and women, do continue to practice traditional marriage and attend masquerade performances.[11] For them, these performances evoke a pattern of social relations—between the old and young, women and men, the living and the dead—which must be maintained, despite conflict and change, if a distinctive Bùnú identity is to continue. These performances are not simply attempts by elders to assert authority or by members of a marginalized ethnic group to counter economic and social neglect with their own cultural solidarity. Along with these interests, these performances also convey a sense of being grounded in the world, of knowing who you are and where you have come from, associated with a particular geographical place and certain activities and things which are taken as given—as *latayé-bayé*, from the beginning. Similarly, everyday fashions made of machine-woven cloth solidly situate Bùnú villagers in the world of the here and now. They set in relief the tension between particular and general identities, individual and community concerns, and differing conceptions of the past and present.

TEN

EXTRAORDINARY
VISION AND THE
TWO SIDES OF CLOTH

I know the time will come when

God shall open their eyes to

know themselves [and the] dust

and ashes and the Ifas which

they worship shall be taken from

their eyes.

James Thomas, September 26, 1858

Ifa is Light.

Business card of Mr. Yusufu Ikusika

Mẹgbóle, Herbalist Doctor, Àkútúpá-

Kírí-Bùnú, 1988

The nineteenth-century CMS Bùnú catechist James Thomas would be pleased by the number of churches that exist in Bùnú District today. Through Bible-reading and prayers, Bùnú women and men have "opened their eyes" to new practices and beliefs, to ọlàjú. Yet Thomas would probably be troubled by the continuing consultations with Ifá diviners by many Bùnú villagers. Rather than rejecting the past, Bùnú villagers have adapted and maintained Ifá divination, continued masquerade performances, and kept cloths for the commemorative funerals of deceased kin along with Christian worship. For many (though not all), this multiplicity of spiritual practices does not contradict Christian belief but rather is a way of addressing different

concerns. Thus, despite the sense of change perceived by many
Bùnú villagers, they have also maintained a sense of continuity.

This continuity has been sustained, in part, through the use of
cloth. While handweaving and cotton production no longer constitute the bases of Bùnú women's and men's wealth as in the past, many
important social relationships continue to be expressed in terms of
cloth.

CLOTH, BODIES, AND KNOWLEDGE

The study of material things like cloth provide a way of grasping the
microscopic ways in which more abstract ideas such as the past, identity, and obligation are constituted in the course of everyday social
life. The bits of red cloth on the road just out of town,[1] the strip of
white cloth tied to a tree, the faded *àdófì* marriage cloth drying on a
line, and the small girl with a doll secured to her back with cloth, all
contribute to the unexamined naturalness associated with a particular way of life. These unassuming pieces of cloth are the vehicles
for socially constituted ideas about other beings, other domains, and
times past. Yet the particular qualities of cloth contribute to people's
perception of their world, as when social relations are described as
webs that are woven and interwoven. Durkheim described this dialectical quality of things that are imbued with ideas but whose qualities, in turn, shape individuals' perceptions. By considering a few
examples of associations made between cloth and the human body in
Bùnú, the ways that ideas, individuals, and things are linked may
more clearly be seen.

The image of the child carrying a doll on her back refers to one of
Bùnú villagers' earliest experiences, being carried as infants on the
backs of their mothers, supported and surrounded by cloth. Known
as "backing," this practice includes certain motions: stooping and se-

Small girl playing, backing doll with cloth.
Àpàá-Bùnú, 1988.

Faded àdófì *marriage cloth hung out in front of a wife's house.*
Àgbèdẹ-Bùnú, *December 1991.*

curing the child's body, then wrapping and tying it with cloth to quite
literally bind the bodies of mother and child together. Through the
habitual, unexamined performance of these actions, feelings of security and well-being merge with particular bodily movements.[2]

The physical act of backing, with mother and child tied together
with cloth, is projected out into the social world in broader, metaphorical ways. In these cases, the image of backing with cloth is used
to represent ideas about protection and support, about gratitude and
obligation, and about affection.[3]

This image is portrayed in several contexts. On the eve of a woman's traditional marriage, the bride (or a woman acting as her surrogate) is said to be "backed" on the way to her husband's house by an
age-mate, covered with a large hooded robe known as an *ìbòrí*. The
idea of support is evident throughout traditional marriage perfor-

Surrogate wife being "backed" by an age-mate on the way to the house of her "husband" during traditional marriage eve. The hooded white satin robe is called an ìbòrí. *Agbede-Bùnú, December 1987.*

mance, as age-mates help dress and sing and sleep with the new bride.

In northern Bùnú, during one phase of traditional marriage performance, the bride wears a particular marriage cloth, *yísalà*, as a baby tie. As she walks in the market, she ties this cloth as if carrying a baby and makes hand motions as if she is patting it. Infertile women may also signal their ambition to carry children by backing objects with cloth, both of which are then given away, i.e., sacrificed. Women give away these things in the hope that the recipients, often lepers or the blind, will, in grateful exchange, grant them fertility.

The imagery of backing is also evident in masquerade performances; for example, the masquerade Òùna "backs" a body as its spirit leaves the earthly domain on its way to the spirit world. And in one masquerade performance, the masquerade known as Nároko briefly carried the masquerade called Egàbọm on its back. This action was in part playful but also expressed the support of Nároko, said to be the husband of Egàbọm.

These bodily actions using cloth, representing support, protection, and reciprocity, also express the way that cloth and people are sometimes symbolically conflated. Cloth may be presented as having some of the qualities of people, while people have certain cloth-like characteristics. For instance, certain cloths are said to hum and to speak like people, a child may be referred to as "my cloth," rolls of cloth may stand for corpses, and madness is equated with clothlessness.

In Bùnú, cloth's symbolic import appears to lie in this intimate association with the body. Like metaphors about the human body which "mediate between the world of material objects and ideas" (Jackson 1989: 146), images of cloth wrapping bodies and tied to trees inform everyday ways of knowing the world. Yet the power of symbols in social life rests on their ability to sustain multiple meanings and interpretations. While cloth may be used to represent ideas of support and gratitude, it can also be employed to express more subversive and ambiguous ideas.

CLOTH HAS TWO SIDES

In Bùnú, the world, like cloth, is described as having two sides—one obvious to everyone, the other only visible to certain individuals. This distinction also applies in cloth use. When an individual wears a cloth, the side facing outward projects its wearer's open sociality, while the side facing inward conceals thoughts and motives known only to the wearer.

The importance of the two sides is also reflected in cloth production. Normally, a woman sees only one side of the cloth she is weaving, while the other side is obscured. However, men weaving the anomalous red cloth, *apọnúpọnyìn*, used in the funerals of kings, were said to be able to see both sides of the cloth as they wove. Indeed, this ability was a prerequisite for learning to weave this dangerous cloth, which was said to hum and call for blood. In order to demonstrate such extraordinary vision, one must have "four eyes," i.e., two pairs, one for each side of the cloth.

The image of a person with four eyes (*olójúmẹrin*) seeing both sides of cloth implies exceptional power more generally. This ability is also associated with the practice of antisocial witchcraft. Not surprisingly, people said to have four eyes (i.e., witches) display other inversions of social behavior. Unlike ordinary people with monovision, people with four eyes can see in the day and night, both near and far, the invisible and the visible, the present and the future. By virtue of this extraordinary vision, individuals with four eyes are acknowledged to have special knowledge. On the other hand, they are also ambiguously evaluated because they are capable of both socially beneficial and antisocial behavior. *Babaláwo* diviners, for example, exhibit this combination of potentially beneficial and destructive behavior. Because of their special sight and knowledge, they are able to divine the future and to know cures. Yet they are also suspected of practicing witchcraft.

Other individuals besides diviners may exhibit this extraordinary vision, their abilities enhanced or hidden through the use of cloth. When *ejínuwọn* women wear *àkì* cloths, they are able to see, as if in a dream, the cause of illness and its cure. The masquerade performer, after donning the medicine-soaked costume of the masquerade Iyelúgbó, is able to see both great distances and invisible enemies, that is, witches and wizards, who also have "four eyes" but disguise themselves by wearing ordinary dress like everyone else.

The problem with people who have extraordinary sight or power is that it is never exactly clear who they are or how their special abilities will be used.

This conflation of sight, special knowledge, and the ambiguous moral associations of the hidden side of social relations is not new in Bùnú. In James Thomas's prayers for the Bùnú people's future that begin this chapter, he contrasts "the time . . . when God shall open their eyes to know themselves," implying lightness and clarity, with vision obscured by "dust and ashes and the Ifas which they worship." He seems to suggest that the knowledge contained in the Bible, available to all who could read, was open and good, while the knowledge of Ifá divination was secret and therefore suspect (see Peel 1978:149). Through the Bible, all had access to ọ̀làjú (enlightenment), this special knowledge supporting an ideal of equality and fellowship in village life, unlike "those with four eyes" whose hidden powers could be used to support the privileges of some at the expense of others.[4]

Ironically, this ideal of village egalitarianism was actually undermined by Christian conversion, which led to differential access to education and subsequent opportunities for employment. People might be equal in the eyes of God but the political and economical inequities of village life became more apparent as those with education were able to enhance their positions. Further, as many of the Bùnú villagers who converted to Christianity following the Omi Mímọ́ movement in the 1930s discovered, unequal misfortune and disease still could not be explained. As Mr. Mẹgbólé's business card (p. 191) suggests, Ifá divination continues to bring light to bear on these perplexing problems for some villagers.

Yet if continuing disparities of wealth and misfortune suggest that some individuals succeed through unholy means, the good fortune of some need not be equated with antisocial self-interest. As with *ọ̀làjú*, such behavior is considered good when individuals are educated and then bring development to their home villagers. *Ọ̀làjú* is bad, however, when, once educated, individuals abandon their villages and kin. Those able successfully to balance the need to give and share with the need to protect and keep their own advantage are likely to be praised for their achievements rather than accused of displaying uncivilized behavior or practicing antisocial witchcraft. The moral evaluation of extraordinary sight, knowledge, and achievement—all potential signs of witchcraft—depends on the situation and the people involved.

To emphasize this point, I conclude with the description of a dispute, essentially a witchcraft accusation, which occurred during my stay in Bùnú. It illustrates several aspects of social life: resentment over disparities in wealth and power, unexplained illness, and extraordinary vision, all associated with witchcraft. It also displays an ambiguous mix of unintended consequences, misinterpretations, polyphonous voices, and indefinite conclusions, making this dispute an excellent example of the contextual nature of interpretations of witchcraft. Further, the dispute itself centered on the wearing of one particular cloth. Throughout this book, I have intentionally downplayed my personal participation as ethnographer. But I have included this dispute along with my part in it because it, more than any other event during my stay in Bùnú, "opened my eyes" to the continuing importance of cloth in Bùnú social life.

The Dispute. In Bùnú in 1987 and 1988 I attended several traditional marriage performances, where I took photographs, some of which I promised to send to the brides. I also took pictures of various people whom I interviewed, planning to send them their pictures as well.

After returning to the States, I sent many of these pictures, in envelopes according to villages, to a friend in Kàbbà to distribute for me in Bùnú.

When I returned to Bùnú two years later, people in one village began asking about one particular photograph. They insisted that I had taken a photograph of one woman and that another woman had appeared in her place. I could not understand what they were saying until I saw the photograph later that day. It was a picture of an older woman I had interviewed about Bùnú cloth. She had access to many different cloths which she showed me, even modeling some of them to demonstrate how they should be worn. In the photograph she was wearing *yísalà*, the traditional marriage cloth, which is only to be worn in the process of performance. What complicated the matter was that I had also taken photographs of a traditional marriage performance in the same village later that year. While I sent the bride several pictures, I did not send her a print of herself wearing the *yísalà* cloth.

Yísalà is used in traditional marriage in northern Bùnú (Kírí) but not elsewhere in Bùnú. It is even rare in northern Bùnú where it was said that only one or two cloths of this type remained. When I was first told about *yísalà* cloth, it was described as a white cloth with a picture of a child drawn on it. To me, it looked more like a long white cloth with a circular reddish blotch in the center. On the trip to the market during traditional marriage performance, this cloth is worn by the bride much as she would wear a baby tie. As she walks, her hand pats the cloth where the imaginary baby would be. Because of its rarity and the belief that it is both dangerous to look at and susceptible to disappearing, its use is closely guarded. After it is worn by the bride at the market, a woman stands by ready to whisk it away to be safely stored. *Yísalà* is not an ordinary cloth and it should not be worn lightly.

When I saw the picture of the older woman wearing the *yísalà* cloth, I knew that the problem was the unauthorized wearing of this cloth. The bride and many other villagers said that the older woman, who had not attended that particular day of the marriage and could not have worn the *yísalà* cloth in any event as she was not the bride, "pushed" the spirit of the bride out of the photograph and appeared there herself. Furthermore, when I took the photograph, I was overheard to have exclaimed about the older woman appearing in the picture. Finally, the photograph explained another unusual occurrence that day which I had noticed myself. As the bride's body was rubbed with red camwood, it had turned black. At the time this was ascribed to her *ejínuwọn* spirit-double troubling her and a small sacrifice had been made. However, with the evidence of the photograph, this occurence was attributed to the spiritual machinations of the older woman.

I retrieved the photograph and the next day a village moot was held, presided over by the king and several village chiefs. All parties stated their positions. I said that I had taken a photograph of the older woman, but, for fear of complicating matters further, that I did not know about the *yísalà* cloth. The older woman denied ever wearing the *yísalà* cloth. The bride and her family stated their argument about the replacement of her spirit, represented by the older woman wearing the *yísalà* cloth, and the bride's subsequent illness. The king asked for the evidence—the photograph—but was surprisingly quiet. Several other people spoke at length, supporting the various interpretations. One Western-educated Bùnú man living outside of Bùnú but who happened to be visiting argued that it was absurd to think that a camera could photograph one woman and that someone else could appear, thus adding another perspective to the case.

I was then asked to promise that when I returned to the States I would send the photograph of the bride wearing the *yísalà* cloth, which I did. The photograph of the older woman was kept by the bride's family as evidence "for future generations." After that, the gathering dispersed though there had been no final judgment about what had happened. The case was left unresolved because the heart of the matter was too dangerous to discuss in a public setting.

In this case, a cloth and a photograph were used as vehicles for indicating resentment felt by the bride and her family toward the older woman and hers. The older woman's son was a wealthy manufacturer and as a result, his mother had more things than many people in the village. Further, she was not only thought to be ungenerous in sharing her wealth with others, but was also described as "syphoning off" the prosperity of others for herself.[5] The primary issue in this case was the disparity of wealth in the village. That the older woman had more wealth than others, who generally shared the same circumstances, led to suspicions that recourse to supernatural power, i.e., witchcraft, was involved. I was similarly implicated in these suspicions because of my special sight—my camera—and my unusual circumstances—my relative wealth, that I traveled alone, that I was a white foreigner.

None of this was voiced by the bride or her family, though other people I spoke with privately agreed that these suspicions and resentments underlay the events. Rather, yísalà was the vehicle through which these sentiments were expressed. The ambiguous ending of the affair and the ominous statement that the photograph would serve as evidence "for future generations" suggest that uncertainty surrounding the causes of inequality is likely to be a source of contention between these and other families for many years to come. It is also likely that people will continue to use cloth "in many ways" in the construction of these arguments and claims.

APPENDIX

Cloth name	Description	Price range[a]	Use
Kẹkẹ[b]	White w/blue stripes	3–8 shillings	Everyday cloth, farm shirts, sold at markets
Àkù	White and blue stripes	5–10 shillings	(Same as keke)
Ọ̀run	White (3 or 4 pieces)	15 shillings	Sold at markets
Fágbò	Light, med., dark blue warp stripes	6–10 shillings	Sold at markets
Àláàgi	White w/blue stripes	3–15 shillings	Sold at markets
Ojúedewó[c]	Med/dark blue warp stripes	8 shillings to 1 pound	Marriage cloth, sold at markets
Arigidi	Narrow white strips (2) w/fine blue warp stripes	1–2 shillings	Sold at markets to cloth traders
Ọ̀já	Single strip, any color		Cloth for carrying babies

Cloth name	Description	Price range[a]	Use
Ọlọ́ba	White, med. and dark blue warp/ weft stripes	10 shillings to 1½ pounds	Commissioned prestige cloth
Àdófì	Black w/white, red warp stripes	4–8 pounds[d]	Marriage cloth by commission
Àtufù	Black w/white, red warp stripes		Marriage cloth by commission
Awẹ̀rẹ̀	Black w/white warp stripes		Marriage cloth by commission
Elésì	Black w/white warp stripes		Marriage cloth by commission
Kẹ́tẹ́kènín	Black w/white warp stripes		Marriage cloth by commission
Ọ̀run patí[e]	White (bast fiber) w/blue, magenta em- broidered edge		Marriage cloth by commission
Ọ̀run padà	White w/red warp stripe		Marriage cloth by commission
Yísalà[f]	White w/reddish blotch and elaborate fringe		Marriage cloth purchased (?)
Mẹ́rí mẹ́kà[f]	Blue w/white warp, weft stripes		Marriage cloth purchased— Bida
Máabò gàndòn[f]	Blue w/white		Marriage cloth purchased— Bida
Obun kero			Marriage cloth, no longer used

Cloth name	Description	Price range[a]	Use
Àkì[g]			
Àkì	Narrow white		*Ejínuwọn* spirit
Ọ̀já	strip, fringe		cloth, by
Àkọjá	tied w/coins,		commission
	cowries, peri-		
	winkle shells		
Ọ̀run padà	Narrow white		Spirit cloth, by
	strip w/small		commission
	black and red		
	stripes in		
	center		
Aṣọ ipò			*Funeral cloths*
Àbatá	Red and tan geo-	3–5 pounds	Sold at Okene
	metric patterns		and Kàbbà, by
	on white (11)		commission
Ìfàlẹ̀	Red and tan geo-	2½ pounds	(Same as *àbatá*)
	metric patterns		
	on white (7)		
Ọ̀já	Single long strip	1½–7 pounds	(Same as *àbatá*)
	of red and tan		
	patterns		
Ẹ̀bẹ	Single short strip		(Same as *àbatá*)
	of red and tan		
	patterns		
Apọ́núpọ́nyìn	Red on both sides		By commission

[a]The range of prices given here reflects the different ages and market experiences of former weavers interviewed. For example, *kẹkẹ* cloth was sold for 3 shillings in 1929, while by 1941, it sold for 6 shillings (Bridel 1929, NAK; Miscellaneous correspondence 1932–1950, NAK).
[b]Handwoven cloths sold in markets were sometimes referred to in general as *kíjìpá*.
[c]*Ojúedewó* cloths were woven in Bùnú; cloths with similar color patterns were also bought from Nupe weavers at Bida.

[d]*Àdófì* prices ranged from 12 shillings ("in the olden days") to 60 náírà (around $7 US) in 1988.

[e]This cloth had not been woven within the lifetimes of any present-day Bùnú weavers. The white thread appears to be a type of bast fiber, though its source is unknown (Boser-Sarivaxévanis 1975).

[f]These three marriage cloths were probably woven by Nupe weavers at Bida. They are only used in marriages performed in northern Bùnú (Kírí).

[g]*Àkì* cloths dyed with camwood a rust-red color are used by the kings of northern Bùnú (Kírí).

NOTES

CHAPTER ONE

Chapter epigraph: A translation of the song that was sung by women in
Àkútúpá-Kírí-Bùnú:

Wọ̀ bá n'éwó, inú a bí ghọn [2x]
Wọ̀ mọ́ ma bìnú ẹni [chorus]
Wọ̀ bá n'áṣọ, inú a bí ghọn
Wọ̀ bá n'ọ́mọ, inú a bí ghọn
N ẹ̀ màsọ se é mọ̀ yéyé.

1. For example, the term *oníkaba* (one who wears dresses) refers to educated women, while the term *aróṣọ* (literally, the people who wear
cloth) refers to uneducated, village women.

2. For information about the role of cloth in social and economic life:
for the Inca, see Murra 1962, 1989; for India, see Bayley 1986 and Bean
1989; for medieval Mediterranean society, see Goitein 1967 and Lombard 1978.

3. Appadurai (1986:5) argues for a focus on things and their social
elaboration though his concern is with things as commodities.

4. Bodily corruption may also be represented by cloth. In Leviticus
14:47–59, for example, mildewed or moldy cloth is referred to as leprous
and unclean. Such cloth was to be taken to a priest and given treatment
comparable to that given to a leper.

5. On the other hand, groups and individuals asserting a new basis of
authority may seek to destroy such objects, as did newly converted
Christians in southern Nigeria during the early part of this century
(e.g., Garrick Braide [Horton 1970]; J. A. Babalọlá [Peel 1968]).

6. Abu 'Ubaydallah al-Bakri, a resident of Cordova, Spain, wrote a detailed account of the Kingdom of Ghana in 1067–68, based on contem-

porary written sources and oral interviews with traders who had traveled there (Levtzion 1973:22).

7. Initially, gifts of colored silks and linen cloths were given by the Portuguese to the king and chiefs of Benin in southern Nigeria in the late fifteenth century. Ryder suggests that a yard of cloth, the "vara acustumada," became a standard unit of value in Benin from which the terms *pano*, *pagne*, and *paan* later derived (1969:57).

8. Ryder estimates that "between 1644 and 1646 the Dutch at Arbo bought at least 16,000 pieces" (1969:93).

9. The price paid for one piece fell, partially explaining the decline in the usefulness of cloth as trade items (Ryder 1969:133). Furthermore, sources of cloth from the north were disrupted by war (Ryder 1969:235).

10. See Adams 1966; Baikie 1856; Barth 1857; Burton 1865; Lander and Lander 1832; Landolphe 1823; Whitford 1967 for lists of cloths used in trade and as gifts.

In Bùnú, missionaries such as the nineteenth-century Bùnú CMS catechist James Thomas recognized the importance of cloth in maintaining economic and social relationships: "January 5, 1863—[In] a little while we met the chief of the Bunnes. . . . I presented the king eight yards of cloth . . . so he received the present with gladness. . . . January 7, 1863—A present of 10,000 cowries was given by the king upon leaving" (1863b/c, CMS).

11. There is also evidence which suggests that cloth woven by central Nigerians such as the Bùnú and Ebira peoples was sold in precolonial Kano (Kriger 1988:14) as well as in southern Nigeria (Boser-Sarivaxévanis 1975).

12. Frobenius 1913, 2:415. Frobenius collected five examples of Kàbbà cloth, which are presently housed in the Staatliches Museum für Völkerkunde, Munich, accession nos. 15-26-51, -52, -53, -54, and -55 (cited in Kriger 1988).

13. See the notebook of A. J. Jepson of J. W. Gill and Company, Manchester, England (1973.856), in the collection of The Art Institute of Chicago, and the collection of C. Beving, Museum of Mankind, London. Charles Beving traveled throughout Nigeria in the early 1900s, col-

lecting cloth, including two pieces of blue and white cloth woven in Kàbbà (nos. 1934-3-7-146 and -147).

14. However, there has been a resurgence of women's weaving recently in southwestern Nigeria, not on broad upright looms but on narrow-strip horizontal (Picton 1991:42) and European floor looms (Renne field notes 1992).

15. In a United Nations report (1968) on West African textile production, it was noted that while handwoven cloth was only a small percentage of textiles consumed, its production had actually increased.

16. Boser-Sarivaxévanis 1972; Eicher 1975; Kent 1971; Lamb 1975; Lamb and Holmes 1980; Picton and Mack 1979; Schaedler 1987; Sieber 1972. For an extended bibliography on African cloth and dress, see Eicher 1969; Pokornowski et al. 1985.

17. For essays that relate cloth to social aspects of Nigerian life, see Ben-Amos 1978, Borgatti 1983, Cordwell and Schwarz 1979, Idiens and Ponting 1980. See Brett-Smith 1984, Dilley 1986, Goody 1982 for other West African examples.

18. The dearth of social analyses of the use of West African cloth may be due to the fact that the preponderance of cloth research has been conducted by researchers with different perspectives. Much of the literature on Nigerian cloth comes from art historical (Aronson 1980, Johnson 1973, Picton 1980, Poyner 1980, and Shea 1975), economic (Bray 1968, Dorward 1976, Liedholm 1982, and Sundstrom 1974), or technical perspectives (Boser-Sarivaxévanis 1969, 1972, 1975; Kent 1972, Menzel 1972, and Murray 1936).

19. While I use the term Bùnú Yorùbá to emphasize their connection with Yorùbá-speaking groups to the southwest, Bùnú people refer to themselves as the Abùnú or Abìnú, and their language as Abìnú, while the district itself is called Bùnú. In order to avoid confusion, I refer to people, language, and district as Bùnú.

20. The northern kingdoms were referred to as Kírí. In this book, I refer to the peoples of the southern, central, and northern (i.e., Kírí) parts of the district as Bùnú District. Archaeological evidence suggests that this area has been populated for several thousand years (Ọbáyẹmí

1976:200) though the antiquity of weaving in Bùnú is uncertain. The earliest archaeological evidence of spinning in Bùnú dates from the sixteenth century (Ọbáyẹmí 1978b).

21. According to a chief in northern Bùnú: "It came to a time when we could not get people for the Nupe to be taken away to Bida . . . [then] they said that we should begin to pay money as well as our locally woven cloth" (T. Moses, Aíyétórò-Kírí-Bùnú).

22. See Eades 1980 and Crowder 1966 for concise background texts on Yorùbá culture and Nigerian history, respectively.

23. See Krapf-Askari (1965, 1966a) for a more detailed account of the Bùnú Yorùbá chieftaincy system.

24. During the nineteenth and early twentieth centuries when Nupe hegemony prevailed, some Bùnú chiefs became Muslims although the majority of the population retained traditional beliefs. Although Muslim worship is not common in Bùnú today, some people, particularly in northern Bùnú (Kírí), are practicing Muslims.

CHAPTER TWO

1. The decline of handspinning in Bùnú District is related to the attendance of young girls in primary school in the early 1950s (see chapter 6).

2. Today few young women know how to spin, whereas formerly it was knowledge required of all women. In the past, demonstrating that a bride could clean, remove seeds, fluff, and spin a certain amount of cotton in one day was part of traditional marriage ritual.

3. The importance of ambiguity in Yorùbá thought is evident in Pemberton's discussion of the trickster deity Eshu, characterized as "a figure of intense activity, of contrasts and reversals, and apparent contradictions . . . 'Eshu turns right into wrong, wrong into right' " (1975:25).

4. It remains to be seen if similar associations are made in other West African societies (e.g., Dogon: Griaule 1965; Ewe: Vermeer 1971; Mende: Boone 1986) where white cloth plays an important part in ritual practices.

5. See Breidenbach 1976; Blier 1987; Boone 1986:236; Jacobson-Widding 1979; Richards 1982; Turner 1967.

6. Among the Ọ̀yọ́ Yorùbá, menstrual blood that is considered to be thin, *aṣẹ́ lílámi*, is referred to as white and is described as *olómi*, watery (Buckley 1985:73–74).

7. Elsewhere in Nigeria and in some parts of Bùnú, members of this cult are known as *ẹlẹ́gbé* (Simpson 1980), *olómi*, and *emèrè* (Abraham 1958:179; Ìdòwú 1962:123). The term *ejínuwọn* is derived from Nupe, *eji*, child, and *nuwon*, water. See Nadel 1954:211–12 for a discussion of the Gwari-Nupe *sogba* cult, from which the *ejínuwọn* cult may have been derived. One woman from northern Bùnú said that this cult was introduced to Bùnú by a Nupe woman called Sogba Kuti.

8. Such individuals are referred to as *àbíkú*, those "born to die." Earlier siblings are believed to be earlier births of the same child who then died, only to be born again (Okri 1991; Verger 1968).

9. Some women said that if a cloth was not completed in one day, a chicken should be killed, or chewed alligator pepper seeds (*atare*) could be sprayed on the cloth (depending on the type) the following day. Others said that the cloth should be removed from the loom and kept in the bush overnight.

10. There is a certain ambiguity about spirit domains in Yorùbá belief. Verger describes *àbíkú* spirits as living in heaven, but while on earth they also take refuge "dans les endroits marécageux ou les rivières . . . ils vont aussi au pied des murs la ou on va vider les ordures" (1968:1454).

11. Bùnú Yorùbá more commonly cite relations with various nature spirits that abide in pools of water, streams (*omi ẹbọra*), rocks, and trees called *ẹbọra*. For a discussion of the influence of Christian writers on descriptions of the Yorùbá conception of a High God, see Verger 1966.

12. *Alálàfunfun-Òkè* may be literally translated as "the owner of white cloth (*àlà funfun*) on the hill."

13. See Nadel 1954:149 on the Nupe use of pots tied with white cloth. In a variation of this procedure in northern Bùnú, two poles are erected and swathed with white cloth to hide the pot.

14. Communication between ancestor and bush spirits is often accomplished through the sacrifice of white things, in particular palm wine (*ẹmu funfun*), white chickens (*adìẹ funfun*), white pigeons (*ẹiyẹlé funfun*), white sheep (*àgbìtàn funfun*), and snails (*ìgbín*).

15. The absorbency of cloth has important everyday implications. One woman explained that if a child urinates on a cloth, one should not wash it or throw it away, else the child will think it too is unwanted and will "go back" (I. Mọ́kànjú, Ọ̀llẹ̀-Bùnú).

16. The theme of carrying a child in front (in the womb) for nine months (Beidelman 1986:179–80) and then carrying it in back supported by cloth for three years is expressed in one popular Yorùbá song:

Ìyá ni wúrà iyebíye	Mother is precious gold
Tí à kó lè f'owó ra	that money cannot buy
Ó l'óyún mí	She was pregnant with me
f'ọ́sù mẹ́san, mẹ́wa	for nine months, ten months
Ó pòn mí f'ọ́dún mẹ́ta	She carried me for three years

17. In the myth about the origins of the spirit cult *òfósì*, associated with women's initiation and marriage, the first *òfósì* women were found in the bush, completely wrapped in white cloth. When unwrapped, they returned to life but speaking a strange, unknown language (Kennett 1931:436).

18. The references to water, slippery skin, and fish here imply a certain ambiguity (Beidelman 1966:386). It is the source of the fertility of women and the earth but moistness also implies slipperiness and the tenuousness of social relations (Beidelman 1986:34).

19. One Bùnú Yorùbá man described the power of this life-giving water: "If you are sick and you drink *omi-mímọ́*, you will be well. And if someone died, it would make him or her come back to life. Anybody that was a witch or a wizard, through prayer, it would come out and they would confess" (O. Ọbárokàn, Àgbẹ̀dẹ-Bùnú).

20. The association of *sìgìdì* spirits with the destructive side of social relations was suggested by the response of an elderly chief to my question of why the Bùnú people did not use these spirits against Nupe horsemen who raided for slaves during the nineteenth century. "We did not use it against the Bida people. We only use it against ourselves" (T. Moses).

21. However, Schneider (1987:431) has noted that qualities of cloth

other than color and patterning may be used to distinguish individuals and groups. "Plain," white cloth, for example, may display a sheerness or sheen that is also significant.

CHAPTER 3

1. Nadel, for example, defined therapeutic practice in general by its "rational intent and objective appropriateness." Nupe medicine is described thus: "Many more treatments are without even this semblance of appropriateness, suggesting merely blundering attempts, unguided even by faulty knowledge" (1954:135). Van Wing, cited in MacGaffey (1977:176), represented the use of medicinal "charms" as "self-seeking and superstitious magic."

2. One Bùnú story tells of a time in the past when people could exchange and wear another person's skin, just like cloth.

3. The entire cloth costume of the masquerade Iyelúgbó is soaked in medicinal substances, imparting on its wearer extraordinary vision ("up to 8 km"), which serves as protection.

4. One Kírí woman described an instance when a woman was caught having taken the corner of another woman's cloth. In a village moot, the accused woman was told to give the family of the woman a goat, palm wine, and millet beer as recompense. She was also told that if anything happened to the woman [i.e, if she got sick or died], "the blame will fall on you" (O. Ezekiel).

5. When a bus stopped in the village with the words *Ènìà l'aṣọ mi* painted on its side, it was explained as meaning that "people [*ènìà*] are my cloth [*aṣọ*]," i.e., that people, like cloth, surround and support one.

6. Clothlessness is one of the surest signs of mental illness in Bùnú. This idea is also expressed in the metaphorical description of corn's leafy covering as "cloth." It is said that "birds laugh at [corn]," insufficiently covered with its "cloth," much as villagers may ridicule the unclothed appearance of the insane. Such corn should be avoided and not eaten.

7. This behavior is similar to descriptions in other parts of Yorubaland of the deity Èṣù, who is said to cause people to quarrel (Pemberton 1975:26). Èṣù is an ambiguous deity, with both beneficent and malevo-

lent qualities. His cap is red on one side and black and white on the other (Pemberton 1975:25), like the bags of Bùnú diviners, which are red on one side and black and white on the other.

8. Èmimọ àgbò (*Pupalin lappacea amaranthaceae*) has sticky, burrlike seeds (see Buckley 1985:213–14). The use of this leaf is probably related to the idea of stickiness—of the mud ball and to evil threats.

9. Such medicine is generally known in Bùnú as *èle* (in Ọ̀yọ́ Yorùbá, it is called *ààlè*; see Fálọlá and Doortmont [1989:326–27]). The use of such medicinal "amulets" or "charms" is common throughout West Africa, e.g., the Kuranko put white cotton above doorways (Jackson 1989:200n). They serve a function similar to objects such as crucifixes and mazuzah, placed at doorways for protection in many Western societies.

10. While such cloths may be any color, it is possible that ideas about black and white threads wrapping medicine are related to the former dress of Bùnú chiefs. Traditionally, important chiefs wore at least two robes, a blue-black robe over a white one.

11. This behavior has been described elsewhere in Yorubaland. "The eating [or sucking of blood] causes a wasting disease to the victim's body. Children and adults alike are eaten by witches. It is said that they also eat the foetus in a pregnant mother's womb, thus causing miscarriage" (Awólàlú 1979:85; see also Simpson 1980:76).

12. The association of older women with witchcraft is expressed in the saying "our mothers, the witches" who, through their former ability to give birth, are thought to have supernatural powers (Drewal and Drewal 1983). The attributions of special powers to women may also reflect attitudes about their economic independence as traders and market entrepreneurs. In Nupe, for example, village women leaders (*sagi*) who acquired their positions by virtue of their own wealth were also believed to be witches (Nadel 1956:149). One older woman told me that formerly women chiefs were associated with witchcraft in Bùnú.

13. In many parts of Africa, extraordinary vision is a characteristic of those associated with divine communication (e.g., by the Kuranko [Jackson 1989:55], the Ndembu [Turner 1967], and the Nupe [Nadel 1954:147]). For example, one Nupe medicine incorporates the use of "a

live chameleon, which contact communicates to the charm the peculiar powers of the animal (which is said to 'see in the dark')." Similar associations are also made in the West, as the terms seer, clairvoyant, and visionary prophet suggest.

14. In other words, for a person to use protective medicine without the corresponding antidote is comparable to using harmful medicine itself. There are several similarities in protective medicines used by the Bùnú and the Kuranko of Sierra Leone, the latter described by Jackson (1989). Among the Kuranko, however, diviners who make protective medicine are not responsible for the harm these medicines may inflict on others. In Bùnú, it appears that diviners *are* held accountable, that their lack of responsibility for consequences contributes to the questionable morality associated with these people.

CHAPTER 4

1. This severing of relations is graphically depicted in dispute settlements, in which chiefs will take the cloths of the two disputants and tear them in half (Ìbéjìgbà 1988:37–38).

2. See Schneider (1978) for an excellent social and economic analysis of sixteenth-century Spanish court preference for black cloth.

3. A range of colors, from blue to lighter shades of bluish-black to black, are obtained according to the number of times thread is dipped in an indigo dyebath. All these shades of blue and black are referred to by one term, *dúdú*, which is translated as black.

4. Black and white threads may be placed on the ground by a woman who has performed traditional marriage to challenge one who has not. A woman who has not performed this ritual cannot walk over these threads, for fear of her life.

5. The Hausa and Tuareg of northern Nigeria and Niger produce indigo-saturated cloths called *turkudi*, which literally serve as money (Lamb and Holmes 1980:95).

6. Bùnú informants said that indigo-dyeing was practiced by particular families; however, it was the knowledge of dyeing that led to this restriction. They emphasized that as many families as could do it successfully did do it.

7. Prices of predominantly black indigo cloths ranged from 5 shillings to 1 pound 10 shillings; skeins of indigo-dyed yarns were sold for approximately 1 shilling 6 pence.

8. To give some sense of what this amount meant in 1929, 3 shillings was the annual tax payment of women. In an assessment report of Kàbbà District in that year, Assistant District Officer Bridel estimated a woman's annual net income to be 14 shillings 6 pence (Bridel 1929, NAK).

9. The collection and preparation of indigo leaves was a source of income for Nupe farmers who sold prepared balls to mainly Yorùbá customers at markets centers at Ìlọrin (Nadel 1956:235). Such indigo balls were probably purchased by Bùnú women at Lokoja, Ọ̀wọ́rọ̀, and northern Bùnú markets.

10. One woman estimated the cost of weaving her *àdófì* cloth, probably during the 1940s, to be: 1 pound for five skeins of 200 lengths each (4 shillings per skein); 7 shillings for red industrial yarn; and 15 shillings for the weaver's labor.

11. Older women's control of young girls' labor, however, was not absolute. One woman described how as a young girl she would hide cotton in her clothes and then throw it into the bush (A. Ikúéndayọ̀, Àpàá-Bùnú).

12. The spinning of a prescribed amount of cotton in one day was formerly part of traditional marriage ritual.

13. This image of the spirit world as a tempting refuge to which some children continually threaten to retreat is admirably portrayed in the novel *The Famished Road* (Okri 1991).

14. Formerly, traditionally marriage was performed when the young wife was brought as a virgin to her husband's house, and the importance of this ritual in controlling the fertility of young women was more obvious.

15. The association of the color black with evil in Yorùbá thought was noted by Westcott (1962:346). The rain forests of southwest Yorubaland differ considerably from the drier savannah to the north, which perhaps explains this negative association. Black does have negative associations in Bùnú as in the association of black nights with danger.

16. Drewal and Drewal's translation, "children are the clothes of men," is imprecise, as *èdá* refers to people in general, not only men (1983:120).

Cloth is conflated with children and people in other Yorùbá areas. Barber (1981:46) cites the *oríkì* poem that states *Mo lè bọ̀sọ ọ́'lẹ̀ kí n fèniyàn bora*, "I could take off my clothes and wrap myself in people."

17. In Sumbanese society, an indigo dyebath has a similar dialectical relationship with fertile women: "Pregnant women may not look at the dye pots, because it is believed that the sight of churning, dark liquids within the pot would dissolve the contents of their wombs and cause immediate abortion. Conversely, menstruating women are barred from the indigo dyeing, since the flow of their blood would make the dyes 'run' irregularly" (Hoskins 1989:150).

18. This description comes from the Ekìtì Yorùbá: "Near Efon, one bush spirit, a former wife of a long-deceased king, told the present king she was going away because her indigo dye pot had been broken by the new road" (Peel 1968:94).

19. Indeed, the *àdófì* cloth might be thought of as the "flag" of Bùnú ethnic identity, in a district constituted by British colonial officials after 1900 and subject to several boundary changes since. In villages throughout the district, women may randomly be seen wearing *àdófì* cloths. When *àdófì* is observed outside the district, it is a sign that the wearer is of Bùnú extraction.

CHAPTER 5

1. Each succeeding rank of chief is acquired through greater expenditures. Chiefs of the first rank acquire the title of *gẹmọ* chief. Those of the second rank are known as *orótà* chiefs. Those of the third rank are known as *olólù* chiefs; the highest title of the third rank is the *olú*, which is translated as king or lord (Krapf-Askari 1966a).

2. A somewhat different relationship between stories and cloth is expressed in the Ekoi story about the Mouse-Woman who weaves "story-children" and to whom the art of storytelling is attributed (P. Talbot, cited in Weigle 1989:177–78).

3. This story summary and others recounted in this chapter have been edited from recordings which have been transcribed in their entirety in both Bùnú Yorùbá and English.

4. See Ṣóyínká 1963 for a modern rendition of this theme (see also Beidelman 1986; Jackson 1982; LaPin 1977). This negative picture does not correspond with the description of senior wives given by Bùnú village women. Rather than discouraging junior co-wives from staying, some women said that senior wives begged their husbands to take other wives (D. Kọ́láwọlé). Some senior wives actively participated in bringing wives for their husbands to marry. Younger (educated) women seemed less interested in having a co-wife, however.

5. *Imọ̀lẹ̀* and *ọ̀fósì* are women's cults associated with worship of *ẹbọra* nature-deities in Bùnú (Krapf-Askari 1965).

6. Unilateral beings are often considered divine or extraordinary (Needham 1980).

7. For example, the Attah of Idah (King of Idah) has consolidated political support through the exchange of royal masquerades with local groups (Miachi 1990:212–13). Hausa rulers secure clients through gifts of handwoven robes (Perani 1989:71).

8. In the story "The Three Brothers and the King's Cloth," rivalry between brothers is also expressed through the use of ranked cloths. The funeral cloth *àbatá* is more expensive and more highly valued than the funeral cloth *ifàlẹ̀*, while neither are as expensive as king's cloth and regalia:

The Three Brothers and the King's Cloth
There was once a woman who bore three sons. One day they decided to go off to war. After preparing, they left, telling their mother that they would return. Much later, the day they promised to return had arrived. After the war, everyone took a cloth [from the defeated?] The eldest took the [red funeral] cloth called *àbatá*. The second took the [red funeral] cloth called *ifàlẹ̀*. The third took the cloth belonging to the *olú*. The eldest then said, "Look at our younger brother who has taken the best cloth!" The second brother agreed. What were they going to do?

They came close to their house. As they went, they began to feel thirsty but didn't see any water to drink. All the streams were dry until they came to the seventh one. When they saw this stream they were very happy. The two elder brothers then decided that their junior should drink first.

As the youngest brother went to drink from the stream, the eldest brother pushed him in and he drowned. The two older brothers then divided up all of the youngest brother's things and added them to their own. Then they started to go to the house.

But their junior brother, who has changed into a bird, arrived at the house first. The mother, who expected their return, had cooked soup and was preparing to make pounded yam. As she started to peel the yams, she heard a bird singing like this:

Mother, don't peel, don't peel
Three of us
We prepared and went to war
The senior of us took *àbatá*
The next took *ifàlè*
I took king's cloth
We prepared to come back from the war . . .
We looked for water and saw water
They pushed me in the water
My face was covered with water
Mother, don't peel, don't peel

This was how the mother discovered that the senior brothers had killed her youngest child (Baba Àbú).

9. Simmel (1971:299) has observed that "the exotic origin of fashions seems strongly to favor the exclusiveness of the groups which adopt them."

10. In a government hearing on a longstanding chieftaincy dispute in Kàbbà held in 1982–83, witnesses from opposing sides supported their claims by disputing the antiquity of each other's crowns and other paraphernalia (Kwara State, Government White Paper, 1983; see Asíwájú 1976).

CHAPTER 6

1. The question of the identity of the original weavers in Bùnú is an open one. There are no patron deities in Bùnú, as there are elsewhere in Yorubaland (Àrèmú 1982). Early explorers (e.g., May

1860; Vandeleur 1898), missionaries, and colonial officials noted the prevalence of women's weaving in the confluence area. In nearby Ìjùmú, women were formerly buried with brass castings of weaving paraphernalia, while men were buried with arrows, suggesting that these gender-specific associations were of some antiquity (Ọbáyẹmí 1989).

2. In Bùnú, men and women are believed to have an equal role in the formation of a child. Men contribute semen and women contribute blood, which combine to form a child. The child is animated, however, by the presence of an ancestral spirit.

3. This connection is also suggested by Òdúyoyè (1972:85), who etymologically relates the name for a girl-child born with a caul with the name of a particular masquerade. However, Òdúyoyè's etymology is noted with some reservation as I could get no confirmation of his statement, at least in Bùnú. The association of cauls with cloth or clothing is not unknown in other parts of the world (Ginzburg 1983:9; Weiner 1985:215).

4. Elsewhere in Yorubaland, this rite was called ẹsẹ̀ n t'aiyé, literally, "foot in the world" (Ìdòwú 1962:181).

5. Since its ancestor spirit could be any one of four grandparents, a child could possess a spirit which was reborn bilaterally. This rebirth was not restricted by gender. Thus, one man was told that he possessed the reborn spirit of his maternal grandmother.

6. While there are no prohibitions against men attending this ritual, the woman who described it and had recently done it for her brother said that only women attended. While the use of marriage things implies that this was largely a women's rite, it is unclear to me who performed it in the past.

7. Several colonial officials and associates took note of these distinctive cloths (Harris 1931, NAK; Byng-Hall and James in Temple 1965:72; Larymore 1911; McCabe 1925, NAK; Niven 1926:297).

8. For example, the Portuguese were trading with Benin in the early sixteenth century (Ryder 1969; Vogt 1975). One trader in 1582 listed suggested merchandise for trade with Benin which included "coarse red

woollen cloth" (Ryder 1969:80). Red woolen cloth could also have reached Bùnú by overland trade networks between the kingdom of Benin and the northeast Yorùbá (Akíntóyè 1969:544). Similarly, these imported red cloths may have come to Bùnú from Benin via Idah (Obáyẹmí 1980:164). Barth (1857, I:518), describing the Kano market, wrote in 1857: "woolen cloth of the most ordinary quality, chiefly red . . . was formerly imported to a great extent [to Kano]; but it has gone out of fashion." Red blankets were also noted in the 1860s in the market town of Egga on the Niger River, north of Lokoja (Whitford 1877, cited in Johnson 1973:362). It is possible that red cloth came from all these sources.

9. Obadiah Thomas was the son of the CMS catechist James Thomas who was born in northern Bùnú, captured and sold as a slave in 1832, and freed and trained in Sierra Leone (see chapter 8).

10. Women are supposed to hide in their houses when Ìró is abroad, but Bùnú women belonging to particular families are exempt from this rule and can even follow the masquerade.

11. I was told of an incident in which a woman attempted to challenge one of the masquerades by giving it bad food, but she was apprehended and subsequently died. See Nadel (1954) for a description of the Nupe masquerade *ndako gboya*, ostensibly introduced to counter the power of older women.

12. The cloths presently used for carrying children (*òjá*) are thick, warp-faced cloths consisting of one long strip with fringes. They were introduced within the last fifty years from outside Bùnú. Older women said that formerly they had used cloth wrappers to carry babies.

13. In this case, the neighboring Ebira make similar color associations, characterizing red as the color of power and achievement and white as an indication of weakness (J. Picton, pers. com.).

14. To give some idea of the amounts involved in the sale of the large *aṣọ ipò* cloth that cost 5 pounds in 1929 (Harris 1931, NAK), an identical amount was levied as the cost of bridewealth repayments in Kàbbà Native Authority court divorce cases in the 1930s.

15. There are several examples of court-sponsored introductions of

special weaving techniques in Africa (Lamb and Lamb 1981; Vansina 1956) and elsewhere (Cort 1989).

CHAPTER 7

1. This situation differed from that resulting from French colonial programs for cotton processing and cloth production in Côte d'Ivoire (Bassett 1988). Among the Baule of central Côte d'Ivoire, women controlled only one phase of cloth production, spinning. Construction of spinning mills by the French affected these women adversely compared to Baule men weavers, who benefited from the introduction of industrially spun yarn (Etienne 1982). In Kàbbà Province, British cotton manufacturers set up gins but not spinning mills. Further, Bùnú women controlled both the spinning and weaving of cotton thread.

2. Describing the Provincial Exhibition held at Lokoja in 1923, the acting resident officer wrote that "there was considerable amount of friendly rivalry among the District Chiefs who vied with each other in sending exhibitions of cotton goods and leather work" (Budgen 1923, NAI). Exhibitions organized to demonstrate handweaving techniques, such as the 1948 "Weaving Exhibition at Okene," were also sponsored by colonial officials (Miscellaneous files 1948, NAK).

3. Thirty weavers from the Bùnú villages Àgbèdẹ and Àpàá were interviewed during the period November 1987 to August 1988. A few Bùnú weavers from Ọ̀llẹ̀, Àkútúpá-Kírí, and Aíyétórò-Kírí were also questioned. The data on Bùnú women weavers applies generally to other Northeast Yorùbá groups—the Ìjùmú, Yàgbà, and Owé—where handweaving was women's major occupation as well (Niven 1926:296).

4. Lloyd noted, however, that the increased number of chieftaincy titles insured the continued demand for handwoven cloth used to make chiefs' gowns in Yorubaland (Lloyd 1953:33).

In a related way, this economic focus has tended to associate commercial handweaving in West Africa with men, while characterizing women's weaving as domestic or "avocational" (Sieber 1972:155). While this is true in some parts of West Africa, it is not the case in parts of southern and central Nigeria. Bùnú women, while interspersing spinning and weaving with domestic duties such as childcare and cooking, said that they wove cloth primarily for sale in local and long-distance markets.

5. Bridel noted that "hitherto the industrial wealth of the District has been reckoned by the income derived by women from weaving; they do not do farm work" (1929, NAK). In a 1935 census of Bùnú District, all adult women in various Bùnú villages were also listed as weavers (Squibbs 1935, NAK).

6. The period discussed is from approximately 1900 until the present. Most of the older women questioned (members of the association Ẹgbẹ́ Ìyá Àgbà) were young, married women during the Holy Water Movement (Omi Mímọ́) led by J. O. Babaloḷá in Kàbbà in 1932. Thus they were probably born during the first decade of this century.

7. Both represent the amount of cloth needed to make a cloth skirt wrapper (R. Ọmọ́sàyìn and C. Ògúníbì, Àpàá-Bùnú). There was considerable variation in the amounts the people remembered paying for imported cloth. One older woman recalled buying ànkàrà cloth "very cheap" at Lokoja, paying only five pence per yard, whereas a Kàbbà cloth trader said that he had sold it for seven and one-half shillings in Bùnú villages.

8. This cloth was referred to as *akwa miri* cloth by the Igbo (Aronson 1989:61; 38, plus plate). There are two examples of *arigidi* cloth in the collection of the Royal Museum of Scotland (accession nos. 1977-173, 1977-173a).

9. This interview with Mr. O. Olúmodì ("Àjìgí") was conducted in Kàbbà by Esther Eniọ́lọ́runfẹ́ in March 1988. Àjìgí also collected *arigidi* cloth from other towns and villages in the area, including Iyah-Gbẹdde, Ódogi, Áiyeré, Ìkàrẹ́, Ogbagi, Íyará, and Kàbbà.

10. Bùnú women remarked that they liked to weave *arigidi* because they could weave it so quickly. Women in Kàbbà said they could weave up to four pairs in a day. One Ìjùmú woman said that while attending primary school in the 1960s near Kàbbà, she wove one pair of cloths a day (Mrs. J. Àjàyí, Kàbbà).

11. Interview with A. Tèmítáyọ̀. Women from Àgbẹ̀dẹ took a similar route after walking west toward Kàbbà (E. Gbodòfé, Àgbẹ̀dẹ-Bùnú). Prices for *aṣọ ipò* cloth ranged from three shillings for one strip (E. Gbo-

dòfé) to as much as three pounds (£3) for an eleven-strip *àbatá* cloth (A. Tèmítáyò).

12. It is likely that Bùnú women formerly also attended the large market at Egga, north of Bùnú on the Niger River. In 1844, members of the Niger Expedition collected cloth samples, including one from Bùnú at Egga (see page 59).

13. One district officer, H. S. Bridel, who realized that the bulk of women's earnings went to rearing their children, remarked that "I can find no justification for this [taxation of women]." In the margin next to this paragraph is the handwritten comment, "Why not?" (1929, NAK). In 1930, at Bridel's instigation, an attempt was made to introduce a graduated tax assessment based on income rather than a flat tax per individual in Kàbbà District. This policy apparently never reached Bùnú District. In the mid-1940s, it was decided that only men should be assessed.

14. See Miscellaneous files 1932–50, NAK. Also, as the tan, hand-spun cotton used in patterning became scarce, the yarn from unraveled burlap sacks was substituted. The resulting jute yarn was dyed a golden tan with *túrí*, the dye extracted by boiling turmeric root (*elégà*) (Dalziel 1937).

15. Atta Ibrahim was appointed as Ebira paramount chief in 1917 and resigned in 1954 (Picton 1980:78). His claim was supported by the Ebira belief that Bùnú weavers cried on their completed cloths, bringing misfortune and death to their potential customers (A. Ibrahim, Okene). One Bùnú weaver said that they did indeed pray that an Ebira person would have died as they carried their cloth to sell at Okene (A. Tèmítáyò).

CHAPTER 8

1. Vandeleur, for example, who was part of the constabulary force that marched through the Bùnú area in 1897, wrote of the Bùnú village of Feraji, where "a great deal of cotton was grown in the fields around, and I noticed women in a house at work on the looms" (1898:193).

2. Elsewhere in Nigeria and West Africa, commodity production and conversion *were* related. For example, in parts of Yorubaland, the intro-

duction of cocoa was closely associated with conversion to Christianity (see Webster 1963). In Senegal, groundnut farming was associated with the founding of a Muslim sect, the Mourides (Hopkins 1973:221).

3. In this chapter, I use annual reports for the entire Kàbbà Division, which included Bùnú District. While Bùnú was less developed and populous than the other three districts (Kàbbà, Gbẹ̀ddẹ̀, and Yàgbà), the economic options of Bùnú villagers were similar.

4. James Thomas 1858, CMS. The Bùnú dialect was distinct from the Ọ̀yọ́ dialect spoken by Bishop Crowther.

5. "[Reverend George Nicol] told me that I must go home and get ready for the Niger mission—on the tenth of September I was admitted in a day School at Wellington that I might be useful on the Bank of the Niger" (J. Thomas 1858, CMS).

6. See James Thomas 1875a, CMS. It is not clear whether a school was ever established.

7. Thomas described him as the "commander-in-Chief of the Bùnú countries residing at Àkpàrá" (1874, CMS).

8. Thomas arrived in Àpàá (Àpàrá) on January 2, 1863, and on the following Sunday gave a short sermon in the Bùnú dialect: "[A] small congregation of which the man [his host] had gathered in his own yard were about 100 men and women besides children and the people paid good attention to hear the word of God . . ." (1863a, CMS).

9. For example, in 1869, Thomas had successfully encouraged Bùnú living in Ọ̀wọ́rọ̀ District to build a small chapel. However, after the congregation lost thirty-five members in a slave raid and the CMS could not redeem them, they refused to return to church (J. Thomas 1869, CMS).

10. Early Annual Reports cite CMS schools at ShokoShoko and Odo-Apẹ̀ by 1914 (James 1914, NAK).

11. The reasons for the British establishment of the Protectorate of Northern Nigeria are complex; however, trade interests, including those of British cotton manufacturers, played an important part in this action (see Àyándélé 1966; Hopkins 1973).

12. The BCGA, organized in 1902, was not only coterminous with the British annexation of northern Nigeria (Duggan 1922:203), but it was also politically linked. In 1904, the BCGA made an agreement with

the colonial government to establish model farms, experimental stations, buying stations, and ginneries in exchange for an annual subsidy from the government and a guarantee of a buying monopoly. Despite these initial commitments and the government subsidy, association personnel complained of the poor transportation system, which they claimed limited the amount of cotton that could be brought to stations and processed. Further, the association was unwilling to increase prices paid to cotton farmers in Kàbbà Division, suggesting instead that colonial officials force farmers to grow cotton. District officers responded by complaining of BCGA policies in annual reports.

13. This acceptance, however, was not the case everywhere. Cotton farmers in neighboring Ọ̀wọ́rọ̀ District were suspicious of British intentions, as revealed in the following incident, described by a district officer: "The Agbaja people were always big cotton growers until ordered by Dr. Cargill to pay half their tribute in cotton. So far from encouraging the cultivation this course made them fear that something was behind such an order, so they practically gave up cotton growing, and even now are suspicious of any orders as to planting, etc." (Ley Greaves 1910, NAK).

14. Because of its geographical location and lack of resources, Bùnú District residents were essentially left to their own devices by colonial officials. This may account for the BCGA's decision to abandon the promotion of cotton in Bùnú and neighboring districts, concentrating on the area around Kano in northern Nigeria, where rail transport was available.

15. One secretary for the Northern Provinces wrote in 1911 that "cash is a commodity, and must be purchased like any other commodity. Now there is an unlimited demand for cotton and there is not such a demand for any other produce which is grown. This fact is not realised by many of the natives and we should do our best to bring it home to them" (Goldsmith 1911, NAK). The extremely low prices set by the BCGA made this unlimited demand irrelevant.

16. This assessment report for Kàbbà District indicates the relative low return on comparably sized plots, although it does not make clear how the practice of intercropping (of cotton with maize, for example) would have affected income.

17. The following table indicates that commodity prices in British currency dropped by half after the 1929 market collapse:

| | Price | |
Commodity	End of 1929	End of 1930
Palm kernels	£9 per ton	£4 per ton
Cocoa	£26 per ton	£15.5s.0 per ton
Benniseed	£8.10s.0 per ton	£4.10s.0

(Source: James 1930, NAI.)

18. For example, Ezekiel Ikúsemoro, son of an important chief in Ọ̀llẹ̀, was the founder of the CMS church in this central Bùnú village. Because many of his older siblings had died, Ezekiel was sent to be raised in southern Bùnú where he was baptized in the CMS church in Odo-Apẹ̀. Returning to Ọ̀llẹ̀, he worked to establish a small church there. Despite opposition, in 1948 he acquired permission to build a small chapel where he conducted services and baptized many of his fellow villagers (funeral notes, Ọ̀llẹ̀-Bùnú).

19. The woman head of the CMS church at Àpàá observed that "in the church, there is nothing secret except if you cannot read. But once you can read, everything is open to you" (M. Ikúsemí). She is implicitly contrasting Biblical knowledge, open to all who could read, with the esoteric knowledge of babaláwo, literally "father of the secret" (see Peel 1968:140).

20. There are also stories about yams, including one describing its introduction by a spirit (àlùjọ̀nú or jènú). This spirit told a farmer to kill his firstborn child, cut it up in small pieces, and plant the pieces in mounds. The pieces later grew into yams. Yams are also said to maintain some of their former human qualities, such as mobility, so that during a drought "yam seeds go to the river and drink. They take fresh air and refuse to come back so that farmers complain, 'Yams don't germinate this year.' But it is nothing else but they have gone to drink water—that's it" (Baba Àbú).

21. Before planting, farmers would look for the leaves of the ètìperonlá plant and one cowrie, then mix them together with the cotton seeds be-

fore planting. The leaves were believed to work like medicine and would make the cotton grow better (M. Bójúwọn, Ọllẹ̀-Bùnú). Ashes were also added to the cotton seeds to prevent them from sticking together during planting.

22. Cotton seed soup (ọbẹ̀ ògìrì) was prepared in two ways. One could boil the seeds, then press out the white inner seed after they cooled. The white inner seed would be ground and then reboiled and added to soup. Or the seeds could be pounded without boiling or cooking. After pounding, they were sieved and then ground and the resulting powder used in soup.

CHAPTER 9

1. In Kàbbà and Bùnú, the shift from handwoven to machine-woven school uniforms came later than to larger cities to the southwest. Peel (1983:133) mentions that handwoven cloth was replaced by its machine-woven counterparts in Ilẹ́ṣa during the 1930s.

2. This school, mentioned in chapter 8, was started sometime in the 1930s, was later closed, and then reopened in 1940 (Miscellaneous files 1930, NAK).

3. While teaching at one Nigerian university, I noticed that neither the staff nor the students wore traditional Yorùbá dress. When I asked the reason, I was told that "you wouldn't feel smart dressed like that," smart referring both to fashion-sense and to intelligence.

4. The most commonly named European cloths were similar in color and design to handwoven cloths. Àpatúpa cloth was a coarse heavy cotton cloth in red, black, and white. Dínrìn was a lighter weight cotton, similar to muslin or poplin, and very white. Àtòrìnbàdàn was a dark blue cotton cloth with white stripes. Olórí cloth was off-white and was used for going to the farm.

5. In the 1930s, Bùnú was also a "fresh" market for the òṣọmààló in the sense that villagers were socially and economically isolated and hence at a cultural disadvantage to the trader who "needed to have the edge of ọlàjú over his customers" (Peel 1983:158).

6. Handwoven cloth was generally measured by spans of an outstretched hand.

7. The roots of the *idìpẹta* (or *igi pòota*) tree were pounded and shredded to make a foamy solution used to wash cloth. When cloth was exceptionally dirty, ashes (*àbẹtẹ*) could be used as well. Both of these methods were labor-intensive. Black soap was also used to wash cloth but not everyone could afford it. Today a range of commercial washing soaps and powders is used.

8. Because of their construction, *àsòsò*, normally worn by men, were also used by women when menstruating. Extra cloth for absorbing blood was inserted under the flap of cloth secured in the back by two ties. Women no longer use *àsòsò* and presently use toilet paper or cotton sanitary pads worn with underpants.

9. Barry Wonder is a successful Nigerian popular singer and General Ibrahim Babangida is the former president of Nigeria. Chief Ọbáfẹmí Awólòwọ̀ was prime minister of the former Western Province and is much revered among the Yorùbá.

10. In her discussion of Senegambian fashion, Heath (1992) examines the ways that dress is part of a complex dialogue in which representations of modernity and tradition are drawn upon in constituting particular identities (see also Layne 1989).

11. Some dissenters have even come back to the fold. "When Christianity came, some people abandoned the masquerades. But as time went on, some came back to it" (A. Ọbajànọ̀).

CHAPTER 10

1. Small pieces of red cloth have been strewn along one section of the road just north of the town of Aíyétórò-Kírí-Bùnú, given out as protection against the harmful intentions of others.

2. This sense of comfort and security associated with backing is described by Ṣóyínká (1988:15): "Of all the women on whose backs I was carried, none was as secure and comfortable as Mrs. B's. It was capacious, soft and reassuring, it radiated the same repose and kindliness that we had observed in her face."

3. In the popular song "Ìyá ni Wúrà" (Mother is gold) (see note 16, chapter 2), listeners are reminded of the time their mothers carried them, both in the womb and on their backs. The song's last lines are:

"Mother, thank you for the work you have done for me, I will never abuse [through neglect] my mother."

4. The association of witchcraft with extraordinary financial and political success achieved at the expense of others is depicted in the person of Madam Koto by Okri (1991).

5. People gave as an example the story of a Yorùbá woman who used to come to the village to trade. The older woman was said always to sit next to the woman at the market. While the older woman sold well, the Yorùbá woman sold nothing and after a time stopped coming to the village.

GLOSSARY

àbíkú. Child believed to have been born and died (born to die)

àbò. A three-piece basket, dyed dark blue, used to carry marriage cloths during traditional marriage

àbò yẹyẹ̀. "Basket" made with broken things, to imitate àbò used in traditional marriage; literally, ridiculous marriage basket

àdófì. Named marriage cloth, predominantly black, which marks the performance of marriage

ahínimọ́ni. When two opposites come together

àjẹ́. Witch; female counterpart to *oṣó*

àkì. A narrow, white handwoven cloth used by *ejínuwọn* women; also the generic name for these cloths

àlùjọ̀nú, jènú. Evil spirit (derived from Arabic, *al'janu*)

ànkàrà. Wax-print industrially produced cloth, formerly imported

apọ́núpọ́nyìn. Type of funeral cloth, described as red on both sides and used only in the burial of kings

aró. Indigo dye

aṣọ. Cloth

aṣọ àtutà. Second-hand clothing

aṣọ dúdú. Black cloth

aṣọ ẹbí. Cloth specially chosen to be worn by all family members at a special event

aṣọ ẹbọra. Spirit cloth

aṣọ funfun. White cloth, used to placate troublesome spirits

aṣọ ipò. Red funeral cloths

aṣọ obitan. Marriage cloths

aṣọ òkè. Type of handwoven cloth, usually woven in narrow strips *aṣọ òyìnbó*. "White people's cloth"; industrially woven cloth, formerly imported

àwọdẹ. Hunter's shirt

baba. Father

babaláwo. Diviner (father of secrets)

dúdú. Black, also dark shades of blue, brown

ẹbọra. Type of spirit, often residing in rocks, trees, and unusual natural sites

egúngún. Masquerader, ancestor

èjìgí. Title chieftaincy position; head of women in Kírí

ejínuwọn. Spirit cult member (literally, Nupe for child of water)

èle. Object used as medicine or charm

èrò. Antidote used for *èle* medicine

funfun. White, also refers to opaque and transparent things

gbé obitan (Yorùbá: *igbéyawo*). Bring a wife ("traditional marriage")

gẹmọ. First title taken by men

ibòrí. Burnous-like robe used in traditional marriage

igbà. Tradition

igbá obitan. Set of three calabashes and a three-part basket, stained dark blue, used in traditional marriage and *pákó* ritual

imọ̀lẹ̀. Former women's spirit cult, similar to *òfósì* but members did not have secret language

inú (Yorùbá: *ilé ọmọ*). Womb; literally, inside

itìjú. Shame, literally, closing the eyes

ìyá. Mother

ìyálé. Senior wife

iyedé. Title of leader of women in Bùnú towns and village without the *èjìgí* title; below the *èjìgí* title

kíjìpá. General name for handwoven cloth; sometimes referred to as *aṣọ ofì*

kóbò. Nigerian currency; 100 kóbò equals 1 *náírà*

náírà. Nigerian currency; in 1988, 8 *náírà* equalled 1 dollar (US) *obitan* or *ebitan* (Yorùbá: *ìyàwó*). Wife; form of chieftaincy title for women

ọdẹ. Hunter

òfósì. Women's spirit-possession cult; restricted by family

ogùn. Medicine, herbal and Western; can also refer to charms used for protection from harm, evil intent

o-kun: Bùnú Yorùbá greeting

ojú. Eyes

òlàjú. Enlightenment, civilization; literally, opening the eyes

olójúmẹ́rin. Clairvoyant; literally, owner of four eyes; a euphemism for witchcraft

Ọlọ́run. God; literally, owner of heaven

olú. King; title of highest ranking chief in some Bùnú villages

omi. Water

omi aró. Water left in exhausted indigo dye bath

omi ẹbọra. Water in which spirits reside

omi mímó or *omi ìyè.* Holy water or life-giving water

ọmọ. Child

ó mú ni mọ pákó. Ritual performed to identify an ancestral spirit reborn in a child spirit

oníṣègùn. Traditional herbalist but not necessarily diviner

orí. Head; destiny

orótà. Chieftaincy title for men, taken after obtaining *gẹmo* title

òrun. Sky, heaven

oṣó. Wizard (male)

òṣọmààló. Yorùbá cloth traders who sold cloth on credit

òwú. Cotton

òyìnbó. White person; the British

pupa. Red

ṣe Ifá. Consult Ifá; divination

yísalà. White handwoven cloth with reddish stain at center, used in traditional marriage in northern Bùnú (Kírí)

BIBLIOGRAPHY

PRIMARY SOURCES

ARCHIVAL

National Archives, Kaduna (NAK):

Bridel, H. S.

    1929 Kabba District Assessment Report. Lok Prof 51/1929.

    1931 Notes on the Owe, Yagba, Ijumu (Gbedde) Clans. Lok Prof
          41/1931.

Cator, D.

    1917 Kabba Division Annual Report, 1916. Ilorin Prof 2/8, no.
          115/1917.

Clark, D.

    1939 Notes on Inspection of Kabba C.M.S. School. Lok Prof 16A/
          1930.

Fitzpatrick, J. F. J.

    1920 Kabba District Half Yearly Report. DCJ 145/1920.

Goldsmith, H. L.

    1911 Letter to Resident, Kabba Province. March 15. File ACC
          16.

    1912 Letter to Resident, Kabba Province. April 17. File ACC 17.

Harris, P. G.

    1931 Burial of an Orota. Notes on the Owe, Yagba, Ijumu
          (Gbedde) Clans. Lok Prof 41/1931.

James, H. B.

    1914 Assessment Report on Bunu District. Lok Prof 15/1914.

Ley Greaves, J. A.

    1910 Kabba Province Annual Report, no. 2, 1910. File ACC 16.

McCabe, A.

    1925 Pot Burials. Lok Prof 161/1925.

Miscellaneous Files

    1929–39 Cotton Cultivation and Seed Distribution, Kabba
           Province. Kad. Min. Agric. no. 7513.

    1930 C.M.S. Mission Schools. Lok Prof 16A/1930.

    1932–50 Local Manufacture of Small Articles. iii. Kabba Cloth.
           Lok Prof 217.

    1948 Development of Local Arts and Crafts—Routine
           Correspondence. Lok Prof 15/s.1.

Squibbs, G.

    1935 Organisation of Bunu District, Kabba Division, Kabba
           Province, 1935. File SNPH 25254.

National Archives, Ibadan (NAI):

Budgen, T. A. G.

    1923 Kabba Province Annual Report, 1923. CSO 26, no. 12941,
           vol. 1.

James, H. B.

    1928 Kabba Province Annual Report, 1928. CSO 26, no. 12941,
           vol. 6.

    1930 Kabba Province Annual Report, 1930. CSO 26, no. 12941,
           vol. 8.

    1931 Kabba Province Annual Report, 1931. CSO 26, no. 12941,
           vol. 9.

Payne, R. S.

    1932 Kabba Province Annual Report, 1932. CSO 26, no. 12941,
           vol. 10.

Rosedale, W. O. P.

    1933 Kabba Province Annual Report, 1933. CSO 26, no. 12941,
           vol. 11.

    1937 Kabba Province Annual Report, 1937. CSO 26, no. 12941,
           vol. 12.

Sciortino, J. C.
1927 Kabba Province Annual Report, 1927. CSO 26, no. 12941, vol. 5.

*Church Missionary Society (CMS) Archives, University of Birmingham:
Niger Mission Papers*

Thomas, James
1858 Journal entry, June 15, CA 3/038.
1859a,b Journal entries, June 13 and July 13, CA 3/038/8.
1863a,b,c Journal entries, January 4, 5, 7, CA 3/038/9.
1867 Journal entry, July 23, CA 3/038/13.
1869 Journal entry, November 24, CA 3/038/16.
1874 Letter, September 30, CA 3/038/19.
1875a,b Journal entries, February 11 and 12, CA 3/038/18.
Thomas, Obadiah
1878 Journal entry, December 29, CA/3/039/2.
Williams, Pythias J.
1880 A Journal of Itinerary to the Towns and Villages Situated on the North, East, and South of Gbede. CA 3/042/4.

*Archival Collection, Union Theological Society (UTS), New York:
Church Missionary Society Documents*

MUSEUM COLLECTIONS

African Textile Collection, Museum of Mankind, London
  Niger Expedition Collection
  Charles Beving Collection

African Textile Collection, Royal Museum of Scotland, Edinburgh
Department of Textiles, The Art Institute of Chicago
  A. J. Jepson sample book

SECONDARY SOURCES

Abíọlá, Florence
  1980 *Tie and Dye*. Unpublished essay, Kwara State College of
        Education, Home Economics Section, Òró-Ìlorin, Nigeria.
Abraham, R. C.
  1958 *Dictionary of Modern Yoruba*. London: University of London
        Press.
Adams, John
  1966 *Remarks on the Country Extending from Cape Palmas to the
        River Congo*. London: Longman. (Originally published 1823.)
Agbor, Ajan
  1989 "Born to Die," *Newswatch* 9:32–33.
Àjàyí, J. F. A.
  1965 *Christian Missions in Nigeria, 1841–1891*. London: Longman.
Ajísafé, A. K.
  1924 *The Laws and Customs of the Yoruba People*. London: Routledge
        and Sons.
Akíntóyè, S. A.
  1969 "The North-Eastern Yoruba Districts and the Benin
        Kingdom," *Journal of the Historical Society of Nigeria* 4:539–
        53.
Ánjórìn, A. O.
  1966 "European Attempts to Develop Cotton Cultivation in West
        Africa, 1850–1910," *Odu* 3:3–15.
Appadurai, Arjun, ed.
  1986 *The Social Life of Things*. Cambridge: Cambridge University
        Press.
Àrèmú, P. S. O.
  1982 "Yoruba Traditional Weaving: Kijipa Motifs, Colour and
        Symbols," *Nigeria Magazine* 140:3–10.
Aronson, Lisa
  1980 "Akwete Weaving and Patronage," *African Arts* 13:62–66.
  1989 "Akwete Weaving: Tradition and Change," in *Man Does Not*

   Go Naked, ed. B. Engelbrecht and B. Gardi, pp. 35–64.
   Basel: Museum für Völkerkunde.

Asíwájú, A. I.
   1976 "Political Motivation and Oral Historical Traditions in
      Africa," *Africa* 46:113–28.

Àyándélé, E. A.
   1966 *The Missionary Impact on Modern Nigeria, 1842–1914*.
      London: Longman.

Awólàlú, J. O.
   1979 *Yoruba Beliefs and Sacrificial Rites*. London: Longman.

Baikie, W. B.
   1856 *Narrative of an Exploring Voyage Up the Rivers Kwo'ra and
      Bi'nue in 1854*. London: J. Murray.

Barber, Karin
   1981 "Documenting Social and Ideological Change Through
      Yoruba Oriki: A Stylistic Analysis," *Journal of the Historical
      Society of Nigeria* 10:39–52.
   1991 *I Could Speak Until Tomorrow: Oriki, Women and the Past in a
      Yoruba Town*. Washington, D.C.: Smithsonian Institution
      Press.

Barbour, J., and D. Simmonds, eds.
   1971 *Adire Cloth in Nigeria*. Ibadan: University of Ibadan Press.

Barth, Heinrich
   1857 *Travels and Discoveries in North and Central Africa*. New York:
      Harper and Brothers.

Bascom, William
   1984 *The Yoruba of Southwestern Nigeria*. Prospect Heights, IL:
      Waveland Press. (Originally published 1969.)

Bassett, Thomas
   1988 "The Development of Cotton in Northern Ivory Coast, 1910–
      1965," *Journal of African History* 29:267–84.

Bayly, C. A.
   1986 "The Origins of Swadeshi (Home Industry): Cloth and
      Indian Society, 1700–1930," in *The Social Life of Things*,

   ed. A. Appadurai, pp. 285–321. Cambridge: Cambridge
   University Press.

Bean, Susan
   1989 "Gandhi and Khadi, the Fabric of Indian Independence," in
   Cloth and Human Experience, ed. A. Weiner and J. Schneider,
   pp. 355–76. Washington: Smithsonian Institution Press.

Beidelman, T. O.
   1966 "Swazi Royal Ritual," *Africa* 36:373–405.
   1983 *The Kaguru*. Prospect Heights, IL: Waveland Press.
   (Originally published 1971.)
   1986 *Moral Imagination in Kaguru Modes of Thought*. Bloomington:
   Indiana University Press.

Ben-Amos, Paula
   1978 "Owina N'Ido: Royal Weavers of Benin," *African Arts* 11:48–
   53, 95.

Blier, Suzanne
   1987 *The Anatomy of Architecture*. Cambridge: Cambridge
   University Press.

Bloch, Marc
   1973 *The Royal Touch*. London: Routledge and Kegan Paul.
   (Originally published 1923.)

Boone, Sylvia
   1986 *Radiance in the Water*. New Haven: Yale University Press.

Borgatti, Jean
   1983 *Cloth as Metaphor*. Los Angeles: University of California
   Press.

Boser-Sarivaxévanis, Renée
   1969 *Aperçus sur la teinture à l'indigo en Afrique occidentale*. Basel:
   Naturforschende Gesellschaft 80/I.
   1972 *Les tissus de l'Afrique occidentale*. Basel: Pharos Verlag.
   1975 *Recherche sur l'histoire des textiles traditionnels tissés et teints de
   l'Afrique occidentale*. Basel: Verhandlungen der
   Naturforschenden Gesellschaft.

Boston, John
   1966 "The Hunter in Igala Legends of Origin," *Africa* 34: 116–26.

Boyer, Ruth
1983 "Yoruba Cloths With Regal Names," *African Arts* 16:42–45,
98.

Bray, Jennifer
1968 "The Organization of Traditional Cloth Production in Iseyin,
Nigeria," *Africa* 38:270–80.

Breidenbach, Paul
1976 "Colour Symbolism and Ideology in a Ghanaian Healing
Movement," *Africa* 46:137–45.

Brett-Smith, Sarah
1984 "Speech Made Visible: The Irregular as a System of
Meaning," *Empirical Studies in the Arts* 2:127–47.
1989 *Fruitful Death: Minianka Women's Shrouds.* Paper presented at
the Eighth Triennial of the Arts Council of the African
Studies Association, Washington, D.C.
1990/91 "Empty Space: The Architecture of Dogon Cloth," *RES*
19/20:162–77.

Buckley, Anthony
1985 *Yoruba Medicine.* London: Oxford.

Burton, R. F.
1865 "My Wanderings in West Africa, by a F.R.G.S.: Parts II and
III. The Renowned City of Benin," *Fraser's Magazine*, vol. 67.

Buxton, T. F.
1967 *The African Slave Trade and Its Remedy.* London: Cass.
(Originally published 1839.)

Byfield, Judith
1989 *Explorations in Oral History: Interviews with Adire Dyers in
Abeokuta, 1988.* Paper presented at the Institute for Research
on Women and Gender, Columbia University, New York.

Caldwell, John
1976 *The Socio-Economic Explanation of High Fertility: Papers on the
Yoruba Society of Nigeria.* Canberra: The Australian National
University.

Church Missionary Society
   1863–65 *Proceedings*. London.
   1887 *The Gleaner Pictorial Album*, vol. 1. London.
   1909 *Proceedings*. London.
Cohen, David W., and E. S. Odhiambo
   1989 *Siaya, the Historical Anthropology of an African Landscape*.
      London: Currey.
Cordwell, Justine, and Ronald Schwarz, eds.
   1979 *The Fabrics of Culture: The Anthropology of Clothing*.
      The Hague: Mouton.
Cort, Louise
   1989 "The Changing Fortunes of Three Archaic Japanese
      Textiles," in *Cloth in Human Experience*, ed. A. Weiner
      and J. Schneider, pp. 377–415. Washington, D.C.:
      Smithsonian Institution Press.
Crowder, Michael
   1966 *The Story of Nigeria*. London: Faber.
Dalziel, J.
   1937 *The Useful Plants of West Tropical Africa*. London: Crown
      Agents for Overseas Governments.
Darish, Patricia
   1989 "Dressing for the Next Life," in *Cloth in Human Experience*,
      ed. A. Weiner and J. Schneider, pp. 117–40. Washington,
      D.C.: Smithsonian Institution Press.
deHeusch, Luc
   1981 *Why Marry Her?* Cambridge: Cambridge University Press.
Dilley, Roy
   1986 "Myth and Meaning and the Tukulor Loom," *Man* 22:256–
      66.
Dorward, D. C.
   1976 "Precolonial Tiv Trade and Cloth Currency," *International
      Journal of African Historical Studies* 9:576–91.
Drewal, Henry
   1977 "Art and the Perception of Women in Yoruba Culture,"
      Cahiers d'Études Africaines 68:545–67.

Drewal, Henry, and Margaret Drewal
1983 *Gelede: Art and Female Power Among the Yoruba.* Bloomington:
     Indiana University Press.
Duggan, E.
1922 "The Cotton Growing Industry in Nigeria," *Journal of the
     African Society* 21:199–207.
Eades, Jeremy
1980 *The Yoruba Today.* Cambridge: Cambridge University Press.
Èbájẹ́mítọ́, John
1985 *Indigenous Technology in Bunu District Since the Nineteenth
     Century.* Unpublished essay, Department of History,
     University of Ilorin.
Eicher, Joanne
1969 *African Dress: A Select and Annotated Bibliography of
     Subsaharan Countries.* East Lansing: Michigan State
     University.
1975 *Nigerian Handcrafted Textiles.* Ile-Ife: University of Ife Press.
Etienne, Mona
1982 "Women and Men: Cloth and Colonialism," in *Women and
     Colonization*, ed. M. Etienne and E. Leacock, pp. 214–38.
     New York: Praeger.
Evans-Pritchard, E. E.
1983 *Witchcraft, Oracles, and Magic Among the Azande.* Oxford:
     Clarendon Press. (Originally published 1937.)
1956 *Nuer Religion.* New York: Oxford University Press.
Fádìpẹ̀, N. A.
1970 *The Sociology of the Yoruba.* Ibadan: University of Ibadan
     Press.
Fálọlá, T., and M. Doortmont
1989 "Iwe Itan Oyo: A Traditional Yoruba History and Its Author,"
     Journal of African History 30:301–26.
Feeley-Harnik, Gillian
1989 "Cloth and the Creation of Ancestors in Madagascar," in
     Cloth in Human Experience, ed. A. Weiner and J. Schneider,

pp. 73–116. Washington, D.C.: Smithsonian Institution
Press.

Fourneau, J., and L. Kravetz

1954 "Le pagne sur la Côte de Guinée et au Congo du XVᵉ siècle à
nos jours," *Bulletin de l'Institute d'Etudes Centrafricaine* 7–8:
5–22.

Fraser, Douglas, and Herbert Cole

1972 *African Art and Leadership.* Madison: University of Wisconsin
Press.

Frobenius, Leo

1913 *The Voice of Africa.* Trans. R. Blind. London: Hutchinson and
Co.

Gilfoy, Peggy

1987 *Patterns of Life: West African Strip-Weaving Traditions.*
Washington, D.C.: National Museum of African Art.

Ginzburg, Carlo

1983 *Night Battles.* London: Penguin Books. (Originally published
1966.)

Goitein, S. D.

1967 *A Mediterranean Society.* Berkeley: University of California
Press.

Goody, Esther, ed.

1982 *From Craft to Industry.* Cambridge: Cambridge University
Press.

Griaule, Marcel

1965 *Conversations with Ogotemmeli.* London: Oxford University
Press.

Heath, Deborah

1992 "Fashion, Anti-Fashion, and Heteroglossia in Urban
Senegal," *American Ethnologist* 19:19–33.

Hertz, Robert

1960 *Death and the Right Hand.* London: Cohen and West.

Hocart, A. M.

1970 *Kings and Councillors.* Chicago: University of Chicago Press.
(Originally published 1936.)

1970 *The Life-giving Myth*. London: Tavistock.

Hopkins, A. G.

1973 *An Economic History of West Africa*. London: Longman.

Horton, Robin

1970 "A Hundred Years of Change in Kalabari Religion," in *Spirit Mediumship and Society in Africa*, ed. J. Beattie and J. Middleton, pp. 14–49. New York: Africana Publishing Company.

Hoskins, Janet

1989 "Why Do Ladies Sing the Blues? Indigo Dyeing, Cloth Production, and Gender Symbolism in Kodi," in *Cloth in Human Experience*, ed. A. Weiner and J. Schneider, pp. 141–73. Washington, D.C.: Smithsonian Institution Press.

Ìbéjìgbá, Solomon

1985 *Traditional Marriage Practices in Bunuland, Kwara State: Olle as a Case Study*. Unpublished essay, Institute of African Studies, University of Ibadan.

1988 *Study of the Traditional Social Mechanisms in Olle-Bunu, Kwara State*. M.A. thesis, Institute of African Studies, University of Ibadan.

Idiens, Dale, and I. Ponting, eds.

1980 *Textiles in Africa*. Bath: The Pasold Foundation.

Ìdòwú, E. Bólájí

1962 *Olodumare: God in Yoruba Belief*. Ikeja: Longman.

Isaacman, A.; M. Stephan; Y. Adam; M. J. Homen; E. Macamo; and A. Pililao

1980 "Cotton Is the Mother of Poverty," *International Journal of African Historical Studies* 13:581–615.

Jackson, Michael

1982 *Allegories in the Wilderness*. Bloomington: Indiana University Press.

1983 "Thinking through the Body," *Social Analysis* 14:127–49.

1989 *Paths toward a Clearing*. Bloomington: Indiana University Press.

Jacobson-Widding, Anita
  1979 *Red-White-Black as a Mode of Thought.* Stockholm: Uppsala
         Studies in Cultural Anthropology.
Johnson, Marion
  1973 "Cloth on the Banks of the Niger," *Journal of the Historical
         Society of Nigeria* 6:353–63.
  1974 "Cotton Imperialism in West Africa," *Journal of the Royal
         African Society* 73:178–87.
  1978 "Technology, Competition, and African Crafts," in *The
         Imperial Impact*, ed. C. Dewey and A. Hopkins, pp. 259–69.
         London: Athlone Press.
Kennett, B. L. A.
  1931 "The Afoshi Dancers of Kabba Division, Northern Nigeria,"
         JRAIGBI 61:435–42.
Kent, Kate
  1971 *Introduction to West African Weaving.* Denver: Denver
         Museum of Natural History.
  1972 "West African Decorative Weaving," *African Arts* 6:22–27,
         67–70.
Kingsley, Mary
  1988 *Travels in West Africa.* Boston: Beacon Press. (Originally
         published 1897.)
Krapf-Askari, Eva
  1965 "The Social Organization of the Owé," *African Notes* 2:9–12.
  1966a "Time and Classifications: An Ethnographic and Historical
         Case-Study," *Odù* 2:3–18.
  1966b "Brass Objects from the Owé Yoruba, Kàbbà Province,
         Northern Nigeria," *Odù* 3:82–87.
Kriger, Colleen
  1988 "The Sokoto Caliphate Textile Industry." Paper presented at
         the annual meeting of the African Studies Association,
         Chicago.
Kuchler, Suzanne
  1988 "Malangan: Objects, Sacrifice, and the Production of
         Memory," *American Ethnologist* 15:625–37.

Kwara State
1983 *Government White Paper Report: Obaro Chieftaincy Stool in Kabba.* Ilorin: Government Printer.

Lamb, Venice
1975 *West African Weaving.* London: Duckworth.

Lamb, Venice, and Judith Holmes
1980 *Nigerian Weaving.* Hertingfordbury: Roxford Books.

Lamb, Venice, and Alastair Lamb
1981 *Cameroun Weaving.* Hertingfordbury: Roxford Books.

Lander, Richard, and John Lander
1832 *Journal of an Expedition.* New York: Harper.

Landolphe, J. F.
1823 *Mémoires du Capitaine Landolphe, rédigés sur son manuscript par J. S. Quesne.* Paris: Bertrand.

LaPin, Deirdre
1977 *Story, Medium and Masque: The Idea and Art of Yoruba Storytelling.* Ph.D. dissertation, Department of African Languages and Literature, University of Wisconsin.

Larymore, Constance
1911 *A Resident's Wife in Nigeria.* London: Routledge. (Originally published 1908.)

Layne, Linda
1989 "The Dialogics of Tribal Self-Representation in Jordan," *American Ethnologist* 16:24–39.

Levtzion, N.
1973 *Ancient Ghana and Mali.* New York: Africana Publishing Company.

Levtzion, N., and J. Hopkins, eds.
1981 *Corpus of Early Arabic Sources for West African History.* Cambridge: Cambridge University Press.

Liedholm, Carl
1982 "The Economics of African Dress and Textile Arts," *African Arts* 15:71–74, 90.

Lloyd, P. C.
1953 "Craft Organization in Yoruba Towns," *Africa* 23:30–44.

Lombard, M.
    1978 *Les textiles dans le monde musulman VIIe–XIIe siècle.* Paris:
          Mouton.
MacGaffey, Wyatt
    1977 "Fetishism Revisited: Kongo Nkisi in Sociological
          Perspective," *Africa* 47:172–84.
Mack, John
    1989 *Malagasy Weaving.* London: Shire.
Mann, Kristin
    1986 *Marrying Well.* Cambridge: Cambridge University Press.
Mason, Michael
    1970 "The Jihad in the South: An Outline of the Nineteenth
          Century Nupe Hegemony in North-Eastern Yorubaland and
          Afenmai," *Journal of the Historical Society of Nigeria* 5:193–
          209.
Mauss, Marcel
    1973 "Techniques of the Body," *Economy and Society* 2:70–88.
May, D. J.
    1860 "Journey in the Yoruba and Nupe Countries in 1858," *Journal
          of the Royal Geographical Society* 20:213–33.
Menzel, Brigitte
    1972 *Textilien aus Westafrika.* 3 vols. Berlin: Museum für
          Völkerkunde.
Miachi, Thomas
    1990 *The Masquerade Phenomenon in Igala Culture: An
          Anthropological Analysis.* Ph.D. dissertation, Institute of
          African Studies, University of Ibadan.
Morton-Williams, Peter
    1960 "Yoruba Responses to the Fear of Death," *Africa* 30:34–40.
Murra, John
    1962 "Cloth and Its Function in the Inca State," *American
          Anthropologist* 64:710–28.
    1989 "Cloth and Its Function in the Inka State," in *Cloth in Human
          Experience*, ed. A. Weiner and J. Schneider, pp. 275–302.
          Washington, D.C.: Smithsonian Institution Press.

Murray, K. C.
  1936 "Women's Weaving Among the Yorubas of Omu-aran in Ilorin
       Province," *Nigerian Field* 5:182–91.
Nadel, S. F.
  1954 *Nupe Religion.* London: Routledge and Kegan Paul.
  1956 *A Black Byzantium.* London: Oxford University Press.
       (Originally published 1942.)
Needham, Rodney
  1980 *Reconnaissances.* Toronto: University of Toronto Press.
Niven, Rex
  1926 "The Kabba Province of the Northern Provinces of Nigeria,"
       Geographical Journal 48:289–302.
  1982 *Nigerian Kaleidoscope.* London: C. Hurst.
Ọbáyẹmí, Adé
  1976 "The Yoruba and Edo-speaking Peoples and Their
       Neighbours Before 1600," in *A History of West Africa*, vol. 1,
       2nd ed., ed. J. F. A. Ajayi and M. Crowder, pp. 196–263.
       London: Longman.
  1978a "The Sokoto Jihad and the 'O-kun' Yoruba: A Review,"
       Journal of the Historical Society of Nigeria 9:61–87.
  1978b "An Archaeological Mission to Akpaa," *Confluence* 1:60–67.
  1980 "States and Peoples of the Niger-Benue Confluence Area," in
       Groundwork of Nigerian History, ed. O. Ikime, pp. 144–64.
       Ibadan: Heineman Books (Nigeria).
  1989 *Nine Centuries of Yoruba Art and Thought.* Paper presented at
       Conference on Yoruba Culture, Center for African Art, New
       York City.
Òdúyoyè, M.
  1972 *Yoruba Names.* London: Blackrose Press.
Okri, Ben
  1991 *The Famished Road.* London: Vintage Press.
Oyèníyì, Hannah
  1979 *Local Weaving at Òrò-Àgọ́.* Unpublished essay, Kwara State
       College of Education, Home Economics Section, Oro-Ilorin.

Peel, J. D. Y.
  1968 *Aladura: A Religious Movement Among the Yoruba*. London: Oxford.
  1978 "*Ọlaju*: A Yoruba Concept of Development," *Journal of Development Studies* 14:139–65.
  1983 *Ijeshas and Nigerians*. Cambridge: Cambridge University Press.
Pemberton III, John
  1975 "Eshu-Elegba: The Yoruba Trickster God," *African Arts* 9:21–27, 66–69, 90–92.
Perani, Judith
  1989 "Northern Nigerian Prestige Textiles," in *Man Does Not Go Naked*, ed. B. Engelbrecht and B. Gardi, pp. 65–81. Basel: Museum für Völkerkunde.
Picton, John
  1980 "Women's Weaving: The Manufacture and Use of Textiles Among the Igbirra People of Nigeria," in *Textiles of Africa*, ed. D. Idiens and I. Ponting, pp. 63–88. Bath: Pasold Research Fund.
  1991 "On Artifact and Identity at the Niger-Benue Confluence," *African Arts* 24:34–49, 93–94.
Picton, John, and John Mack
  1979 *African Textiles*. London: British Museum.
Pokornowski, Ila; Joanne Eicher; Moira Harris; and Otto Thieme
  1985 *African Dress II: A Select and Annotated Bibliography*. East Lansing, Mich.: African Studies Center.
Poyner, Robin
  1980 "Traditional Textiles in Owo, Nigeria," *African Arts* 14:47–51, 88.
Renne, Elisha
  1990 "If Men Are Talking, They Blame It on Women," *Feminist Issues* 10:37–49.
  1992a "*Aso Ipo*: Red Funeral Cloth from Bunu," *African Arts* 25:64–69, 102.

1992b "Polyphony in the Courts: Child Custody Cases in Kabba District Court, 1925–1979," *Ethnology* 31:219–32.

Richards, Audrey
1982 *Chisungu*. London: Tavistock. (Originally published 1956.)

Ryder, A. F. C.
1965 "A Reconsideration of the Ife-Benin Relationship," *Journal of African History* 4:25–37.
1969 *Benin and the Europeans, 1485–1897*. New York: Humanities Press.

Schaedler, Karl-Ferdinand
1987 *Weaving in Africa South of the Sahara*. Munich: Panterra [English edition].

Schneider, Jane
1978 "Penguins and Peacocks," *American Ethnologist* 5:413–47.
1987 "The Anthropology of Cloth," *Annual Review of Anthropology* 16:409–48.

Schneider, Jane, and Annette Weiner
1986 "Cloth and the Organization of Human Experience," *Current Anthropology* 27:178–84.

Schon, J., and S. Crowther
1970 *Journal of an Expedition up the Niger in 1841*. London: Cass. (Originally published 1843.)

Shea, Phillip
1975 *The Development of an Export Oriented Dyed Cloth Industry in Kano Emirate in the Nineteenth Century*. Ph.D. dissertation, University of Wisconsin.

Shenton, R., and L. Lennihan
1981 "Capital and Class: Peasant Differentiation in Northern Nigeria," *Journal of Peasant Studies* 9:47–70.

Sieber, Roy
1972 *African Textiles and Decorative Arts*. New York: MOMA.

Simmel, Georg
1950 *The Sociology of Georg Simmel*. New York: Free Press.
1971 *On Individuality and Social Forms*. Chicago: University of Chicago Press. (Originally published 1904.)

Simpson, George
   1980 *Yoruba Religion and Medicine in Ibadan.* Ibadan: Ibadan
         University Press.
Smith, Fred
   1982 "Frafra Dress," *African Arts* 15:36–42, 92.
Ṣóyínká, Wọlé
   1965 *The Interpreters.* London: Heinemann.
   1988 *Aké: The Years of Childhood.* Ibadan: Spectrum. (Originally
         published 1981).
   1989 *Ìsarà: A Voyage Around Essay.* Ibadan: Fountain.
Spitzer, Leo
   1974 *The Creoles of Sierra Leone.* Madison: University of
         Wisconsin Press.
Steiner, Christopher
   1985 "Another Image of Africa: Toward an Ethnohistory of Cloth
         Marketed in West Africa, 1873–1960," *Ethnohistory* 32:91–
         110.
Sundstrom, Lars
   1974 *The Exchange Economy of Pre-Colonial Tropical Africa.* New
         York: St. Martin's Press.
Temple, O.
   1965 *Notes on the Tribes, Provinces, Emirates, and States of the
         Northern Provinces of Nigeria.* London: Cass. (Originally
         published 1919.)
Turner, Victor
   1957 *Schism and Continuity in an African Society.* Manchester:
         Manchester University Press.
   1967 *The Forest of Symbols.* Ithaca: Cornell University Press.
   1969 *The Ritual Process.* Chicago: Aldine.
United Nations
   1968 "The Textile Industry in the West African Sub-Region,"
         Economic Bulletin for Africa 7:103–25.
Van Allen, Judith
   1976 "'Aba Riots' or Igbo 'Women's War'?" in *Women in Africa*, ed.

N. Hafkin and E. Bay, pp. 59–86. Stanford: Stanford
University Press.

Vandeleur, Seymour

1898 *Campaigning on the Upper Nile and Niger*. London: Methuen.

Vansina, Jan

1956 *The Children of Woot*. Madison: University of Wisconsin
Press.

Verger, Pierre

1966 "The Yoruba High God," *Odù* 2:19–40.

1968 "La société *egbé ̀orun* des *àbíkú*, les enfants qui naissent pour
mourir maintes fois," *Bulletin de l'IFAN*, serie B 30(4):1448–
87.

1973 "La notion de personne et ligne familiale chez les Yoruba," in
La Notion de Personne en Afrique Noire, ed. G. Dieterlen, pp.
61–71. Paris: CNRS.

Vermeer, D.

1971 "Geophagy Among the Ewe of Ghana," *Ethnology* 10:56–72.

Vogt, John

1975 "Notes on the Portuguese Cloth Trade in West Africa, 1480–
1540," *International Journal of African Historical Studies*
8:623–51.

Webster, James

1963 "The Bible and the Plough," *Journal of the Historical Society of
Nigeria* 2:418–34.

Weigle, Marta

1989 *Creation and Procreation*. Philadelphia: University of
Pennsylvania Press.

Weiner, Annette

1985 *Inalienable Wealth*. American Ethnologist 12(2):210–27.

1987 "Toward a Theory of Gender Power: An Evolutionary
Perspective," in *The Gender of Power*: ed. M. Leyenaar et al.,
pp. 41–77. Leiden: Vakgrvep Vronwen Studies FSSW.

1989 "Why Cloth? Wealth, Gender, and Power in Oceania," in
Cloth in Human Experience, ed. A. Weiner and J. Schneider,

pp. 33–72. Washington, D.C.: Smithsonian Institution
Press.

1992 *Inalienable Possessions.* Berkeley: University of California
Press.

Weiner, Annette, and Jane Schneider, eds.

1989 *Cloth and Human Experience.* Washington, D.C.:
Smithsonian Institution Press.

Westcott, Joan

1962 "The Sculpture and Myths of Eshu-Elegba, the Yoruba
Trickster," *Africa* 32:336–54.

Whitford, John

1967 *Trading Life in Western and Central Africa.* London: Cass.
(Originally published 1877.)

Wittgenstein, Ludwig

1978 *Philosophical Investigations.* Berkeley: University of California
Press.

INTERVIEWS QUOTED

Baba Àbú, Aíyétórò-Kírí-Bùnú

Madam Mary Adé, Àpàá-Bùnú

Madam Janet Àjàyí, Kàbbà

Baba Aláró, Gìrò-Kírí-Bùnú

Chief Ezekiel Àyìnmódè, Ọ̀llẹ̀-Bùnú

Mr. O. Baiyéré, Tẹdó-Kírí-Bùnú

Chief Johnson Baiyésheá, Àgbẹ̀dẹ-Bùnú

Madam Grace Baiyéshéa, Àgbẹ̀dẹ-Bùnú

Chief Michael Bójúwọn, Ọ̀llẹ̀-Bùnú

Madam Margaret Ekúndayọ̀, Àpàá-Bùnú

Madam Ọmọ́lójú Ezekiel, Aíyétórò-Kírí-Bùnú

Madam Elizabeth Gbodòfé, Àgbẹ̀dẹ-Bùnú

Madam Arimat Ibrahim, Okene

Chief Philip Ikúéndayọ̀, Àpàá-Bùnú

Madam Alice Ikúéndayọ̀, Àpàá-Bùnú

Madam Mary Ikúsemí, Àpàá-Bùnú

Mr. B. Jethro, Ìsàdó-Kírí-Bùnú

Chief Jimoh Ayegboka, Odo-Apẹ̀-Bùnú

Madam Naomi Joseph, Aíyétórò-Kírí-Bùnú

Madam Deborah Kọ́láwọlé, Àgbẹ̀dẹ-Bùnú

Iya Mọ́kànjú, Ọ̀llẹ̀-Bùnú

Madam Roda Mọni, Àpàá-Bùnú

Chief Tolúfá Moses, Aíyétórò-Kírí-Bùnú

Madam Elizabeth Nua, Àpàá-Bùnú

Madam Deborah Ọbadémowó, Àpàá-Bùnú

Madam Iyegere Ọbájáfà, Àpàá-Bùnú

Chief Alèdáre Ọbajànọ̀, Àpàá-Bùnú

Madame Comfort Ọbajànọ̀, Àpàá-Bùnú

Chief Gabriel Ọbàlò, Àpàá-Bùnú

Chief E. Ọbalúhà, Ọ̀llẹ̀-Bùnú

Chief O. Ọbárokàn, Àgbẹ̀dẹ-Bùnú

Mr. Funsho O. Ọbásàjú, Kàbbà

Madam Comfort Ògúníbì, Àpàá-Bùnú

Chief Benjamin Ọlọ́runípa, Ìgbo-Bùnú
Mr. James Olówósaiyé, Àpàá-Bùnú
Chief Zachias Olú, Àpàá-Bùnú
Chief Ọlọ́rúntóba Olúkòtán, Àpàá-Bùnú
Mr. O. Olúmodì, "Àjìgí," Kàbbà
Madam Comfort Olútìmáyìn, Àgbèdẹ-Bùnú
Madam Mofẹ́ Ọmọ́le, Àgbèdẹ-Bùnú
Madam Ruth Ọmọ́sàyìn, Àpàá-Bùnú
Chief Mark Owónaiyé, Òllè-Bùnú
Madam Alùmọ́nyìn Tèmítáyọ̀, Aíyétórò-Kírí-Bùnú
Madam Mary Zaccheus, Àkútúpá-Kírí-Bùnú

INDEX

Bold italic numbers refer to illustrations